Profiles and Portraits of
AMERICAN
PRESIDENTS

Profiles and Portraits of
AMERICAN
PRESIDENTS

—◆—

Margaret Bassett

With an Introduction by Dr. Henry F. Graff

New and Updated Edition

DAVID McKAY COMPANY, INC.

NEW YORK

Library of Congress Cataloging in Publication Data

Bassett, Margaret Byrd, 1902-
Profiles and portraits of American presidents.

Bibliography : p.
1. Presidents—United States—Biography. 2. Presidents
United States—Portraits. I. Title.
E176.1.B23 1976   973'.0992[B]   76-16022
ISBN 0-679-50618-7

Manufactured in the United States of America
Designed by The Etheredges

CONTENTS

THE PRESIDENCY *by Dr. Henry F. Graff*   vii

THE PRESIDENTS

GEORGE WASHINGTON   1

JOHN ADAMS   7

THOMAS JEFFERSON   13

JAMES MADISON   19

JAMES MONROE   25

JOHN QUINCY ADAMS   31

ANDREW JACKSON   35

MARTIN VAN BUREN   41

WILLIAM HENRY HARRISON   45

JOHN TYLER 49

JAMES KNOX POLK 55

ZACHARY TAYLOR 61

MILLARD FILLMORE 65

FRANKLIN PIERCE 69

JAMES BUCHANAN 73

ABRAHAM LINCOLN 79

ANDREW JOHNSON 87

ULYSSES SIMPSON GRANT 93

RUTHERFORD BIRCHARD HAYES 99

JAMES ABRAM GARFIELD 105

CHESTER ALAN ARTHUR 109

STEPHEN GROVER CLEVELAND 115

BENJAMIN HARRISON 121

WILLIAM MCKINLEY 127

THEODORE ROOSEVELT 133

WILLIAM HOWARD TAFT 141

THOMAS WOODROW WILSON 145

WARREN GAMALIEL HARDING 153

JOHN CALVIN COOLIDGE 159

HERBERT CLARK HOOVER 165

FRANKLIN DELANO ROOSEVELT 173

HARRY S. TRUMAN 185

DWIGHT DAVID EISENHOWER 193

JOHN FITZGERALD KENNEDY 201

LYNDON BAINES JOHNSON 211

RICHARD MILHOUS NIXON 221

GERALD RUDOLPH FORD 235

PRESIDENTIAL REFERENCE

LAWS GOVERNING THE PRESIDENCY 239

SALIENT FACTS ABOUT EACH PRESIDENT 245

SELECTED BIBLIOGRAPHY 297

vi

THE
PRESIDENCY

———⋖◉⋗———

The presidency of the United States, as a repository of both power and prestige, is unique in the world. Its occupant is chief of state, head of government, and commander of the armed forces. Beyond these formal roles, well-rooted in the Constitution, are powerful ones, which were unplanned for, and yet have been played by the Chief Executives since the beginning of our national history. The Presidents have frequently been our moral leaders, the fountainheads of patriotism, the principal source of information and news, and our pace-setters in everything from personal courage to cultural tastes. Above all, they have provided the dramatic emphases of our story as a people.

The office of President is a continuous one in the legal sense, but the special qualities its incumbents have brought in turn to it invest it with its vibrancy and, indeed, its majesty. Each new President exhibits a style of behavior, a quality of insight and determination, and a measure of personal magnetism that marks his place in history—ours and the world's. When a man yields up the keys of this office to his successor, there is heard no equivalent of the ancient cry, "The King is dead! Long live the King!" Presidents are not interchangeable or standardized parts of our political system, and we are instinctively sure that we would not have them so.

The Presidents who parade before us, in turn, cannot escape being subject to constant public scrutiny and criticism, and then, historical evaluation. How we judge the individual Chief Executives is, of course, a matter of our own politics, our sense of the past, and the fact that we are Americans. Some appear larger than life—and some smaller. It seems unavoidable that we make our President into what we want him to be. We ascribe to him the qualities we prize most in ourselves. The effect has been that the President often seems to reflect the America of his time with an uncanny precision, which, considering the vagaries of the political obstacle course he runs to reach the White House, is truly remarkable. It makes of the presidency a delicate, indispensable instrument of republican government that far surpasses anything in the most optimistic dreams of the Founding Fathers.

As we examine the portraits on the pages that follow, we are struck forcibly by the fact that we have met these men before. Every schoolchild, if he learns nothing else of American history, learns the names of all the Presidents and fixes in his mind the faces of the most important of them. One thing, therefore, he is made aware of early: our nation is still so young that, unlike the Kings of France or the Sultans of Turkey, the Presidents of the United States each occupy a niche and are identified with a record that the well-informed citizen must consult. One day, as our history lengthens, it will no longer be possible to know in intimate detail the lives of the Presidents any more than the ordinary well-informed person today can know, let us say, the lives of the Saints. Until then, however, the careers of our Chief Executives, like their faces, will be recognized individually.

The history of the presidency, nevertheless, is no mere kaleidoscope of faces changing in endless procession. Even now the men who have served as our Chief Executives and whose deeds are celebrated here are beginning to fall into definable groups.

Four of the first five Presidents—Washington, Jefferson, Madison, and Monroe—were Virginia "aristocrats." They had had a vigorous part in creating the new government and they were uncompromisingly committed to making it a success—in Washington's memorable words, to establishing "a standard to which the wise and honest can repair." The society out of which they sprang did not fully embrace "the people." Its spokesmen generally regarded the ownership of property as a basic requirement for voting and for holding office, and they never used the word "democracy" in a benign sense, preferring to think of it as a synonym for mob rule.

If these viewpoints seem repellent or even incomprehensible today, it must be remembered that joined with them was a deeply felt obligation to participate in unselfish public service as a way of life. This kind of dynamic for power motivated also John and John Quincy Adams of Massachusetts, who added to the Virginia ideal a pessimism about human nature, drawn from their New England heritage, that sometimes made both father and son seem crabbed and uncharitable. Most important, the first six Presidents, like Old Testament patriarchs, served their conception of what constituted the public good without currying popularity or enslaving themselves to that remarkable master, whose power had not yet been discovered, "the will of the majority."

The inauguration of Andrew Jackson in 1829 began a new phase in the history of the Executive Office. Jackson was the beneficiary of the discovery of "the people," who in larger numbers than ever before were going to the polls to express electoral choices. Never thereafter would public policies—including especially those emanating from the White House—be presented as being what the nation ought to have, but instead, as what the people want.

Yet in the thirty years that followed Jackson's advent it was not always easy for a President to pander to or satisfy this emerging "democratic spirit." The tendency was for citizens to look to Congress rather than to the Chief Executive for the satisfaction they required. Although a number of the first fifteen Presidents were held in high esteem everywhere in the expanding country (and Washington and Jackson were revered figures), there was a widespread fear of government, expressed as a fear of a strong executive branch. The American recollection of George III faded slowly.

The Civil War and the herculean part that Abraham Lincoln played in it brought a change. A President, it seemed, could combine humanity with power, wage a modern war relentlessly but magnanimously, and preserve the constitutional structure under mortal attack. Lincoln's presidency became a new and inspiring model for occupants of the office. His immediate successors, however, were both products and victims of the rapid industrialization of America and the postwar letdown in the morality of public officeholders. As you look at the faces of these bearded men you may want to ponder the phrase of William Allen White, the Kansas editor, who saw them as "masks in a pageant."

The opening of the Twentieth Century coincided almost exactly with the accession of Theodore Roosevelt to the presidency. T.R. entered the national scene on the wings of America's seemingly easy victory over Spain in 1898. He brought youthfulness, unquenchable energy, and a keen sense of the direction in which "public opinion"—a phenomenon produced in part by the emergence of mass journalism—was leading the nation. He created the pattern that still is dominant in our conception of how a Chief Executive ought to comport himself, modified, to be sure, by the favorites who came after him—Wilson, Franklin Roosevelt, Eisenhower, Truman, and Kennedy.

From T.R.'s time to the present, the Presidents have been moving closer and closer to the people they serve. Although Lincoln was the first who was widely photographed, it was not until the newspaper halftone became a commonplace after 1900 that the President's face could regularly be seen in every home and with a variety of expressions. Then came the motion picture, which could show the President in action, the radio, which could bring his voice to every hearthside, and the television set, which could make him a veritable visitor in every living room. Moreover, the transcendent events that have occurred on the scene beyond our water's edge have made the Presidents of the United States world figures, whose comings and goings are of moment everywhere. Their policies, their family life, even their physical condition, have a reach into every corner of the earth. And when they leave the immediate scene they are remembered in foreign lands, not only through the statues and street names that daily recall their labors, but in programs and utterances like the Monroe Doctrine in the Nineteenth Century and the Truman Doctrine in our own, the Fourteen Points of Woodrow Wilson, the Four Freedoms of Franklin Roosevelt, Dwight Eisenhower's Atoms for Peace, and many others. Jefferson's prediction—"The election of a President of America, some years hence, will be much more interesting to certain nations of Europe, than ever the election of a King of Poland was"—has been gloriously fulfilled.

This collection of presidential portraits is a dignified and worthy tribute to the lofty office upon which they focus. In the individual pictures each of us may glimpse a moment of our history caught imperishably by the artist or the photographer. Collectively they and the character sketches accompanying them reveal the attitudes and qualities we as a people prize as our proudest heritage. This heritage is at the heart of our faith in the institutions and continuity of what John F. Kennedy liked to call "the Great Republic."

HENRY F. GRAFF

GEORGE WASHINGTON

FIRST PRESIDENT

On one of the obscure pages of history are detailed the wayside demonstrations and municipal welcomes that delayed Washington four days on his trip from Mount Vernon to New York to become President of the United States. At Philadelphia, as he passed under a laurel arch "a civic crown was, unperceived by him, let down upon his head by a youth ornamented with sprigs of laurel, who was assisted by machinery"; and at Trenton there was "a party of matrons leading their daughters dressed in white, who carried baskets of flowers in their hands and sang, with exquisite sweetness, an ode composed for the occasion" while they strewed flowers before him.

It is not hard to imagine the object of such exuberant affection, polite but impassive, pleased but thinking how unpopular he might be four years thence. For Washington was depressed by the prospect of the presidency, feeling unsure of his ability to conduct what he called "this experiment intrusted to the hands of the American people." At his inauguration, on

1

April 30 of 1789, after taking the oath of office on the balcony of Federal Hall, with a huge crowd spread out on the streets and roofs around him, he stepped inside to the Senate Chamber to deliver his inaugural address, and we have this description: "It was a very touching scene and quite of a solemn kind, his aspect grave, almost to sadness; his modesty actually shaking; his voice deep, a little tremulous, and so low as to call for close attention."

In spite of his incurable diffidence in the glare of public attention, Washington had been involved in politics since he was elected to the Virginia House of Burgesses at the age of twenty-six. When Patrick Henry startled the Burgesses—and all the American colonies—by rising in his buckskins to denounce the British Parliament's Stamp Act of 1765 and warn George III that he too, like Tarquin, Caesar, and Charles I, might be dethroned, Washington was not one of those who cried "Treason!" Cool and slow-thinking, he talked things over with his close friend George Mason, and joined the group that was willing to take the lead in resisting taxation. By 1769 he had reached the conclusion that he would not hesitate to take up arms, if necessary, to defend the liberty that was his right. When the first Continental Congress was called, he was one of the seven Virginia patriots representing that state.

The Continental Congress looked upon Washington as its military expert. His soldiering, however, had been done as a young man, and for the past sixteen years he had been preoccupied with his plantations. He stood straight, like a soldier, big-boned and tall—six feet according to the measure he sent to his London tailor—with a pale face lightly marked by smallpox and an uncommonly straight nose. In Congress he leaned heavily on the privilege of a soldier and farmer to be seen and not heard, although his understanding and judgment were second to none.

George was a younger son of a prosperous Virginia planter who died before he could provide a proper education for him. Augustine Washington, the father, left the finest part of his 5,000 acres to his eldest son, Lawrence, another property to his second son, and the small Ferry Farm near Fredericksburg to George, then eleven, the eldest child of his second wife. George spent part of the next few years with his mother and his little brothers and sister at the Ferry Farm, part with his half brothers. Lawrence took a particular fancy to him and made him his residuary legatee, so that due to Lawrence's early death and that of his only child, George came into the Mount Vernon and other properties at twenty-two.

In the meantime he learned surveying and at sixteen was in the Shenandoah Valley mapping Lord Fairfax's estate. Following the death of his brother Lawrence, he managed the Mount Vernon lands and was in command of the district militia. The French and Indian Wars took him to the Ohio frontier and raised him to the rank of colonel. He liked soldiering and the frontier life. He rode magnificently, enjoyed physical exertion, had complete personal courage and never understood how anybody could be a coward. His two brushes with the enemy on the frontier were woeful defeats, that of his own making at Great Meadows in 1754, and, with the blundering Braddock, near Fort Duquesne the next year. Returned from the wars in 1758, he settled down to his plantations, the House of Burgesses, and marriage with a spirited little widow, Martha Custis.

It is said that Washington was difficult to paint. Perhaps this is why in many of his portraits he is a bland and wooden figure. Actually he was a hearty man, could be roused to anger and to pound the table with a mighty oath, although his self-control was proverbial. His taciturnity and formality as President dropped away when he was in the midst of his friends and relations at Mount Vernon. He thoroughly enjoyed plantation life, its responsibilities and its pastimes—dancing, cards, raffles, barbecues, and the long southern house parties. He was a shrewd farmer, with an eye to improving the uses of land, the efficiency of his overseers, and the maintenance of the plantations. At the time of his death he was reputed one of the richest men and largest landholders in the country.

As commander of the American troops in the Revolution, he was wise, and sometimes brilliant, as in the strikes at Trenton and Princeton in the winter of 1776–77. He endured much in the way of criticism for being overcautious, but without his tenacity in keeping his army in the field for six long years, it is conceivable that the Revolution would have broken up into little clots of local resistance, a process that would have doomed it.

After the war, Washington fully expected to retire to Mount Vernon. He worried about his properties and longed to be at home, and he was in fact left in peace for a short time. He was required to preside over the Constitutional Convention in 1787, where, even as the constitutional provisions for the presidency were being written, it was commonly said that he should be the first to fill that office. The electors, each of whom had two votes, all cast a vote for him, making his election unanimous. Their second votes were divided, the greater number going to John Adams, who therefore became Vice President. Diffident as he was about his own capabilities, Washington set a magnificent standard for American presidents in holding his contentious and self-serving countrymen on a reasonably steady course. He was profoundly disturbed by the appearance of factionalism, and it was his fear of disunity that impelled him to serve a second term, to which he was again unanimously elected.

The "Farewell Address," which Washington wrote with the help of James Madison and Alexander Hamilton and published in the autumn before he left office, delivered to the American people some severe thoughts on the political turbulence of his second four years. It stands today, not as advice on what government policy should be, but as advice on political attitudes and discipline.

While he was in office Washington took no part in politics. He could not think as a party man, nor could he let himself be too distracted by party tantrums. Instead he had the courage to force the American people to stay out of the wars in Europe, in spite of the intrigues of the pro-French Republican party and the pro-British Federalists. In dealing with the British, he persuaded the people, and the Senate, to accept the best possible conditions he could get in the Jay Treaty, though the treaty was received in America with more anger than approval. When he retired from the presidency, he was a greater man and more beloved than on the day he passed under the laurel arches on his way to assume the office.

Washington lived less than three years after his retirement. The celebrated funeral oration delivered before Congress by one of his closest friends, General Henry ("Light-Horse Harry") Lee, coined the popular summary of his life: "First in war, first in peace, first in the hearts of his countrymen."

HIGHLIGHTS OF HIS ADMINISTRATION

⋙ Establishment of a sound financial basis for the Federal government under a proposal by Secretary of the Treasury Alexander Hamilton to assume the Revolutionary War debts of the states and, with the Federal debt, refinance the whole at par.

⋙ Establishment of a national bank to handle Federal bonds, notes, and deposits.

⋙ Taxes for revenue, including one on spirituous liquors that provoked the "Whisky Rebellion" of 1794 among the farmers of the Monongahela Valley in Pennsylvania.

⋙ Choice of a site on the Potomac for a Federal City, the capital to be Philadelphia until 1800.

⋙ Declaration of American neutrality in the war declared by France against England and Spain. Washington demanded recall of the French minister, who sought to use the United States as a base for French military and privateering operations. British seizures of American ships carrying French goods or sailing to French ports caused severe losses by the American merchant marine and provoked indignation in the United States that was a constant threat to neutrality.

◆§ Battle of the Fallen Timbers, August 20, 1794, in which General "Mad Anthony" Wayne decisively defeated a force of Indians and Canadian rangers on the Maumee River, near Lake Erie, leading to a peace agreement with the Indians that opened the northwest to settlers.

◆§ Treaty with England negotiated by John Jay, partially composing the differences between the United States and England. It provided for British evacuation of frontier posts in the American northwest but did not satisfy American demand for a halt to the seizure of American ships at sea. It was signed on November 19, 1794. Received badly in the United States, especially by pro-French elements, it barely passed the Senate.

◆§ Treaty with Spain, signed in October 1795, which stabilized the Florida border and gave the southwestern frontier a commercial outlet by way of the Mississippi and New Orleans.

◆§ The emergence of political parties. To Washington's profound regret, two factions appeared with the debate on Hamilton's fiscal policies and the war between England and France. Hamilton and the party he called Federalist attracted the commercial and business interests, the upper strata of society and those who were by self-interest or merely association pro-British. Jefferson organized the Republican party that appealed to the farmers, the workingmen, and the liberals who sympathized with republican France. Each party had extremists and their intrigues sometimes threatened national unity.

JOHN
ADAMS

SECOND PRESIDENT

John Adams, in one of his frequent moments of self-criticism, wrote in a letter: "I have never sacrificed my judgment to kings, ministers, nor people, and I never will. When either shall see as I do, I shall rejoice in their protection, aid, and honor; but I see no prospect that either will ever think as I do, and therefore I shall never be a favorite with either."

Such was the wry boast of the "Father of Independence," the Boston puritan who brought the Declaration of Independence, composed by Thomas Jefferson, to the floor of the Continental Congress, defended it, and guided it to passage. As Daniel Webster said of that performance, his "power, both of thought and of expression . . . moved us from our seats."

Obviously Adams is no authority on Adams, except in the subtle interpretations of a psychologist. Personally a tactless and vain man, his great moral vision of public duty could light a fire in him that made him a shining patriot. In this manner he took the issue of British colonial taxes, which he considered illegal, and debated it into the cause of liberty. By 1770 he was the intellectual leader in Boston of this cause, so secure in his reputation that he made a great gesture of legal morality and defended the British Captain Preston and his soldiers when they stood trial for murder in perpetrating the "Boston Massacre."

With all his unique personal qualities, Adams was in many ways a typical product of frontier society in New England. His father was a farmer, and also the village shoemaker in Braintree (now Quincy) just south of Boston. A family tradition was that the eldest son should be given an education and thus a chance to raise his station in life, if it were financially possible. The preferred station was the ministry, and with this in view, Adams was sent to Harvard. Shortly after graduation, however, he convinced himself that the ministry was not for him and turned to the law. His decision was apparently the right one, for in a comparatively short time he built up one of the largest law practices in Massachusetts and handled the legal business of several wealthy and prominent men.

Physically Adams was not impressive. A small man, he grew fat with middle age—his enemies delighted to refer to him as "His Rotundity." He had the good fortune to marry a woman with many of the warm, personal qualities that he lacked and with equal intelligence. It was an extremely happy marriage, and the man who had the reputation of being the most ungracious person in public life was at home the tenderest husband and father. Through his prolonged absences from home, husband and wife kept up a correspondence that shows them both in an engaging relationship. The letters of Abigail Adams have long been considered one of the charming commentaries on American history.

Adams was one of the Massachusetts delegates to the First Continental Congress in 1774 and was a member of Congress until 1777. He served laboriously on its committees, most notably as chairman of the Board of War and Ordnance. By a stroke of genius, in 1775 he chose Washington to lead the military effort of the Revolution and persuaded Congress to put him at the head of the valiant but untrained army of militiamen then besieging Boston.

Congress sent Adams to France as one of its three commissioners in 1777, but characteristically, he made an independent review of the operating efficiency of the commission and advised Congress that it did not need three men to do the work that could be done by one. Congress took his advice and turned over the commission's work to a single member, not Adams, but Benjamin Franklin, who was also the highly successful minister to France. Adams was delighted to return home.

Diplomatic missions in Europe were to absorb most of Adams's efforts for the next decade. In 1780 he was eminently successful in Holland in obtaining recognition of American independence and substantial loans to Congress. Two years later he was one of the American commissioners in Paris negotiating peace with England. In 1785 he was sent as minister to England, in which difficult and lonely post he was at least consoled by having his family with him. The English, who at first received him very politely, proceeded to ignore him as best they could. Finally he resigned, in 1789.

Adams's election as Washington's Vice President was something of a misfortune to Adams and to Washington. To be the runner-up in the contest for the presidency, that is, to be elected Vice President, was to be relegated to comparative uselessness. Adams detested his sole official duty, which was to preside over the Senate. Neither the duty nor the Senate was important enough for his capacities. At the same time, Washington was deprived of an adviser or diplomat who could have been enormously useful to him.

In the self-discipline with which he accepted whatever public service was required of him, Adams ranks with Washington. But he was also a proud and jealous man. In a bitter partisan campaign in 1796, he was elected President by only three electoral votes, Jefferson having the next greatest number of votes and becoming Vice President. The narrowness of his margin humiliated Adams.

Since, like Washington, he was a Federalist, he retained Washington's cabinet. It was some time before he realized that he did not command its loyalty. Nor, in fact, did he have any appreciable support from the members of his own party. Alexander Hamilton, though now retired to private life, continued to dominate his party. This extraordinary man, a West Indian immigrant in his youth, a parvenu who rose to statesmanship in Washington's administration, played an almost wicked part in Adams's career. An egotistical man who disliked to yield control of the Federalists to its titular head, and who disliked Adams personally, Hamilton controlled Adams's cabinet, until in 1800 the President became partly aware of the treachery and dismissed his Secretary of State, Timothy Pickering. Adams's defeat for re-election that year and the demise of the Federalist party resulted from the revelation of Hamilton's intrigue within the party against Adams.

With all his political disappointments, Adams made a good President. Inheriting from Washington the hazards of neutrality in the war between England and France, but with France now the troublemaker, he stood

9

fast against the war hawks at home and the provocations abroad. In the end, in a typical Adams moment of spontaneous decision, he opened negotiations with France and ended the state of tension that was close to a declared war. He should be credited with promoting naval construction, a program that unfortunately his successor, Jefferson, neglected.

Adams was the first President to live in the fine new President's House, but there was no comfort or satisfaction in it for him, either physically or spiritually. He was bitter over his defeat for a second term, so bitter that he refused to take part in the inauguration of Jefferson, slipping out of Washington early in the morning of the day his opponent took the oath of office. He lived to be ninety years old and to see his son, John Quincy, President, dying, like Jefferson, on the 50th anniversary of the Declaration of Independence.

HIGHLIGHTS OF HIS ADMINISTRATION

◆§ The dispute with France over French seizure of "neutral" American ships, provoking the "X,Y,Z Affair." This was an attempt to negotiate the dispute, foundering on a devious maneuver by the French minister Talleyrand to secure a large American loan plus something for his own pocket. The American commissioners sent to France were not received by Talleyrand because they declined to comply with his terms. Publication of their correspondence on the affair intensified the war fever in the United States, with the popular cry: "Millions for Defense, but not One Cent for Tribute."

◆§ Sea fights during the undeclared war with France, in which the Americans checked French depredations on American ships in the Caribbean. In one notable action, on February 9, 1799, the new American frigate *Constellation* captured the French frigate *L'Insurgent* off Nevis Island in the West Indies.

◆§ Signing of a convention with France in 1800, in which peace was re-established.

◆§ The Sedition, Naturalization, and Alien laws. These acts were passed in an effort to control political disaffection. The Sedition Act extended the common interpretation of sedition to include false or malicious writings against the President or Congress in order to arouse hatred

10

toward them. The Naturalization and Alien Acts aimed at control of the influx of radical foreigners. The Republicans attacked the laws as violations of personal liberty and free speech. Madison drew up Resolutions, passed by the Virginia legislature, and Jefferson composed Resolutions, passed in Kentucky, asserting the right of the states to oppose the Federal government in a matter interpreting the Constitution.

THOMAS JEFFERSON

———◄◉►———

THIRD PRESIDENT

The political ascent of the common man owes as much to Jefferson as to
any other statesman. He was not only the chief author of the Declaration
of Independence, but his ideas for improving the human institutions of
government, civil law, and education have become imbedded in the faith
on which American democracy rests. Many of these took form in his revision of the legislative code of Virginia: separation of church and state;
universal suffrage; public education from primary grade to university;
humane objectives in the criminal code; retirement from public law of
the concept that large estates could be kept together by entailing their
inheritance to eldest sons. He also foresaw at this time the rise of the
Negro problem and urged abolition of slavery and the deportation of slaves.
In his Northwest Ordinance of 1784 he provided a pattern of laws used
in the government of territories from 1787 on, although his most important
proposal, that slavery be excluded from western lands after 1800, was
rejected.

During the preparation of the Constitution, Jefferson was absent, as minister to France, but he approved of it, except that he criticized the lack of a bill of rights, a lack that was later remedied by the Bill of Rights amendments. In the sorely controversial issue over the powers of the states versus the power of the central government, he believed in a strong federation; but since his entire political philosophy rested on popular responsibility at local levels, he advocated state sovereignty in certain areas of law and administration.

Although a poor public speaker and no debater, Jefferson was a skillful organizer and in his own quiet, withdrawn way could be a deadly opponent. His Republican party, into which he drew the farmers and workingmen, the "producers" of the country, was destined to have a much wider appeal than Hamilton's Federalists, based on a select class of wealth and privilege. It was to remain fundamentally the party of the people and states' rights, progenitor of the Democratic party.

Jefferson was an enigma to many people, especially those who could not understand his warm concern for human beings in the mass. He was by nature a man of strong attachments, to his family, to Virginia, to the idea of a united nation, and as gradually was to appear, an expanding nation. His birth was not different from that of many another Virginia farmer. His father, although a plain, uneducated man, had married into the rich and prominent Randolph family, but moved from his plantation in tidewater Virginia to the west, settling near Charlottesville. Young Tom grew up to be tall—six foot two—red-haired, and as he lost his ungainly boyish look, quite handsome. He followed the pattern for young men of his position: education at William and Mary College in Williamsburg; a law career combined with the care and improvement of the plantations inherited from his father; membership in the Virginia House of Burgesses. He enjoyed the social life of Williamsburg, where he spent much of his time and where he was married.

In the mounting spirit of protest of the early 1770's against the tax laws of the British Parliament, Jefferson took the lead with Patrick Henry and other "radical" young Virginians in giving the protest form and purpose. He was elected to the Second Continental Congress, and after his notable service there in 1776, returned to Virginia, where he thought there was greater need for his services in mustering the state's resources to supply Washington's army. He did this so effectively that when the British army moved into Virginia in 1781, there were not enough men left equipped to defend their native soil. The state legislature and Jefferson, then governor, fled from the capital at Richmond just before it was burned by

14

the British, and took refuge in Charlottesville. Tarleton was sent in pursuit and nearly caught up with Jefferson at his residence, Monticello. It was the last year of the fighting, for Cornwallis surrendered at Yorktown that October.

Jefferson was one of that flying squad of statesmen who served the new republic wherever they were required, not by choice but by necessity. It was extremely hard to find qualified men who would take government jobs, put aside their private affairs in these uncertain times, and do so at a stingy government salary. Jefferson was crushed by the death of his wife in 1782. Yet he was back in Congress the following year. Then a plum was offered him, a mission to France to negotiate commercial treaties. Shortly he replaced Benjamin Franklin as American minister to France, a post that he found extraordinarily congenial. His personal charm and his wide-ranging interests in the French scene made him highly acceptable to Frenchmen, and he reciprocated the regard. He was delighted to pursue his interest in architecture, gathering material which he was to use later to embellish Monticello. Toward the developing phases of the French Revolution, although officially aloof, he found himself taking the position of the benign but conservative friend, suggesting moderation. French republicanism was far too radical and violent for him.

Jefferson's four years as Washington's Secretary of State served to harden his own republicanism and turn his thoughts to the organization of a party. Alexander Hamilton, then Secretary of the Treasury and in the midst of his brilliant reorganization of Federal finances, aroused his opposition. The two men were born to be antagonists, with no understanding or tolerance of each other. Jefferson regarded Hamilton's policies as a pernicious attempt to convert the republican form of government provided by the Constitution into a centralized government in the hands of a rich and privileged class. He found this disrespectful of the Constitution and contemptuous of the rights of the people. Washington, with Olympian fairness, tried to work with both men and keep a pacific atmosphere in the cabinet, but he was personally closer to Hamilton and generally in any dispute gave him the decision. Jefferson left the cabinet at the end of 1793, wisely deciding that his continuance in the government was useful to no one.

Like Washington returning to Mount Vernon, Jefferson always returned eagerly to Monticello. The care and improvement of his 10,000 acres led him to explore scientific farming, and the mansion gave him, over a long and satisfying period of years, the chance to practice his

15

avocation of architect. Then too the next three years at Monticello were busy politically, as he assumed the leadership of a new party. His term as Vice President in John Adams's Federalist administration saw the rise of the Republican party and the decline of the Federalist party, foundering in the animosity between Adams and Hamilton. In the 1800 presidential election, the Republicans intended to vote for Jefferson as President and Aaron Burr as Vice President, but the electoral law still did not recognize a separate vote for each of these offices. Jefferson and Burr received the same number of electoral votes, which meant a tied election that must be decided by the House of Representatives. Hamilton had the votes in the House to throw the election either to Jefferson or to Burr. He wisely preferred Jefferson as President in spite of his antipathy toward him.

Jefferson, the first President inaugurated at Washington, ended what he considered the kingly pomp of Washington and Adams and introduced a democratic simplicity in official manners. His re-election in 1804 was by a handsome margin. The Twelfth Amendment had now simplified the count by specifying a vote for President and one for Vice President. At the end of his second term, with his friend Madison ensconced in the presidency, he retired to Monticello, where for the next sixteen years he occupied himself with the design and building of his great liberal college, the University of Virginia. He was proud to be chosen its rector, and, happily, lived long enough to see the central buildings completed to the point where students could be enrolled. Business misfortunes and excessive hospitality to the hordes of admirers who wished to visit him reduced him to poverty, and he was finally forced to accept public contributions in order to live out his days at Monticello. He, like John Adams, died on the 50th anniversary of the Declaration of Independence.

HIGHLIGHTS OF HIS ADMINISTRATION

◦§ The purchase of Louisiana from France for $15,000,000, increasing the public domain by 140 per cent, in 1803.

◦§ The Lewis and Clark exploration of the Northwest, in 1804–06.

◦§ The successful war against Tripoli, 1804–05. By an American naval operation combined with a land attack by an adventurous American, William Eaton, with a small private army, its Pasha was induced to bow to American demands that he abandon his practice of levying tribute on American shipping.

❧ The treason trial of Aaron Burr, in 1807, in which he was acquitted.

❧ The embargo on American shipping to foreign ports, 1807–09, in an attempt to avoid entanglement in the war between England and France.

❧ The *Chesapeake-Leopard* Affair, the most inflammatory incident in the prelude to the War of 1812. The British *Leopard*, in 1807, caught the American frigate *Chesapeake* off its guard, fired at close range, and forced it to surrender. Three sailors were taken off the American ship on the ground that they were British deserters.

JAMES MADISON

———◄◉►———

FOURTH PRESIDENT

When he rose to speak in the Constitutional Convention at Philadelphia in 1787, he was so short that the delegates could scarcely spot him among the big men of the Virginia delegation. His voice was so thin that even the reporter had to strain his ears. He spoke merely from notes written in a minute hand on slips of paper, with hardly a gesture and no flowers of oratory. Yet every delegate leaned to attention, for "the great little Madison" had the floor. As John Marshall said, "If convincing is eloquence, he was the most eloquent man I ever heard." James Madison was, of all the Revolutionary statesmen, the authority on government.

When the Virginia delegation brought to the Convention the plan that became the pivot of discussion, it was one outlined by Madison. As the delegates settled down to take up the Constitution article by article, he was the member most constantly in attendance, rising to his feet a dozen times a day to explain, to inform, and to direct the debate. Not only was he the most knowledgeable political scientist present, but his powerful mind gave him the wisdom to interpret his knowledge along the lines most useful to the matter in hand. In addition, with remarkable industry, he kept full notes on the proceedings, which constitute the best record we have of the Convention.

Bringing the Constitutional Convention into being was in a sense a personal triumph for Madison, though he was too canny a politician to push himself to the front in a movement that depended for its success on the co-operation of many men. The need for reforming the Federal government was apparent to Washington and most thinking people, but state jealousies were an obstacle. Madison was then a member of the Virginia legislature and one of the prominent exponents of a stronger central government. The possibility of approaching it indirectly through the commercial interests of the states occurred to him after he had brought Virginia and Maryland together to harmonize their customs rules along the Potomac. He persuaded the Virginia Assembly to suggest to all the states a meeting at Annapolis to discuss general trade regulations. Only five states sent delegates and the convention disbanded in three days, but it supplied a platform from which an address was issued to all the states calling for a constitutional convention at Philadelphia to take up all their common problems. The initiative was thus handed to the states with consummate tact, and the appeal succeeded.

In the popular pastime of awarding titles to the founding fathers the only candidate for "Father of the Constitution" is Madison. It is not enough for him, for he was a man of interesting and unusual talents, aside from his genius as a lawmaker. He first appeared in politics at the age of twenty-five, when through the influence of his father, he was elected to the Virginia Convention that met in 1776 to organize a government for the new state. In the midst of the wealthy and conservative men who now took this grave step, "Jemmy" Madison was a timid young man who rose to his feet only once, to offer an amendment on religious freedom. Although the son and heir of an important landholder of Orange County, he looked more like a pale and sickly scholar, which in fact he was. He took to scholarship as a boy and had been interested in practically nothing else. As an undergraduate at Princeton his only indiscretion was an attempt to eliminate sleep so that he could study longer. After he reduced it to three hours a day, his health broke down. He was now at home recuperating, restless and lonely, not sufficiently fulfilled in his studies and in the task he had assumed of tutoring his little brothers and sisters, physically unfit for military service in the Revolution, and by taste unfit to enjoy the pastimes of Virginia country society.

Politics proved the answer. He became a professional in it of the most intelligent kind, combining political science and law with practical skill in bringing men and issues together. For ten years he was a member of either the Virginia legislature or the Continental Congress. He worked with Alexander Hamilton to secure both a strong Federal constitution and its ratification by the states. In the latter effort, he and Hamilton produced the best interpretation of the Constitution in "The Federalist" papers, of which Madison wrote twenty-nine. Elected to the First United States Congress, he was Washington's floor leader in the House of Representatives, and on a personal basis, the only man outside of his cabinet whose advice Washington regularly sought. It was in these circumstances that Madison sent to the President, who expected to take leave of public life after one term, the passages that Washington later incorporated into his "Farewell Address."

Personally Madison was good-humored and without vanity. He got on well with almost everybody, and his wife, the irresistible Dolly, was perhaps the most popular and celebrated in the social graces of all the Presidents' wives. The Madison plantation, Montpelier, beautifully situated in the rolling country east of the Blue Ridge, commanded more of Madison's time and affection as he grew older. Like Jefferson at Monticello, he spent a great deal of money enlarging and decorating the mansion, and loved to have company there.

With Jefferson's withdrawal from the Washington administration, following the split with Hamilton, Madison gravitated to Jefferson and the Republicans. He became leader of the Republican opposition in the House, in which role he very nearly defeated the bill to finance the Jay Treaty with England. When Jefferson became President, Madison became his Secretary of State and served as such for eight years. It was assumed that he was Jefferson's choice for the presidency in 1808, and he enjoyed an easy nomination and election. He took office in the most perilous times. The war between France and England threatened to destroy American commerce or force America to abandon a neutral status. With an aroused anti-French faction and an equally angry anti-British faction dividing American politics, steering a peaceable middle course was becoming increasingly difficult.

Madison was a pacific man. He lacked the sternness to bully factions, and in relation to England and France he trusted too much to the power of economic weapons. Faced with French and English decrees that interdicted American shipping on the entire coast of western Europe, he tried to manipulate nonintercourse to obtain relaxation of the decrees by one side or the other. He chose to believe Napoleon's unscrupulous promises and thus favored France, while he imposed nonintercourse on England. The effect was to make England appear the chief villain and to intensify American feeling against her. At the same time, with the elections of 1810, there appeared in Congress a new crop of Republicans, young and aggressive, led by Henry Clay and John C. Calhoun, who demanded war with England. Madison yielded to them and embarked on a war that was futile, that the country was in no way equipped to fight, either in men, weapons, or money.

When the War of 1812 was over, the loss column showed a large national debt, the destruction of the government buildings in Washington, the near disaffection of New England; the credit column showed some military lessons learned through defeats, some brave naval engagements for the history books and Andrew Jackson, the hero of the battle for New Orleans. In retiring from the presidency to the solace of Montpelier, Madison was forced to look beyond the war and congratulate the American people on the Constitution.

HIGHLIGHTS OF HIS ADMINISTRATION

⊌§ The War of 1812, declared June 18, ended by the Peace of Ghent, without advantage to either England or the United States, on December 24, 1814. The most famous naval engagements were the American victories on Lake Erie and Lake Champlain; at sea the defeat of the British *Guerrière* by the *Constitution*, the capture of the British *Macedonian* by the *United States*, and the loss of the *Chesapeake* to the British *Shannon*. The worst land defeat was the capture of Washington by the British; the greatest land victory was the Battle of New Orleans, fought after peace had been signed.

⊌§ Tippecanoe. Here, Governor William Henry Harrison of the Indiana Territory crushed Indian resistance organized by Tecumseh and his brother, the Prophet, in 1811.

⊌§ Disaffection in New England. The stubborn radicals of the Federalist party, in a spirit of opposition to the Republicans and the Virginia dynasty in Washington, proposed separation of New England from the Union. A minority group, they stiffened New England's resistance to the War of 1812 so that Madison's call for help with money and

22

militia was generally refused. The Hartford Convention of December 1814, to which Massachusetts, Connecticut, and Rhode Island sent delegates, proved to be the first step in a move toward disunion. The Peace of Ghent, following in the same month, terminated the movement.

◆§ Re-establishment of a national bank, the Second Bank of the United States (opened in January 1817), found necessary to stabilize currency and handle government obligations. It was chartered for twenty years. Four-fifths of its capital and its board of directors were private. It was not taxable, but it paid the Treasury a bonus for its privileges.

JAMES MONROE

FIFTH PRESIDENT

In the severe political relapse that followed the war with England, the election of a calm and conciliatory President well expressed the mood of the people. James Monroe was able to move into a renovated President's House, whose scorched walls had been covered with a thick coat of white paint, and he set himself to renew the will of Americans to live together. Remembering the success of Washington's grand tours, and considering that the war warranted a look at the military and naval establishment, he set off in the summer of 1817 on what was originally billed as a private inspection of national defenses in the northeast. The private inspection quickly unfolded into a public progress that drew great crowds. New Englanders in particular turned out to see the President, the first one to come among them in some years. The response was so enthusiastic that a newspaper coined the phrase "Era of Good Feeling."

Monroe was at this time a man with fifty years of public office behind him. He had not the intellect or forcefulness of the presidents before him, but he was a good man with a friendly manner. Jefferson had said of him, "He is a man whose soul might be turned wrong side outwards without discovering a blemish to the world." He passed through his first term so blamelessly that his second election lacked one vote of being unanimous. A New Hampshire elector explained that he did not think anyone but Washington should have the honor of a unanimous vote.

The President was the fourth Virginian to serve, but not of the planter aristocracy. His father owned a small farm, near the Rappahannock River, in Westmoreland County. As a boy, James walked several miles through a natural wilderness to a country school, often in company with another lad, named John Marshall. By good fortune, since he lost his father early, James's mother had a brother who was a judge and an influential man in Fredericksburg. This uncle was good to the boy, paid his bills at the College of William and Mary, took him into his home, and in general, treated him as a son.

The call to arms in 1775 was answered readily by young Virginians, for the state was crackling with patriotic sentiment. Monroe, aged seventeen, went north to join Washington's Continental Army with the 3rd Virginia, as a second-lieutenant. Three years of soldiering brought him up to the rank of major, got him a wound at Trenton and a handsome commendation from Washington. Returning to Williamsburg in the hope of recruiting more troops, he found Virginia drained dry. After a few frustrating and restless months, he was appointed aide to the governor, Thomas Jefferson. It was the connection that determined Monroe's future. Jefferson, who had the least possible use for military trappings, proposed to teach the young man law, and the offer was eagerly accepted. Congenial to the study of law was election to the state legislature. Thus Monroe became one of Jefferson's first political converts, as he was to remain the most loyal and amenable.

Winning elections was so easy to Monroe that he decided to drop his law practice and make a career of officeholding. By this time he had rolled up a respectable record of elections, to the Virginia legislature, the Continental Congress, and finally the United States Senate. To be closer to his great patron, he moved from Fredericksburg to Charlottesville and bought land near Jefferson's Monticello, where he planned a mansion to be called Ash Lawn and to be built after Jefferson's designs. By this time he was married, having captured the heart of a haughty young miss from New York, and he enjoyed the social and financial prestige that had been his goal since boyhood.

Though of a careful and sensible disposition, it was probably unlikely that Monroe should pass unscathed through the political strife of the mid-1790's. As a supporter of Jefferson's young Republican party, he was bound to share its hates and loves, and when Washington chose him as minister to the French Republic, which would accept no American minister but a Republican, he was bound to show where his sympathies lay. Washington chose Monroe in the hope that, though pro-French in sympathy, he would be cool enough to uphold American neutrality. In the war between France and England that was of first importance. To maintain neutrality, Washington constantly resisted pressures by French and British partisans at home, while he sought to persuade England to stop interfering with American ships at sea. If he could hold relations with France steady and negotiate a suitable agreement with England, he would save the United States from being drawn into the war.

Monroe began his duty in France with a flowery speech to the French Convention and an exchange of embraces with its president. Reproved by the nervous State Department for this display, he still assured the French government that nothing would disturb traditional American good will toward France, certainly not John Jay's treaty negotiations then going on in London. When the terms of the Jay Treaty were released, they were far more conciliatory to England than he had been led to expect. Washington pointed out later that it was his duty to defend it to the French, regardless of his own opinion. The President also suspected him of furnishing the Republicans at home with information to use in political attacks on the Federalists. Recalled as minister, Monroe returned to Philadelphia the center of a swirling controversy. Blaming Federalist foreign policy and the personal enmity of Secretary of State Pickering for his recall, he set about preparing a 500-page vindication of his conduct in France.

This was Monroe's only political misadventure in his long career. It showed that he was not made for controversy. A lesser quarrel with Alexander Hamilton after his return from France was handled with more dignity. In this affair Hamilton accused him of releasing a five-year-old story of a blackmail attempt against Hamilton based on his relations with a woman. Monroe had been one of three men who investigated the incident, since it involved charges against Hamilton's public integrity, cleared him, and agreed to keep the whole thing quiet. The story appearing in print at the time of Monroe's recall convinced Hamilton that Monroe had released it in a spirit of political vindictiveness. Monroe said this was not true. Whether or not he knew how the story leaked out, or whether he was in any way responsible, he never said.

Remaining in Virginia during the regime of Federalist John Adams, Monroe was returned to public life by President Jefferson, who entrusted him with several diplomatic missions. Among these was one as special envoy to help negotiate the Louisiana Purchase. As Jefferson's retirement from office drew near and the question of who should succeed him was raised, attempts were made to lure Monroe into declaring his candidacy. As he was sure that Jefferson favored Madison, Monroe resisted the temptation, and had his reward on Madison's retirement. He was more especially sure of the Republican nomination in 1816 because of his prominence in Madison's cabinet, as Secretary of State, and in the darkest days of the war with England after the burning of Washington, as interim Secretary of War.

"Tall and eel-like Monroe" was one unkind but witty description of the fifth President. He took himself too seriously, lacked humor, and was sentimental about his Revolutionary background. But he conducted an admirable administration. It was a time of rising nationalism and he was in sympathy with it, but he kept it temperate. With nationalism came a surge toward territorial expansion, and he triumphed in buying Florida from Spain, which also eliminated the chronic Indian-Spanish troubles on that border. He had not, to be sure, an answer to the bank panic of 1819 that trailed years of depression behind it. But discovering that the Second Bank of the United States had become involved in the speculation that led to the panic, he reorganized the bank in the hope that its controls on banking would function better in the future. His most productive policy, perhaps, was in choosing a strong cabinet, and in using it, as had Washington, to the fullest extent. The credit for the Monroe Doctrine belongs to his Secretary of State, for John Quincy Adams supplied both the boldness and the imagination to produce such a large gesture in international politics.

HIGHLIGHTS OF HIS ADMINISTRATION

ê The Monroe Doctrine, incorporated in Monroe's annual message of December 2, 1823, developed from a suggestion by British Foreign Secretary George Canning that in view of the probability that the Holy Alliance in Europe would try to help Spain recover her possessions in the Western Hemisphere that had revolted and established their independence, the United States should join England in declaring that they were opposed to such a move. Canning's interest was entirely selfish, resulting from British commercial interests in South America and tentative interest in acquiring Cuba. Secretary of State Adams would not be drawn into such an agreement with England, but he saw the value of a broad statement along the same line undertaken on

American initiative. The key sentences in the Doctrine: "We should consider any attempt on their [European powers'] part to extend their system to any portion of this hemisphere as dangerous to our peace and safety . . . we could not view any interposition for the purpose of oppressing them [governments who have declared their independence], or controlling in any other manner their destiny, by any European power in any other light than as a manifestation of an unfriendly disposition toward the United States."

⋅§ The Seminole War, in which Andrew Jackson was sent against the Seminoles who in 1817 were raiding American lands, recently ceded by the Creeks, north of the Florida border. He pursued the Seminoles into Florida, and boldly exceeding his instructions, occupied that part of Florida, sending the Spanish governor and garrisons off to Cuba. The United States restored the occupied territory to Spain, much to Jackson's indignation.

⋅§ Purchase of Florida from Spain for $5,000,000, negotiated in 1819. Territory inaugurated July 17, 1821, with Andrew Jackson as governor.

⋅§ The Missouri Compromise, result of the first debate in Congress over extension of slave territory west of the Mississippi. It provided that Missouri be admitted as a state without restriction on slavery, but that slavery be prohibited north of 36° 30′ north in the rest of the Louisiana Purchase lands.

JOHN QUINCY ADAMS

SIXTH PRESIDENT

John Quincy, like his father, John Adams, had a long, illustrious career as a statesman, but not primarily in the presidency. He wanted to be President, in fact, he wanted it so much that he abandoned his lofty attitude that the office should be spontaneously offered to him, as it had been to Washington, and scratched humbly for votes. In the 1824 election, none of the four candidates came up with a majority, Adams being second to Andrew Jackson in electoral votes garnered. Lack of a majority threw the election into the House of Representatives, according to the provisions of the Twelfth Amendment. The House was now required to choose among the three candidates with the greatest number of votes. The fourth candidate, who had been eliminated but who still had some of the votes in his pocket, was Henry Clay. By securing the states under Clay's control in the House plus two more states, Adams was elected by one vote, having thirteen of twenty-four states.

To be even a "minority President" was more than most men wise in politics would have expected of him. He was not only hopelessly stiff and ungracious on public occasions, he treated individuals as if they were issues instead of warm-blooded, sensitive human beings, thus making enemies out of men who might have been his friends. He should have been more impressionable, for he had been given every opportunity to adapt himself to the amenities of public life. At the age of ten he went along on his father's first mission to France and for the next eight years enjoyed somewhat precociously the blessings of being John Adams's son. Besides being given the opportunity to study at the University of Leyden, he went to Russia at fifteen as secretary to the American minister and served as his father's secretary in his ministry to England at eighteen. The Harvard instinct was strong, however, and John Quincy returned home to complete his education there. He then studied law and set up a practice in Boston.

Washington appointed Adams minister to the Netherlands, an auspicious beginning to a distinguished diplomatic career, which he suspended at his father's advice when Jefferson was elected President. There was nothing at home that could match the excitement of Europe, however, not even the four years he served in the United States Senate during the period of precarious neutrality in the war between France and England—a policy which had his support. Madison restored him to the diplomatic orbit, sending him as minister to Russia for five years, and placing in his hands the peace negotiations that ended the War of 1812 with England. When Monroe set about assembling his cabinet in 1817, Adams was minister to England. Monroe brought him home and appointed him Secretary of State, an office in which he added considerable dignity and luster to the Monroe administration.

In the prime of life when he became President, John Quincy Adams was short and stout, with a bald head and black eyes that grew rheumy from the immense amount of correspondence and paperwork he handled with his own pen in the White House. He always rose before dawn and read a chapter in the Bible. Then he set out on a brisk walk to the Capitol and back, if it were winter, or, if the weather were warm, took a sunrise swim in the Potomac. Unwilling, or temperamentally unable, to delegate authority, he filled his day with administrative chores, great and small, and saw practically any visitor who wanted to see him. In the evening he wrote in his *Diary*, the record of his life and thoughts that he began in boyhood and kept for sixty years.

Although reputed to be a cold and harsh man, Adams was easily touched by expressions of admiration and friendship. Overburdened with theory and the speculations of an analytical mind, he could, under the

beneficent influence of appreciative company, turn into a lively con-
versationalist, full of wit and allusion to a wide range of interests. The
presidency gave him little chance for such company. He worried constantly
about his wife, who was delicate and nervous, and about the eldest of his
three sons, an unstable young man on whom he lavished volumes of good
advice. He abandoned his own political career largely to chance, though
he might have used the politicians who agreed with him, such as Henry
Clay and Daniel Webster, to shape a personal organization.

In his first annual message, Adams proposed a grand plan for national
improvements including a Department of the Interior, a Naval Academy,
a system of roads and canals, a uniform system of weights and measures,
and other government institutions. In only one area of public concern was
there any congressional action and this resulted in the "Tariff of Abomina-
tions" passed in 1828, purporting to be a protective measure but actually a
patchwork of rates designed for political effect. With many matters
awaiting attention, the business of government was laid aside while the
factional opposition concentrated on destroying him and putting Andrew
Jackson into office at the next election.

The anti-Adams campaign was highly effective under the management
of Martin Van Buren, Senator from New York. Every message to Congress
or administrative act of Adams was turned to his disadvantage by the
Jackson men. The appointment of Clay as Secretary of State, immediately
following the election, was made to appear the result of a corrupt deal
between Clay and Adams to get Adams elected; Adams's policies of internal
improvements and a protective tariff were made to appear as tyrannical
schemes to centralize government at the expense of the states; even Adams's
personal honesty was attacked in whatever way would destroy his credit
with the people. This witches' brew of trumped-up prejudices and passions
produced the unsavory election of 1828, in which Andrew Jackson and his
Democratic Republicans were swept into office.

After his defeat at the polls, John Quincy Adams, now sixty-one,
thought to retire to his farm; but no sooner had he got the Adams mansion
in Quincy refurbished and livable than the Anti-Masonic party begged
him to become their candidate for Congress from the Plymouth district.
Elected in 1830, he served seventeen years, perhaps the most illustrious
years of his life. Known as "old man eloquent," independent and belligerent,
he fought a winning battle for the right of the anti-slavery forces to be
heard. His lofty moral attitude combined with his skill in parliamentary
dramatics made him the most picturesque figure in Congress. He died
from a stroke of apoplexy suffered at his seat in the House just after he
enunciated a "No" on a roll call.

ANDREW JACKSON

———◆———

SEVENTH PRESIDENT

For the first time, in 1828, the American people knew what it was to have power at the polls. With a new interest in politics, stimulated by a broadening of the right to vote and a popular candidate to vote for, they turned out at the presidential election three times as strong as in 1824. As a result, Andrew Jackson swept to an overwhelming victory over John Quincy Adams, the man he was firmly convinced had stolen the election from him four years earlier. When he was sworn in on the east portico of the Capitol the following March fourth, looking out upon the thousands who had swarmed into Washington, he devoutly believed that he had been given a mandate by the people. This belief, actually no more than a faith in his own leadership, was his whole political philosophy. As he put it in a rough draft of his inaugural address, "a government deriving all its powers from the will of the people" had chosen him.

Americans loved him for many picturesque and forceful qualities— his personal courage, his military sagacity, and not the least, his fine, dignified appearance. He was at the time physically frail, suffering from

35

intestinal trouble and old duelling wounds, and mentally distressed by the recent death of his beloved wife; but years back, in his Indian-fighting days, his soldiers had nicknamed him "Old Hickory," and it aptly expressed his ability to endure. As he mounted his horse to ride from the Capitol to the White House, a tall, thin man in black, with a craggy face, intensely blue eyes, and an unruly shock of white hair, the crowd fell in behind him. There followed a presidential reception such as the White House has never seen since, in which perhaps as many as 20,000 people shoved and fought to get in the door and at the refreshments. In the midst of a "regular saturnalia," the President escaped through a side door, but the riot continued until someone thought to place tubs of punch on the lawn, when enough of the guests went out the windows to lessen the pressure.

Andrew Jackson was purely a man of the people, with most of the prejudices and many of the antique beliefs of simple folk. His extreme sense of personal honor, enough to kill a man in a duel for an insult, his knightly feeling for womanhood, his highly colored language and emotions, all related him to the unschooled but highly moral frontier society from which he sprang. He was born in the community of Waxhaw in South Carolina, just south of the North Carolina line. At thirteen he played his part in the American Revolution, when the British invaded that sternly patriotic corner of the south. He fought them at the Battle of Hanging Rock and was later captured and imprisoned. There is a story that he defied a British officer who ordered him to get down on his knees and black his boots, and for his valor received a sabre blow that left a scar on his head and hand. The Revolution took the lives of his two brothers and his mother, the last from the pestilence of the British prison ships in Charleston Harbor, where she went to nurse the captives.

After the war, Jackson studied law and was admitted to the bar in North Carolina. A little later he took a trip with a friend to the western counties, those that were to become Tennessee. At Nashville he was told there was a fine opening for a young lawyer, so he decided to hang out his shingle there. The fees were good and there was plenty of rich land to be bought. In a few years he was a wealthy planter, a legal power for peace and order as solicitor for the district around Nashville, a citizen of such eminence that he was sent to the Tennessee Constitutional Convention, to the United States House of Representatives and to the Senate. The last two posts he held briefly and with little interest. In 1801 he was both judge of the Tennessee Supreme Court and major general in the state militia.

It was a liberal frontier society, where rough justice, bad grammar, personal quarrels, and robust pastimes such as gambling, cockfighting, and running fine horses were accepted. Jackson had all these inclinations. Shortly after arriving in Nashville, at the age of twenty-four, he made an impetuous marriage to a woman who had been previously married. His enemies later hounded him with the story that he had run off with another man's wife. Nothing could be further from the truth, or more out of character in a man so circumspect with women. But he had married on the mere report coming out of Virginia that Rachel Donelson's husband had divorced her. He was an eager lover and Virginia was a long way off. Two years later he discovered that the report was greatly exaggerated and only the first legal step had been taken toward a divorce. Since Rachel had been living with Jackson, she was now divorced on the ground of adultery. A second marriage was performed, but Jackson was deeply humiliated by the affair.

He retired from the state supreme court in 1804 and devoted himself to his private finances, which were in a bad way. In order to get out of debt he was forced to sell most of his land and move to a small farm with a log house. This property, with careful management and a brick house built many years later, became the famous "Hermitage."

It is probably no overstatement to say that Jackson's authentic genius lay in the military direction. His training, management, and command of the militia were in every way professional. His campaign against the Creeks in 1813–14 showed him cool-headed, disciplined, and above all, respectful of efficient military management. His defense of New Orleans against a well-trained British expeditionary force demanded more military science than was ever learned in Indian-fighting. This makes his victory there on January 8, 1815, more remarkable, particularly in consideration of Jackson's losses, 13 killed and wounded, against British losses of 2,000 killed, wounded, and captured.

The Seminole expedition of 1818 was handled with characteristic dispatch and the Indians beaten into submission in three months. The complications from this campaign were diplomatic, for General Jackson had exceeded his authority in occupying Spanish territory, dispatching the Spanish governor and garrisons to Cuba, and summarily executing two British adventurers who, he deemed, had incited the Indians to war. The Monroe administration was placed in a delicate situation, and in the cabinet debates on what to do about it, the Secretary of War, Calhoun, thought Jackson deserved to be censured. Jackson firmly believed that he had the authority to do precisely what he had done, and Monroe dared not attack the popular general.

Jackson's capacity for the presidential job was an open question in March 1829. The Adams Republicans had expressed their opinion of it during the campaign by presenting the Democratic-Republicans with a jackass as a party symbol. There is no doubt that Jackson felt his inexperience, for he drew about him the friends he trusted, the advisers in his campaign, a "kitchen cabinet." The official cabinet was selected on the basis of political harmony and included, besides Van Buren, the New York politician, as Secretary of State, men under the influence of the Vice President, John C. Calhoun. Jackson had one personal friend in it, the Secretary of War John Eaton, and it was Eaton who unintentionally caused the first disturbance in the administration.

Van Buren called it "Eaton malaria" and it revolved around the social acceptability of Eaton's wife, a celebrated Washington charmer with an unconventional past. The wives of all Jackson's official family snubbed her. Jackson, with characteristic chivalry, demanded that they change their attitude. The more he forced the issue, the more stubbornly the ladies snubbed her, none more so than the aristocratic Mrs. Calhoun. Van Buren, who was a widower, looked on with amusement and pleasure because he detested Calhoun and welcomed anything that would lessen his influence with the President. It was a petty squabble, but it contributed to the event Van Buren hoped for. When some of the anti-Calhoun men around Jackson ferreted out proof that Calhoun wished to reprimand him in 1818 for invading Spanish Florida, the President turned against his Vice President. A reorganization of the cabinet in 1831 removed all Calhoun men from the administration. It also removed Secretary and Mrs. Eaton from the scene. Van Buren, who had kept clear of intrigue with the utmost care, now became Jackson's favorite and candidate for the vice-presidency in 1832.

Jackson entered the White House without any stated program. He met the issues as they came up. He disapproved of local internal improvements at Federal expense; he was prepared to use force against South Carolina in the nullification controversy; he proved an implacable enemy to the Bank of the United States; and he showed the frontiersman's distrust of the Indians by a wholesale removal of the tribes to the far west. He introduced the "spoils system," or as he preferred to call it, rotation in public office. In the field of foreign diplomacy, he successfully collected some longstanding indemnity claims against France, persuaded Great Britain to reopen the West Indies to American trade, and was cautious in relations with the new Republic of Texas. He left the White House in 1837 as popular as when he entered, handing the mantle to his favorite, Van Buren. In retirement at the Hermitage he continued to dominate his party and remain a personal idol to millions of Americans.

HIGHLIGHTS OF HIS ADMINISTRATION

⋙ The Hayne-Webster Debate, not related to Jackson, but one of the most famous debates in American history. It started from resolutions to restrict western land sales, proposed in the Senate, December 29, 1829, and grew into a massive debate (delivered by installments) on states' rights, upheld by Robert Hayne of South Carolina and refuted by Daniel Webster of Massachusetts.

ᴈ§ Nullification: an attempt by South Carolina to resist the tariff laws of 1828 and 1832. A state convention on November 24, 1832, passed the South Carolina Ordinance of Nullification, declaring these laws would not be binding as of February 1, 1833. The legislature authorized the governor to call out the militia to protect citizens refusing to pay duties. Jackson sent seven revenue cutters and a warship to Charleston Harbor and proclaimed, on December 10, 1832, "The laws of the United States must be executed." At his request, a Force Bill was brought up in Congress, January 21, 1833, that would authorize him to call out the Army and Navy to enforce acts of Congress. The dispute was settled by an agreement to reduce the tariffs and withdraw the nullification ordinance.

ᴈ§ War against the Bank of the United States. On the ground that the Bank was unconstitutional, Jackson vetoed the bill to recharter it, in 1832. In 1833 he began diverting government funds to state banks.

ᴈ§ The first national conventions to nominate candidates for the presidency: The Anti-Masonic party, at Baltimore, September 1831; National Republican party, at Baltimore, December 1831; Democratic party, Baltimore, May 1832.

ᴈ§ Black Hawk War. Sauks and Fox under Chief Black Hawk were driven from their lands at the mouth of the Rock River in Illinois, pursued north and destroyed at the Battle of Bad Axe in Wisconsin, in 1832.

ᴈ§ The Georgia Cherokees' appeal to the Supreme Court to force Georgia to respect their rights to tribal lands. The Court handed down a decision in their favor. Jackson ignored the decision, saying: "John Marshall has made his decision. Now let him enforce it!" In 1835 the Cherokees agreed to sell their lands to the Federal government and move west.

ᴈ§ The Seminole War. Resisting removal westward, a band of Seminoles with some fugitive slaves under the command of Osceola fled into the swamps of Florida in 1835 and fought off United States troops. Osceola was captured by a ruse in 1837 and died the next year in Fort Moultrie at Charleston. In December 1837, Colonel Zachary Taylor defeated the Seminoles at the Battle of Lake Okeechobee. Most of the Indians agreed to move west in 1842.

MARTIN VAN BUREN

EIGHTH PRESIDENT

Below Albany and along the Hudson were once the Dutch farms and villages of New York. In this country, at Kinderhook, east of the river, Martin Van Buren was born at the end of the American Revolution, the son of a farmer and tavern keeper. At fourteen he began studying law with one of the town's attorneys, serving at the same time as an apprentice law clerk, and even taking civil cases before the justices of the peace. There is a story that he argued a case at fifteen, when he was so small that he stood on a table to address the jury. Perhaps this is slightly exaggerated, but it is certain that he never grew very tall. He was "Little Van" then, as he was thirty-odd years later when he bounced along on top of a horse, riding with President Andrew Jackson on their daily constitutionals.

With law went politics. Young Martin accepted the complexities of New York politics as he did those of the law. His affable manners pleased the older men, while his industry and his readiness to go along with the party organization soon made him its master and one of the leading Republicans in the state. He was elected to the state Senate, and during the seven years he spent in Albany, became leader of the "Albany Regency," the machine that controlled Republican party politics and patronage. The spoils system was then well developed in New York, as it was in other states, though it was not thought to be necessarily corrupt. Van Buren dominated the Republican, or Democratic-Republican, party for many years. In one of the elections, when he was an elder statesman, the abbreviation of Old Kinderhook was used as the code name of Democratic clubs in New York. A Whig misunderstanding of "O.K." and a wisecrack that it was probably Jacksonese for "Oll korrect" gave Americans their handiest slang term.

Van Buren was in the United States Senate, as was Jackson, during Jackson's first campaign for the presidency. While Jackson resigned and returned to the Hermitage after his defeat, Van Buren stayed on, and according to John Quincy Adams, became the master strategist of the second Jackson campaign. Largely this campaign was a coldhearted attack on Adams. The "Red Fox of Kinderhook" was not one to draw attention to himself, and his activities were mostly behind the scenes. In the fall of 1828 he was elected governor of New York, but somewhat against his inclination, he was persuaded to resign that office two months after he was sworn in, to take a place in Jackson's cabinet of mediocrities. The old hero, whose habits of command sometimes made courtiers of his followers, wanted a man of solid character and superior political experience close to him. Van Buren justified Jackson's confidence; gave him good and disinterested advice; even opposed him to save him from impolitic action. Little Van never lost Jackson's confidence. After serving as his Vice President for his second term, he went into the Democratic National Convention of May 1835 with Jackson's blessing and was nominated unanimously for the presidency. His election over the Whig William Henry Harrison was by a handsome majority of electoral votes but a narrow margin in the popular vote.

Van Buren's term in office is associated with an economic disaster so general that hardly any person, whether he was banker, farmer, manufacturer, capitalist, or mill hand, came out of it whole. It began immediately after the inauguration in 1837, with a bank panic, set off by a sudden and extraordinary demand for specie payment. Banks that had not enough specie to meet their obligations closed, starting a chain reaction that spread all across the country. A speculative boom, especially in western lands, had led most banks to extend their obligations far beyond their resources. The flow of investment was stopped down, throwing hundreds of thousands out of work in the industrial centers. Farmers suffered from a drop in the price of cotton and a wheat crop failure in the preceding year. Van Buren called a special session of Congress, but neither Congress nor the President had any suggestions to relieve the emergency, although the Treasury took care of its own immediate problem by issuing $10,000,000 in temporary notes. It was two years before those banks that survived the crash resumed specie payment and more than four years before the country pulled out of the depression.

Van Buren deserves credit for his plan to secure government deposits without resorting to a national bank, an "independent treasury" or sub-treasury banking system. The Sub-Treasury Act had difficulty getting past the Whigs and friends of private banking in Congress, but it was enacted in 1840 and proved an efficient basis for Federal finance. Van Buren made an excellent President and might have been re-elected in more normal times.

After his defeat in 1840, the Democrats refused to nominate him in 1844 because he took an unpopular position in opposing the annexation of Texas. In 1848 he became even more unpopular with the Democrats when he fused the splinter groups opposed to the territorial extension of slavery in the Free Soil party and ran as its candidate for President—with Charles Francis Adams, son of John Quincy, for Vice President. The effect was to split the New York Democrats, enabling the Whigs to carry the state and win the election. Van Buren died in the second year of the Civil War, having spanned the interval between union and disunion.

HIGHLIGHTS OF HIS ADMINISTRATION

ی§ The Depression of 1837, described above.

ی§ The Sub-Treasury Act, passed in 1840, setting up sub-treasuries in five cities.

ی§ The *Caroline* Affair. A rebellion in Upper and Lower Canada in the fall of 1837 evoked such sympathy among Americans in neighboring New York and Vermont that Van Buren thought it necessary to make a formal proclamation of neutrality. This did not prevent the Canadian William Mackenzie from running freedom fighters and guns from the United States across the Niagara River in the steamer *Caroline*. The Canadian government seized the vessel one night at the American shore. It was set on fire and put over Niagara Falls.

While Van Buren unsuccessfully demanded reparation, a Canadian named McLeod was arrested in New York, and charged, on his own loose boasts, with having taken part in the raid and killed an American. The British government demanded McLeod's release, which Secretary of State Daniel Webster refused. On trial McLeod was acquitted, and the whole matter was dropped.

43

WILLIAM HENRY HARRISON

———————<◦>———————

NINTH PRESIDENT

After their miserable showing in the presidential election of 1836, the Whigs decided they needed two things: a national organization and a candidate with popular appeal. The man who had run best in the recent campaign, General William Henry Harrison, was a westerner but he was also a national hero, like Andrew Jackson. He was under no handicap of sectional jealousies, and he was not known to have offended anybody by his political opinions. Possibly he would have some of Jackson's magic with the voters. By the time the Whig National Convention of 1839 met at Harrisburg, Pennsylvania, there was a well-coördinated movement among the practical politicians in the party to nominate Harrison.

The bulk of the delegates were probably for Henry Clay, the greatest of the Whigs and certainly, of all the statesmen of that period, the one who should have been President. But he was twice a loser for the presidency, and his chances for the nomination this year were disposed of on the ground that as a slave-owning southerner he could not get the northern vote. The Harrison men devised an ingenious scheme to control the convention and keep the delegates from stampeding to Clay. The polling of votes was delegated to three men from each state, who met privately in committee off the convention floor. As soon as this committee had arrived at a majority vote—for Harrison—they so reported to the convention. In order to catch the Southern vote, the vice-presidential nomination was given to John Tyler of Virginia.

A disgusted Clay supporter voiced his opinion of the candidate after the convention in a way that tickled the Democratic press. Give Harrison, he said, a pension of $2,000 a year and a barrel of hard cider and he would rest contentedly in his log cabin with coonskin nailed to the door, the rest of his life. The Harrison managers pounced on this jibe the moment the Democrats put it into circulation. It provided precisely the touch they wanted. In addition to the alliterative slogan of "Tippecanoe and Tyler Too" that rang through the campaign, the log cabin became the Harrison symbol in every imaginable form; the cider barrel was standard equipment for party rallies and picnics; and the coon became the Whig mascot.

It was a rollicking, gay campaign, with parades, barbecues, and gigantic rallies, often with Harrison himself delivering a speech, and lots of singing. Never before had there been so many campaign songs and so many thousands of songbooks. The gimcrackery Americana was enriched by Harrison badges of every description and log cabins in infinite styles, notably a glass container put out by a Philadelphia distiller and labeled "E. C. Booz Old Cabin Whiskey." There were campaign newspapers breaking out in every direction like measles. The most popular of these was young Horace Greeley's weekly *Log Cabin*, which claimed a circulation of 80,000. John Quincy Adams called the campaign the "Harrison Whirlwind." It swept "Little Van" back to "Old Kinderhook" and the "Hero of Tippecanoe" into the White House—with an army of eager job-hungry Whigs following close behind him.

William Henry Harrison was a good soldier and an honest gentleman who met the demands of frontier life successfully. By 1841, when he became President, he was sixty-eight and long retired from his public career to the life of a country gentleman at North Bend, Ohio, a few miles west of Cincinnati. His large rambling house overlooking the Ohio was a landmark for travelers passing on the river. Behind the clapboards of one section was the shell of the two-story log house he had lived in during his early years in the west, preserved for sentimental reasons. In one of his guest rooms he kept a copy of *The Lives of the Signers of the Declaration of Independence*, a reminder that he himself was the child of one of those gentlemen.

Harrison was the youngest son of Benjamin Harrison, the Virginia Revolutionist and friend of Washington, master of Berkeley Plantation on the James River. William Henry complied with his father's wishes and took up the study of medicine, but he had no liking or aptitude for it. On his father's death, he persuaded President Washington to give him an ensign's commission in the army, and in 1791 marched out of Philadelphia with a detachment of recruits for the northwest frontier. He was stationed at Fort Washington, a blockhouse post overlooking the dozen or so cabins that were Cincinnati. There he learned Indian fighting from General Anthony Wayne and served as his aide-de-camp at the Battle of the Fallen Timbers. After he married, he resigned from the army, bought land at North Bend, and began to develop his farm.

President John Adams appointed him governor of Indiana Territory in 1801, and in this capacity he secured several million acres of Indiana lands for white settlers, and snuffed out the incipient revolt of Tecumseh and his brother The Prophet at the Battle of Tippecanoe in 1811. After the first reverses to American arms at Detroit in the War of 1812, Harrison was given command of the northwest forces, recovered Detroit and defeated the Canadians at the Battle of the Thames. Harrison had had a little political experience as a member of Congress and had proved that he was not supple enough for the diplomatic life in a brief period as American minister to Colombia.

It seemed, as his wife said, that the old hero might have been left in peace on his Ohio farm. He served exactly one month of his term. The cause of his death was presumed to be pneumonia, aggravated possibly by an overabundance of medical attention in the way of bleeding, blistering, cupping, and dosing.

JOHN
TYLER

---◄●►---

TENTH PRESIDENT

When for the first time a Vice President succeeded to office on the death of a President, it was not clear to all the people that he was legally a full-fledged President. Some thought John Tyler was only "acting President." In a few short months, the opposition in his own party were making a play on those words and sneering at him as "accidental President." The Whigs were finding out that Tyler was a Whig only by some peculiar definition of his own and not according to the leadership of the great Henry Clay. In choosing "Tyler too" to run with "Tippecanoe" at the national convention in 1839, the Whigs had taken for granted that any man who campaigned for Clay's presidential nomination by the convention was a sincere Clay Whig. Tyler in fact worked for Clay to the bitter end and was reported in tears when Clay lost the nomination to William Henry Harrison. Given the vice-presidential nomination as a sop to Clay and the southern Whigs, Tyler was expected to stay in line. Yet he did not stay in line. Looking back, history knows him best as the President who changed parties in mid-term.

49

John Tyler was neither a complex nor a remarkable man. He was personally ambitious, which led him to be excessively tolerant and expedient; but at the point when any other man would have felt totally committed, his personal opinions took over and he was quite likely to reverse himself on the basis of some principle or other that could not be compromised. "Honest John" was the type of man who drives practical politicians to distraction because sooner or later he is going to be stubbornly impractical.

He was well educated and conditioned for political priggishness. Born at Greenway Plantation on the James River in Virginia, he had been brought up to be proud of Virginia, Thomas Jefferson, and states' rights, to support the Constitution only in its most limited and literal interpretation, and to be suspicious of almost everything else. After graduating from William and Mary College at seventeen, Tyler studied law with his father, a United States district judge. Within two years he was admitted to the bar and practicing the art of oratory on juries. At twenty-one, he was a member of the Virginia House of Delegates, starting on his way up in politics. In the next twenty-five years, he was elected to Congress, to the governorship of Virginia, and to the United States Senate. In 1836 he had run for the vice-presidency of the States' Rights Whig ticket.

From the beginning of his career, Tyler made it plain that he was arrogantly conservative. His course can be traced by his objections to all variances from the cautious standards of an aristocratic Virginian. He distrusted Andrew Jackson's courting of the common people in 1824 and therefore supported John Adams for the presidency. But when Adams produced his elaborate program for Federal subsidy of internal improvements, physical, economic, and social, he recoiled in horror from this plot to centralize government and fell into the arms of the Jackson Democrats. Once Jackson was in the White House, opening the door to the spoilsmen and the plebeian rabble, Tyler objected to him as a dictator and "abominably unfashionable." From that point, he began to take on the color and conformation of a Whig.

The only world that really suited John Tyler was his own personal world of a Virginia plantation and its social suburbs in the fashionable resorts north and south. Within the confines of his taste he was a good-humored man with a great capacity to amuse and be amused. He loved to play the fiddle and go to parties. On the whole, he was a gentle master, so that his slaves were a happy lot. He had no lack of friends and relations to keep his house full, and presided gracefully over one of the last strongholds of the antebellum, feudal South. Married twice, he fathered fifteen children, the last one born when he was seventy years old. It is interesting that Tyler and his children span most of United States history, since he was born during Washington's administration and his youngest child died during the Truman administration.

When President Harrison died, Vice President Tyler was at his plantation in Virginia, not having been informed of the President's illness. A messenger, riding through the night, got him out of bed at sunrise and told him that he was President. Traveling by horseback and boat, he made the distance to Washington in twenty-one hours and was sworn in on April 6, 1840, at Brown's Hotel. He did not arrive so easily at determining how he was to handle the presidency, whether to be bold and assert his leadership or to be cautious and let the Whig leadership in Congress take over.

In the end, he passed the initiative to Congress. Senator Clay seized it with alacrity. His first move was to bring up a bill to establish a third United States Bank. Tyler found it necessary to oppose the bill and vetoed it, explaining his objections. Congress revised the bill, trying to meet his objections, and again he vetoed. The anger of Clay and almost every Whig in and out of Congress was understandable, for the stubbornness of a man who would not yield a little to the counsels of his own party was beyond belief. The cabinet, held over from the Harrison administration, resigned in a body, except for Secretary of State Webster, who stayed because he was in the midst of negotiating with Great Britain a settlement of the Maine-Canada boundary. Two days later, a little more than five months after he became President, Tyler was formally read out of the Whig party.

Tyler hoped to be strong enough to build up his own leadership, but having neither the force of character nor issues to do so, he mustered to his cause only a handful of discontented Jackson Democrats. Toward the end of his administration, he became concerned about the fate of Texas. On information that Great Britain was quietly trying to secure commercial and political privileges in the young republic, Tyler hastened to offer the Texas president, Sam Houston, a treaty of annexation. Houston accepted and the treaty was signed on April 12, 1844. But it could not be got past the Senate. Not until the fall election that year was it clear that the country at large was in favor of annexation, when the Democrat Polk was elected President on his support of it. Tyler was then inspired to propose to Congress that annexation be put in the form of a joint resolution, which required a simple majority for passage, instead of the two-thirds vote in the Senate required for a treaty. By this device annexation of Texas was achieved in the last days of his term.

Attempting a third-party movement, Tyler had himself nominated for the presidency at a "Democratic-Republican" convention in May, 1844. By that summer he realized it was no use and withdrew. In June he was married for the second time, his bride thirty years his junior, a lively, ambitious daughter of a prominent New York family. On the following March fourth, the Tylers left Washington without attending the inauguration of the new President and retired to Sherwood Forest, a plantation not more than two miles from the house in which Tyler was born.

He emerged once more as a person of some national importance when the Peace Convention that met in Washington in February 1861, to try to reconcile the South and the North on the eve of the Civil War, chose him its president. When he died in January 1862, no notice was taken in Washington of his death, for a few days earlier, he had taken his seat as a member of the Confederate House of Representatives.

HIGHLIGHTS OF HIS ADMINISTRATION

❧ The tariff bill of 1842, restoring the rates of 1832 before the compromise that ended the nullification controversy.

❧ The Webster-Ashburton Treaty of August 9, 1842, defining the Maine-Canada boundary.

❧ The "gag rule" in the House of Representatives, by which anti-slavery petitions were tabled without being read, repealed in December 1844.

❧ The *Princeton* disaster, on February 28, 1844. A gun, the "Peacemaker," exploded during an official junket aboard the new steam frigate, arranged to demonstrate its Ericsson propellers and the Peacemaker. Eight people were killed, including the Secretaries of State and the Navy and Tyler's prospective father-in-law.

❧ The joint resolution providing for the annexation of Texas, signed by Tyler, March 1, 1845.

JAMES KNOX POLK

In Mecklenburg County, North Carolina, on May 31, 1775, a handful of farmers formally severed their relations with the British Crown. According to local tradition, some of these men were named Polk, and one of these had a son, Samuel, who later on emigrated to the Duck River Valley in Tennessee, where he became a prosperous farmer and raised a family of ten children. The eldest of these was James Knox Polk. At the time the family emigrated from Mecklenburg County, James was about eleven, old enough to help with the wagons and probably do a man's work in clearing the new land. Then he left the farm to get an education, become a lawyer, and go into politics.

Polk studied law in Nashville with a good friend of Andrew Jackson, Felix Grundy, who naturally took his pupil out to the Hermitage to meet the great man. Bright, industrious, and loyal, Polk was soon a rising young man in the Democratic party, close enough to Jackson to be nicknamed "Young Hickory," later on, when he was running for President.

He was no sooner admitted to the bar, than he was combining the practice of law and the practice of politics in Columbia, Tennessee. Elected to the Tennessee House of Representatives, he sponsored a law to prohibit duelling. Two years later he was in Washington as a Congressman. He spent fourteen years in the House, the last four as Speaker, a period that overlapped Jackson's presidency at both ends.

Tennessee was now split politically between Jackson's Democrats and the Whigs. So Polk quit the House and went home to run for governor and to help rebuild his party. He was elected for a term, but running for re-election in 1840, went down to defeat in the Democratic debacle of that year. Two years later he tried again and was again defeated.

Personally Polk seemed cold. He was thin, about average height, had a melancholy face, and was generally serious. Nevertheless, he warmed up on the stump, and though he had no use for oratorical trimmings and was inclined to be a little long-winded, he was considered a good convincer, and in fact, was hailed by his followers as the "Napoleon of the Stump." He married the daughter of a wealthy merchant, a strait-laced woman who did not believe in such frivolities as dancing. From his law practice and his plantation he made a reasonable fortune. By 1844, he was considered a good possibility for the Democratic vice-presidential nomination in that year's election.

The presidential nominee was expected to be Van Buren. At least this was so until President Tyler in April sent to the Senate a treaty for the annexation of Texas. This was a bomb thrown among the politicians. For some time what to do about Texas—now independent of Mexico for eight years—had been a highly dangerous issue that most candidates running for office would have liked to avoid. For, so closely was it bound to the slavery question, since Texas was slave territory, and so constantly did it confuse sectional prejudice with party policies, that no one knew which was the "right" side to take. Both Van Buren and Henry Clay chose to oppose Texas annexation, and lived to regret it. Van Buren lost the Democratic nomination, and Clay lost the election.

In the Democratic convention Polk was brought forward to break a deadlock when the Southern delegates instructed for Van Buren refused to give him their votes or switch to one of his opponents in the balloting. Polk's candidacy was such a happy solution that his nomination was made unanimous. Clay, nominated by the Whigs for the third time, asked: "Who's Polk?"—perhaps the first time this barb had been thrown at a dark-horse candidate.

The voters showed that Polk's stand on Texas was what most of them wanted. In April he had said clearly, positively, and sincerely that he was for the "re-annexation of Texas," and he thought that if the United States did not hasten to take Texas into the Union, it would become a commercial dependency of Great Britain, possibly even a British colony. With the election of Polk, President Tyler considered that he had a popular mandate on the admission of Texas. In the last weeks of his administration he pushed through Congress a resolution admitting it as a state.

With the matter of Texas out of the way, President Polk turned his attention to a much larger scheme. The entire Far West, from the Oregon country, for some years claimed by both the United States and Great Britain, south through California and eastward through that vast area called New Mexico, to the Rockies and the Mississippi watershed, should in his opinion be secured to the United States. Securing it he considered both a prudent and a practical policy. It would be prudent to anticipate the occupation of the area by Americans, by now emigrating westward in considerable numbers, and thus provide the means of extending over them "the jurisdiction of our laws and the benefits of our republican institutions." On the practical side, he could not foresee any difficulties that diplomacy, money, or a very limited military effort could not handle. He was correct in judging the Mexican provincial control of California and New Mexico to be feeble and easily dissipated, but he underestimated the spirit of the Mexican government, and the military effort which he hoped would subdue that spirit turned into quite a war.

Nevertheless, Polk had the rare satisfaction of accomplishing in his administration all that he had planned. Refusing to run for a second term, he retired to Nashville. There, while supervising improvements about the house and grounds of a new home, he fell ill of chronic diarrhea and died at the age of fifty-three.

HIGHLIGHTS OF HIS ADMINISTRATION

◄§ The Walker Tariff Act of 1846, reducing rates to a strictly revenue basis. This remained in effect until 1857.

◄§ The Oregon boundary settlement: Polk offered the British minister in Washington a boundary along the 49th parallel, simply an extension of the boundary line existing east of the Rocky Mountains. The minister turned it down. Polk then asked Congress to pass legislation that would: terminate the joint British-American administration of Oregon; authorize the building of American forts there; proclaim the extension of American laws over the area. While Congress debated his request, the British reconsidered and submitted a treaty accepting the 49th parallel boundary, on June 6, 1846, which Polk signed.

Purchase of California and New Mexico: In November 1845, Polk sent John Slidell on a special mission to Mexico to buy California and New Mexico. The price for California was to be $20,000,000 or $25,000,000, depending on whether southern California would be included in the purchase. The price for New Mexico (roughly the area between California and the Rockies, south of Oregon and north of Mexico) was to be $5,000,000. Slidell was also to persuade Mexico to recognize the Rio Grande as the Texas-Mexico border. The Mexican Government refused to receive him.

On the apparent failure of Slidell's mission, in March 1846, Polk ordered General Zachary Taylor, encamped on the Nueces at Corpus Christi, to advance to the Rio Grande. On April 25, a Mexican detachment ambushed an American patrol. Polk notified Congress of what he called an act of invasion and asked for a declaration of war. Taylor crossed the Rio Grande and proceeded southward with actions at Palo Alto, Resaca de la Palma, the capture of Matamoras, Monterey, and Victoria, completing the campaign with a decisive victory at Buena Vista on February 23, 1847.

General Winfield Scott, landing an army of 12,000 at Vera Cruz, beginning on March 9, 1847, advanced toward Mexico City, with actions at Cerro Gordo, Contreras, Churubusco, Molino del Rey, and at the rock of Chapultepec. The campaign was intermittent to allow Nicholas Trist, chief clerk of the State Department, to try to negotiate peace. Mexico City surrendered on September 17. Robert E. Lee, George B. McClellan, and Ulysses S. Grant were young officers with Scott. The peace of Guadalupe Hidalgo was negotiated by Trist, on February 2, 1848. The United States agreed to pay $15,000,000 for California and New Mexico and to assume all American claims against the Mexican government, while Mexico ceded Texas with the Rio Grande boundary.

The occupation of California. Colonel Stephen W. Kearny was ordered to march from Fort Leavenworth to California. He started in June 1846, arrived at Santa Fé on August 18, and raised the American flag there. Traveling west by the Gila Valley and the Colorado, he reached San Diego after American control had been established in California. American settlers in the Sacramento Valley had taken it upon them-

58

selves to raise a white flag with a bear and a star on it, and to proclaim the Republic of California, on June 14, 1846. Commodore Sloat had initiated the seizure of California ports as soon as war was known to have begun on the Rio Grande.

The Wilmot Proviso. Representative Wilmot, Democrat of Pennsylvania, introduced this during the debate on the bill to appropriate money to finance the peace treaty with Mexico. It provided that none of the territory acquired by that treaty would be open to slavery. The House passed it, the Senate defeated it. It was again defeated in 1847.

ZACHARY TAYLOR

TWELFTH PRESIDENT

Zachary Taylor was the fourth general to become President, and not the least distinguished. In the War with Mexico, he commanded a ten-month campaign that produced a succession of victories, although handicapped by a government capricious in its conduct of the war and politically jealous of his success. Toward the end of the campaign, his army was cut in half to help mount General Scott's invasion of southern Mexico. Consequently his last and greatest victory, at Buena Vista, on February 23, 1847, was the more astounding in that his total force was 4,700 against Santa Anna's 20,000. Taylor never forgave President Polk for taking his men away from him, or Winfield Scott for getting them.

Polk's reluctance as a Democrat to offer a Whig general the opportunity to make a hero of himself was understandable. The Whig party, fondly remembering its success with William Henry Harrison, could hardly wait to get its hands on "Old Zack" Taylor. Long before the fighting was done in Mexico, the General was being distracted by letters requesting that he run for the presidency on the Whig ticket. This kind of publicity seemed to him not only out of time and place but a threat to the morale of his army. He therefore refused to become involved in politics. "My duty to the army," he later explained, "and to the Republic whose battles we were waging forbade me assuming a position of seeming hostility to any portion of the brave men under my command."

With or without his permission, the Taylor-for-President movement was well underway long before the old hero was back in his house at Baton Rouge in the fall of 1847. The facts of his army record were picked up and publicized. He had entered the regular army in the wave of public excitement following the British attack on the American naval ship *Chesapeake* in 1807, and had served nearly forty years, distinguishing himself in the War of 1812, accepting the surrender of Chief Black Hawk after the Battle of Bad Axe in the Black Hawk War, and commanding the troops that defeated the Seminoles in the Battle of Lake Okeechobee in 1837. He had been brought up on the Kentucky frontier, though born in Virginia. He was a shrewd, imperturbable officer, in absolute command of his men's respect, as witness his army nickname, "Old Rough and Ready."

In appearance Taylor was short, muscular, with the bowlegs of a horseman and the lined, weathered face of the old campaigner. He affected civilian dress, loose and shabby, in battle—at Buena Vista it was a brown overcoat, and when he was in camp at Corpus Christi before the Rio Grande campaign, he could be spotted by his floppy straw hat. He was famous for these eccentricities and others, such as his tobacco chewing, his habit of sitting with his feet cocked up on a table, his attachment to his warhorse "Old Whitey," whom he took to Washington later and grazed on the White House lawn. In spite of his army habits, he was at home with the planters of Mississippi and Louisiana, spending as much time as possible at "Cypress Grove," a cotton plantation of about 2,000 acres on the Mississippi. Besides this, he had other investments that made him a comparatively wealthy man. One of his boasts was his long indifference to politics. He had, he claimed, never cast a vote.

The Whig convention in 1848 was not unanimous for Taylor, but on the fourth ballot he got a majority and was nominated. The campaign had some of the color of the Harrison campaign but did not get into as high a gear. In the election he would have lost, had not Van Buren and the Free Soil party won enough Democratic votes in New York to subtract that state from the Democratic column and give it to Taylor.

Before Inauguration Day 1849, the political climate was heavy with the coming storm over slavery. Congress adjourned March fourth after three months of angry debate over the question of whether the new western territories should be restricted in that respect and whether the slave trade should be banned in the District of Columbia. Taylor's inaugural address was searched for any clue as to his position on slavery and found to be on the whole "negative." In the sixteen months of his presidency, Taylor did not take the lead on this issue. Henry Clay returned to the Senate after eight years in retirement to propose his compromise of 1850. "Old Zack," certain only that he was for union, followed the counsels of Senator William H. Seward, the radical young Whig from New York, and opposed Clay's resolutions.

Matters of patronage and deep distress over a cabinet scandal, in which his Secretary of War, Crawford, appeared to have profited in his private capacity as attorney for the Galphin Claim against the government, shadowed much of the old hero's short time in office. He died on July 9, 1850, from an attack of gastroenteritis, or "cholera morbus," brought on by indulging his appetite for raw fruits and vegetables and iced drinks in the heat of summer.

HIGHLIGHTS OF HIS ADMINISTRATION

◦§ The beginning of the California gold rush.

◦§ Clay's compromise resolutions on slavery introduced in the Senate, January 29, 1850: California to be admitted as a free state; Utah and New Mexico to be created as territories without restrictions on slavery; assumption of Texas's debt contracted before annexation, Texas to give up her claim to part of eastern New Mexico; prohibition of slave trade in the District of Columbia, though slavery itself was not to be forbidden there without the consent of Maryland; more effectual fugitive-slave laws; Congress no longer to assume the right of forbidding slavery in interstate commerce. Clay's speech lasted nearly two days.

On March 4, Calhoun answered with a speech delivered for him, he being too feeble. He saw no hope in compromise. It was either withdraw the North's demand for abolition or let the South secede in peace.

On March 7, Daniel Webster made his last great speech, in which he supported Clay's appeal for compromise, arguing that the northern abolitionists should not drive the South into secession.

◦§ July 5, 1850, ratification of the Clayton-Bulwer Treaty, in which the United States and Great Britain agreed that any interocean canal in Central America would be neutral and that neither country would extend its territory in that area.

MILLARD
FILLMORE

——⟶◆⟵——

THIRTEENTH PRESIDENT

The tolling of bells at midnight, July 9, 1850, announced the death of the President. At noon the following day, in the House of Representatives, before the Congress and the assembled dignitaries of the United States Government, the Vice President succeeded to that office. The succession of a vice president upon the death of a president has a natural drama, regardless of the persons or the issues involved. In this case, Millard Fillmore, a handsome New York lawyer of conservative and temperate inclination, succeeded Zachary Taylor and brought surcease from sectional strife over slavery.

Fillmore had been since his election to the House of Representatives twenty years before a follower of Henry Clay. During the three months before Taylor's death he had presided, as Vice President, over the Senate debates on Clay's compromise resolutions to reconcile the North and the South, and he had seen them reach a point of deadlock. President Taylor opposed compromise, under the influence of Senator William H. Seward, a radical Whig who considered it a matter of conscience to press for abolition even to the point of disunion. Clay made no secret of his satisfaction at the passing of Taylor. With the active support of Fillmore, his compromise legislation now passed Congress. For a few years the imminence of secession was postponed and the Fillmore administration brought harmony to the country.

Millard Fillmore, in the opinion of the political writers of the time, was a mild and persuasive politician, with a logical mind; a good advocate but no orator. His appearance was always favorably mentioned, for like McKinley, he looked precisely as a statesman should. He was a little taller than average, of a massive figure, with regular features, a fair complexion, and a "Grecian mouth." He was born on a wilderness homestead in Cayuga County, New York, and had neither the money nor the facilities for a proper education. His father was part of the movement westward from New England, begun in the case of the Fillmore family by a sailor of Ipswich, Massachusetts. When Millard was fifteen, he was apprenticed to a fuller, a cloth finisher. The work was not to his taste, however, and before he was nineteen he had bought his time from his master and was studying law, supporting himself by teaching and surveying. By the time he was thirty, he had formed a law partnership in Buffalo that became one of the most successful in that part of the state.

Politics attracted Fillmore and he went to the state legislature, where he distinguished himself by working for the repeal of the law that imposed imprisonment on debtors. In the decade between 1833 and 1843 he served four terms in Congress. There he identified himself with northern industrial and business interests. As chairman of the House Ways and Means Committee, he introduced the tariff bill of 1842 that restored the protective rates yielded in settlement of the nullification dispute with South Carolina ten years before.

The Fillmore administration shone in the last fine glow of two elder statesmen, Henry Clay and Daniel Webster. In remaking the cabinet, the President appointed Webster Secretary of State, a post he held until his death in the autumn of 1852. Webster's best production in that office was his "Hulsemann Letter" addressed to the Austrian chargé d'affaires in reply to a protest over the cordial reception given by the United States to Louis Kossuth, the Hungarian revolutionary. In it he expressed with typical elegance the inalienable right of Americans to favor revolutionary movements in foreign countries without moving an inch from a posture of neutrality.

The honor of running for an elected term in the presidency was denied Fillmore through the bitter opposition of Seward. Nevertheless, it required 53 ballots in the Whig convention to beat him. He retired to Buffalo and his law practice. In 1856 he was nominated for President by the American party, or Know-Nothings, an eccentric chauvinist faction dedicated to the defense of Americanism against foreigners and the Roman Catholic Church. He got the votes of one state, Maryland.

HIGHLIGHTS OF HIS ADMINISTRATION

&§ Enactment of Clay's compromise plan in: the admission of California as a free state; organization of the New Mexico and Utah territories, without the Wilmot proviso, free to become states with or without slavery; assumption of Texas's debt, incurred in her revolt from Mexico, by the Federal government; abolition of the slave trade in the District of Columbia; a new, severe fugitive-slave law.

&§ The opening of trade with Japan: in 1852 Commodore Matthew C. Perry and a naval squadron was sent to deliver a letter to the Emperor of Japan proposing that he sign a diplomatic and commercial treaty with the United States. This proposal was accepted and the treaty signed in 1854.

FRANKLIN PIERCE

FOURTEENTH PRESIDENT

Of all the Presidents, few had such a magnetic personality and such an easy success as Franklin Pierce. None had such an unfortunate career in the presidency. His name was tossed into the Democratic National Convention of 1852 when, after 33 ballots, none of the three leading candidates could muster the two-thirds vote for nomination. Probably he was known to only a handful of the delegates, but his friends rounded up a bloc of votes for him and he was nominated on the 49th ballot.

When the news reached the Pierces in New England, Mrs. Pierce fainted. A delicate and nervous woman, she detested having her husband in politics, and he had obligingly quit running for office ten years back. Living the complacent life of a country lawyer in Concord, New Hampshire, these many years, had given him the opportunity to groom state politics to his liking, however, and he had been successful enough to be called boss of the Democratic party in that state. His affinity for politics was inherited. His father, an overbearing Revolutionary War hero, had made himself conspicuous as a Jeffersonian Republican and Jackson Democrat, and after collecting the title of general in the militia, went on to become governor. His point of departure in his career was a fifty-acre farm and a log house in Hillsborough County, where Franklin was born. An unlettered man, he saw that his son got a proper education, sent him to Bowdoin College in Maine, and polished him off with a law course.

A graceful, easygoing young man, Franklin made a good trial lawyer, with a talent for handling juries. At the same time, he was equally appealing to the politicians and the voters. His only handicap was a weakness for alcohol, against which he struggled most of his life. His intellectual powers were not great, his instinct to please rather than to oppose made him seem weak, and an exasperating difficulty he had in making up his mind when the decisions were important wore down the patience of his partisans. As a rigid party man, he felt it necessary to defend slavery on the ground that it was covered by the constitutional guarantee of property.

In spite of his limitations, Franklin Pierce's popularity carried him smoothly upward in politics. Four years in the state legislature were followed by two terms in the United States House of Representatives and five years in the Senate. He was not conspicuous in Congress, but he made many friends in the Democratic party, especially in the Southern wing, such as Benton, Polk, and Jefferson Davis. With the outbreak of the Mexican War his Washington friendships served him well. He secured a commission as a brigadier general and joined Winfield Scott's army about midway in its drive from Vera Cruz to Mexico City. He made an honest and brave effort to distinguish himself, but his inexperience and a knee injury when his horse fell with him robbed him of the glory he had hoped to win. Still, he came home as *General* Pierce.

Pierce won the 1852 election by a huge majority, with 27 states, to 4 for his recent commanding officer, Winfield Scott. The Democratic party had re-formed solidly on the Clay slavery compromises of 1850. Pierce's personal satisfaction in the election, however, was struck a dreadful blow just two months before his inauguration. He and his wife and their only surviving child, a boy of eleven, were caught in a train wreck and the boy was crushed to death.

Arrived in Washington, Pierce chose a weak cabinet, thus depriving himself of good advisers, which he of all Presidents needed so badly. His second misfortune was to follow the pro-slavery line by giving his support to the Kansas-Nebraska Bill. This act repealed the Missouri Compromise of 1820 and introduced the ingenious rule of "popular sovereignty" in deciding the slavery status of new territories, in effect scrapping all past efforts to reconcile North and South. Pierce was immediately accused of playing traitor to the Democratic platform. The ensuing battle for Kansas between the slavery and anti-slavery settlers excited and confused the President, no less than the rest of the country. His lack of wisdom and firmness permitted the Union to divide with astonishing rapidity. He was so woefully discredited by his own party that he was refused a renomination.

During the Civil War, from his retirement in New Hampshire Pierce freely attacked Lincoln and the war, until he had not a political friend left. On the day following Lincoln's assassination he was threatened by an angry mob, but he made such a valiant speech that none in the mob could believe him seriously disloyal, so the crowd went home. Meanwhile Pierce had had his own problems. Finally a widower, he succumbed to his weakness for liquor, then turned to religion and ended his days in the mellow dignity of a forgotten statesman.

HIGHLIGHTS OF HIS ADMINISTRATION

❧ The Kansas-Nebraska Act, originally the bill to create Nebraska Territory, introduced in the Senate, January 1854, by Stephen A. Douglas as chairman of the Committee on Territories. The bill had been modified in committee to permit the people who settled the territory to determine whether it should permit or prohibit slavery—the doctrine of "popular sovereignty." Before final passage, the territory of Kansas was included in the bill, and the Missouri Compromise of 1820 was specifically repealed. The slavery dispute burst forth into new virulence as a result of the bill.

❧ "Bleeding Kansas": Pierce appointed a pro-Southern governor of Kansas Territory, but two governments were organized, one of anti-slavery immigrants from New England, one of pro-slavery men from Missouri. Guerilla war broke out between the two elements. A Federal marshal and his posse in arresting anti-slavery leaders at Lawrence sacked the town. Abolitionist John Brown murdered five men of a pro-slavery settlement at Pottawatamie Creek.

❧ The Gadsden Purchase, December 30, 1853, for $10,000,000, of land from Mexico to permit the building of a transcontinental railroad.

71

JAMES BUCHANAN

FIFTEENTH PRESIDENT

He was perhaps the finest constitutional lawyer of his day, a first-class diplomat, a devout patriot, and a consummate practitioner in the art of politics. Yet the judgment of history has been hard on James Buchanan, as it usually is on those who chose to appease in a crisis that proved to be soluble only by rougher action. In his seventieth year, as the Southern secession gathered momentum, he was steady in resisting pressure to bring force to bear against the South.

Actually, he was simply the last of the "Southern" Presidents, one who, though a Pennsylvanian, had for all his thirty-five years in politics identified himself with that tradition. It should be remembered that up to his time all the distinguished Presidents except the two Adamses had come out of the south. The Civil War proved him wrong, but fortunately it does not prove him necessarily dull or weak.

Buchanan was born during Washington's first term as President, the son of a Scotch-Irish immigrant, in York County, Pennsylvania. His father was a storekeeper in Mercersburg, who made a success in business, his mother a bright, lively woman with intellectual tastes. There were eleven children born, of whom eight grew up. James, like his brothers and sisters, received the best education available in the neighborhood. He studied law and was admitted to the bar at twenty-one. He practiced in Lancaster, but soon had a state-wide reputation.

Before he was forty he had made enough money in his practice to enable him to retire and give himself entirely to politics. At this time he was already something of a politician, having served in the state legislature and for ten years in the United States House of Representatives. Jackson sent him as minister to Russia in 1832 to negotiate a commercial treaty, a matter that had proved too difficult up to that time. Buchanan secured a satisfactory treaty, returned home, and was elected to the Senate in 1834.

In the next twenty years Buchanan was recognized as an expert on the judicial system and foreign affairs—he was Polk's Secretary of State and minister to Great Britain under Pierce—and the undisputed boss of the Democratic party in Pennsylvania. For years he had longed for his party's presidential nomination and had been, three times, passed over, but in 1856 he had some reservations about accepting the honor. He told a friend before the Democratic convention: "I had hoped for the nomination in 1844, again in 1848, and even in 1852, but now I would hesitate to take it. Before many years the Abolitionists will bring war upon the land. It may come during the next Presidential term."

Whatever his hesitation, there was no doubt that he still wanted the presidency in 1856. Moreover, he had confidence that he could prevent the "Brothers' War" he saw looming up ahead. The new Republican party put into the field the colorful but insubstantial John Charles Frémont with the slogan "Free Soil, Free Speech and Frémont" and it walked away with a good share of the northern vote, New England, New York, and four middle western states. But enough conservatives in the north preferred Buchanan and he won, though narrowly even in his own state. The main issue of the campaign was the battle for Kansas, and each side exploited it to the fullest possibilities of propaganda. Another influence was Harriet Beecher Stowe's *Uncle Tom's Cabin*, a book that had been in circulation for four years, appealing directly to a sense of the human pathos of slavery.

Buchanan viewed the abolitionists as "ignorant enthusiasts," like many others in history who have "spread devastation and bloodshed over the face of the earth." He hoped for the eventual ending of slavery, for he

74

was not Southern enough to see any good in the institution. In the meantime he stood firmly on the Constitution, arguing that slavery was a problem for the slave states and should so remain. Believing that it could be settled by law, he awaited impatiently the Supreme Court's decision on the Dred Scott case. When it was handed down it confirmed the Southern argument and in effect protected slave property. He cherished the delusion that the law had spoken and ended the dispute. Actually the decision merely inflamed the dispute further. Buchanan was ineffectual in the crisis because he reduced it to a matter of law and order. Even the importance of Lincoln and his clarion-clear statement of the slavery issue in his debates with Douglas escaped him.

To one determined in the legalistic point of view the growing fury of dispute, the fanaticism of John Brown, the madness of the "fire-eaters" in the South and the "black Republicans" in the North, were signs of a disorder that hopefully would pass. When Lincoln was elected in 1860 and secession was imminent, Buchanan spent his days debating with himself and his cabinet what the legal course should be. He did not believe the Southern states had the right to secede, nor could he see that the Federal government had the right to force them back into the Union if they did secede. When South Carolina started the procession out of the Union, followed by six more states, and the Confederate States of America was established with Jefferson Davis as president, Buchanan did precisely nothing.

There was a considerable body of public opinion in the north that the South should be allowed to go in peace. Congress had tried and failed to devise a compromise slavery amendment to the Constitution, and a "Peace

Convention" called by Virginia had also failed of a solution. In the south, there were left two minute patches of Federal soil, Fort Pickens at Pensacola and Fort Sumter at Charleston. Buchanan feared to reinforce them lest he increase the spirit of rebellion and precipitate secession in the rest of the south. One attempt was made to get men and supplies to Fort Sumter on a merchant ship, but when she was fired on by the batteries at the entrance to Charleston Harbor, she turned around and sailed away.

Thus, feeling that he had done his best to keep the peace and that the dilemma was not of his own making, Buchanan gladly turned over the government to Abraham Lincoln.

HIGHLIGHTS OF HIS ADMINISTRATION

~§ The Dred Scott Decision. The question: was the slave Scott automatically made free when his master took him from his home in Missouri to Illinois and Minnesota, free territory; and was he a citizen of Missouri? Having been sold to a citizen of New York, he was suing in Federal court under the law that allowed Federal jurisdiction in cases between citizens of different states. The decision (6 to 3) delivered by Chief Justice Taney: The Constitution recognized the right of property in slaves and the Missouri Compromise was unwarranted in destroying that right; Scott was not a citizen of Missouri since his citizenship was decided by the law in the state of his residence and Missouri law did not recognize him as a citizen.

The six justices in the majority were Democrats, five of them southerners. The three justices in the minority were a Republican, a Whig, and a northern Democrat. The Whig and the Republican gave a well-reasoned minority report. Since the court divided along political and sectional lines, the decision merely added fuel to the slavery debate.

~§ The Battle for Kansas. A constitution, passed by a convention representing the pro-slavery people in the state meeting at Lecompton, failed to pass the United States Congress. The English Bill, a compromise passed by Congress, offering a gift of land if Kansas accepted it, was sent back to Kansas for approval. Kansas voted it down. The territory was peaceably admitted as a state in 1861.

~§ The Lincoln-Douglas debates. In 1858 the Illinois Republicans nominated Lincoln for the Senate seat of Stephen A. Douglas, Democrat, running for re-election. In accepting the nomination, Lincoln stated bluntly that the nation could not exist half slave and half free. In joint debates with Douglas he was clear and uncompromising on abolishing slavery, and forced Douglas to negate the Dred Scott decision, losing thereby the support of the South.

John Brown's Raid. This fiery-eyed abolitionist with eighteen men seized the United States arsenal at Harper's Ferry, on October 16, 1859. Colonel Robert E. Lee, with Lieutenant J.E.B. Stuart and a detachment of marines, captured him. He was tried and hanged, on December second.

ABRAHAM LINCOLN

---◄◉►---

SIXTEENTH PRESIDENT

The Republican party in 1860 had wider support, more verve, a better list of candidates for the presidential nomination, and a better chance of defeating the Democrats than on its trial run four years earlier. It also had a great wooden building, called "The Wigwam," for its nominating convention in Chicago, with room for upwards of 10,000 of the general public to watch the proceedings. The leading candidate, the one with the largest personal following in the party and the man who certainly deserved his party's highest honor, was William H. Seward of New York. When the convention got down to the business of balloting, it was plain that Seward lacked the votes to win. In the opinion of the general public that packed the balcony, the man to nominate was the lawyer from Springfield, the man who out-talked Douglas in '58, "Honest Old Abe." On the third ballot the convention made the people in the balcony uproariously happy by nominating Lincoln. A cannon on the roof of the Wigwam boomed and the crowds outside joined the cheering.

79

Seward, the accomplished politician and defeated favorite, called him contemptuously the "prairie statesman" and Lincoln's campaign managers welcomed any picturesque phrase that emphasized the commonness, the rusticity of the man. They steered the campaign as close to the Jacksonian and log-cabin tradition as they possibly could, while Lincoln himself stayed at home receiving visitors but making no speeches. His campaign speeches had been made long since, beginning in 1854, when he undertook to campaign for one Richard Yates running for Congress in Illinois and including the debates with the little Democrat Stephen Douglas in 1858. In the Douglas debates he had been running for Douglas's seat in the United State Senate and he had lost the race. But it was the Lincoln speeches that still echoed across the nation and it was Lincoln who had forced Douglas to give up his claim to leadership in the Democratic party.

The six years of his great speeches summed up with classic simplicity Lincoln's arguments against slavery. They indicted the South for retrogressing in its handling of the slaves; they posed the issue politically as one capable of reasonable solution; and they rejected the emotionalism of the radical abolitionists. With a distilled clarity, and without the rolling periods of rich language generally loved by orators, they made excellent reading, as they still do. For instance, in a speech at Peoria in 1854: "Near eighty years ago we began by declaring that all men are created equal; but now, from that beginning, we have run down to the other declaration, that for some men to enslave others is a 'sacred right of self-government.' These principles cannot stand together. They are as opposite as God and Mammon." And in accepting the Republican nomination for the Senate in 1858: " 'A house divided against itself cannot stand.' I believe this government cannot endure permanently half slave and half free. I do not expect the Union to be dissolved—I do not expect the house to fall—but I do expect it will cease to be divided. It will become all one thing or all the other. Either the opponents of slavery will arrest the further spread of it, and place it where the public mind shall rest in the belief that it is in course of ultimate extinction; or its advocates will push it forward till it shall become alike lawful in all the States, old as well as new, North as well as South."

The emergence of genius is as mysterious when it appears in politics as it is in other forms of art. Abraham Lincoln was born about as humbly as possible. Every shred of evidence relating to his family and early life has been tenderly gathered together and interpreted. Much of it is good reading and good, honest folklore. The simple facts are that he was born on an upland farm near Elizabethtown, Kentucky, of a poor frontier family that never took hold of the land and settled down. When he was seven they moved on to Indiana and began clearing a quarter section deep in the forest near a crossroads that became known as Gentryville. Here his mother died and Abe acquired a stepmother, a kind woman who sympathized with the boy's restless desire for knowledge. The opportunities for education were almost nil—Lincoln later estimated that he had had not more than twelve months of schooling in all his life—but occasionally the boy got hold of a book, and no matter what it was, he read it avidly. At the same time he grew remarkably tall (six feet, four inches) and strong. He was a great hand with an axe or a plow, but he was also very gentle, a great talker, and somewhat lazy.

When Lincoln was twenty-one he helped his family move to Illinois and build a cabin on the Sangamon River, then set out to make his own living. He came to rest for a few years at New Salem, a nondescript little settlement near Springfield, which a few years later was abandoned. Here he clerked in a store and tried to operate a store of his own, a financial disaster that kept him in debt for seventeen years. He met the young toughs of Clary's Grove and wrestled their leader, Jack Armstrong. He fell in love with Anne Rutledge and went through a period of black melancholy when she died. He was debating whether he should become a blacksmith or aspire to the law, for which he feared he had too little education, when he ran successfully for the Illinois legislature, where he was to serve for the next eight years.

The legislature opened up a new life. He was soon borrowing law books, licensed to practice and part of a law firm. In 1837 he moved to Springfield, the year after it became capital of the state, an event that he had helped to bring about in the legislature. Here for the first time he enjoyed the society, and approval, of educated people. Physically he was ungainly—at first impression downright ugly—with overlong arms, large hands and feet. His hair was black and untidy and his swarthy face rested usually in an expression of melancholy. But he won people with his immense kindness and a patent honesty that he was inclined to mix with humor. As a lawyer, he might not be particularly learned, but he had a pointed way of putting his case and an analytical mind that disrobed an argument of its sophistry with unerring skill. He was popular among men as a good talker and a great storyteller. With women he was inclined to go into emotional somersaults, but finally, after five years in Springfield and an interrupted engagement, he capitulated to Mary Todd, a very eligible young girl who set her heart on him.

For several years after marriage, Lincoln devoted himself to a deeper study and practice of law, interrupted only by a single term in the United States House of Representatives, as a Whig. The slavery issue, which

81

had been quiescent after the Clay compromises of 1850, suddenly burst into flame with the passage of Douglas's Kansas-Nebraska Act. This act, an unwarranted victory for the pro-slavery South, repealed the Missouri Compromise of 1820 that had declared the northwest territories free, and theoretically at least, made them available for settlers with slaves.

The effect on Lincoln was to arouse him from the complacency of his prosperous life, stirring up his political antagonism to Douglas and his sense of outrage at the Southern attack on the principle of human fairness, a cornerstone of his own temperament. In the fall of 1854 he took to the stump and became a candidate for the Senate, but lost as a Whig in a strongly Democratic state. In 1856 he took a hand in organizing the Republican party in Illinois and barely escaped being the vice-presidential candidate with the glamorous Frémont on the Republican ticket that year. It is certain that all his political instincts were now alive and he looked ahead, sometimes with confidence, to an office he was peculiarly fitted to occupy.

Lincoln's inaugural address was extraordinarily mild. He tried to reassure the South on its rights and persuade it that it was easier to get on with the North inside the Union than outside. While he bent every effort to constrict the geography of secession and keep in the Union the states that had not seceded, he made not the slightest motion toward military preparation. Never a man to be hurried, he waited for Virginia to make up her mind, while he was plagued to decide what to do about Fort Sumter, isolated, with its Federal garrison, on Charleston Harbor in South Carolina, the first state to secede. By the end of March, Lincoln decided, though most of the cabinet disagreed, that Sumter had to be held as a matter of principle, and he ordered a relief expedition to it.

The Confederate government now hesitated between war and peace, and Major Anderson in the fort offered to surrender in three days if he was not provisioned or ordered to hold on by Washington. Anderson was the precipitant to Jefferson Davis's worries. The Confederate president was trying to decide whether secession would succeed better with a clash of arms. In the end he took the war gamble, ordering General Beauregard, Confederate commander at Charleston, to fire on the fort if there was an attempt to reinforce it. Some of Beauregard's officers took matters in their own hands and began the bombardment on April twelfth.

There was an enthusiasm in the North for the war. Men enlisted readily in the first draft call, and the militia regiments turned out in their fine uniforms, marching gaily off to war with the cry "On to Richmond!", confident that they would roll right over the "secesh" army and settle matters in a hurry. It was not to be. Lincoln lacked good military advice and good general officers. After the brave new army was thrown back disgracefully at the Battle of Bull Run on July twenty-first in the first summer, the word was "more training." Lincoln selected a young West Pointer named George McClellan to train the army. This he did, magnificently, but he never led it to victory. In all, the army that started out for Richmond was in the hands of five successive commanders and was a very different army before it marched into Richmond nearly four years later. It was not until March of 1864 that General Ulysses S. Grant came from his successful western campaigns to supply the kind of over-all military command that could win the war.

In the long search for a winning general, Lincoln showed restraint and patience. The same qualities made him a superb civil administrator. He had in his cabinet several able but difficult men. These he handled with the authority of a dictator and the understanding of a house mother, and was rewarded by their becoming hard-working department heads. He was concerned at all times that the war objective should be understood: to restore the Union. He did intend that slavery should be abolished, with compensation if possible, but the restless and mischievous abolitionists who accused him of going too slowly on slavery were severely and plainly reprimanded. However, he came to believe that the moral position of the war effort at home and abroad required a move toward emancipation. Therefore, in September 1862, after the Union army turned back the Confederate invasion of Maryland at Antietam, Lincoln issued the preliminary emancipation proclamation.

The 1864 presidential campaign came in the last gloomy summer of the war. More than a few people, including pontifical Horace Greeley of the New York *Tribune*, doubted that Lincoln could be elected unless the Confederate armies were beaten speedily. For once Lincoln agreed with him. The North was mortally dispirited and even here and there disaffected. But Sherman's capture of Atlanta on September third was a tonic and by election day there was a general confidence that the war was going to be won. Lincoln, renominated by the Republicans, or the "National Union party," was handsomely re-elected and with him as Vice President, Andrew Johnson of Tennessee. His second inaugural address included the unforgettable paragraph beginning: "With malice toward none; with charity for all; with firmness in the right, as God gives us to see the right, let us strive on to finish the work we are in; to bind up the nation's wounds. . . ."

83

On April fourth Lincoln, with Admiral Porter and a guard of sailors, inspected evacuated Richmond. Five days later Lee surrendered to Grant at Appomattox. On the evening of the fourteenth the actor John Wilkes Booth entered the President's box at the Ford Theatre and shot the President in the head. Leaping from the box to the stage, he waved a knife and yelled "Sic semper tyrannis!" and ran past the actors off the stage into the night. The President was carried unconscious to a rooming house across the street where he died shortly after seven the next morning. His funeral was extraordinary and moving. As the train carrying his body moved slowly westward, people from the towns and the farms all the way to Springfield stood beside the tracks, crying.

HIGHLIGHTS OF HIS ADMINISTRATION

The Civil War. The first shot was fired at Fort Sumter on Charleston Harbor, April 12, 1861, the fort surrendering after 34 hours. The states that made up the Confederate States of America were South Carolina, Georgia, Alabama, Mississippi, Louisiana, Florida, Texas, Arkansas, Virginia, North Carolina, Tennessee. The border states Missouri, Kentucky, Maryland, and the western counties of Virginia (West Virginia) stayed in the Union. Confederate General Robert E. Lee surrendered at Appomattox Court House, Virginia, April 9, 1865, and the rest of the Confederate armies surrendered in the succeeding weeks, the last May twenty-sixth. Casualties: 360,000 Union soldiers died; 258,000 Confederate soldiers died: 500,000 wounded on both sides.

The *Trent* Affair. Confederate agents Mason and Slidell, on their way to London and Paris on the British mailship *Trent*, were taken off and brought back to the United States by the American naval ship *San Jacinto*. Great Britain claimed violation of a neutral ship. Lincoln maintained the right to search British vessels but released Mason and Slidell and the tension between the two countries eased.

Great Britain's permitting the secret building of ships for the Confederate navy in British shipyards. Lincoln protested through the American minister Charles Francis Adams. After laborious representations by Adams the practice was stopped, but the *Florida* and *Alabama*, Confederate raiders built in England, destroyed $15,000,000 worth of Union ships and cargo.

✑ Financing the War: In 1861, a 3 per cent income tax was declared on incomes over $800, and a direct tax and a quarter-billion-dollar loan authorized.

The Legal Tender Act of February 25, 1862, making "Green-backs" or Treasury notes legal tender for all dues except imports and interest on the public debt, and a half-billion-dollar loan. More green-backs were authorized by Congress later. Also further loans.

The National Banking Act, of February 25, 1863, amended 1864: a national banking system by which member banks invested a third of their capital in government bonds and were allowed to issue notes up to 90 per cent of the value of those bonds. A minimum of capital stock and of cash reserves was set and stockholders were held responsible for a proportion of the bank's debts. This system drove most of the old state banks out of business.

✑ The preliminary emancipation proclamation, September 23, 1862, that all slaves in states in rebellion would be free on January 1, 1863. On January first a final proclamation, by military authority, declared free slaves in all the South except Tennessee and the parts of Louisiana and Virginia held by Union armies. Because the proclamation was probably not legal under civil law, the Thirteenth Amendment to the Constitution was introduced in Congress, March 28, 1864. It had passed both houses by January 31, 1865. It was declared ratified on December 18, 1865.

✑ The conscription law of March 3, 1863, drafting all male citizens between ages twenty and forty-five. Badly written, it permitted those with money to buy off from a particular summons or to provide a substitute to fill their places in the roll. It was hardest on the poor. On July thirteenth, draft riots began in New York and lasted for four days, during which a thousand were killed or injured and a number of buildings were looted and burned.

✑ Dedication of the Military Cemetery at Gettysburg, November 19, 1863, for which Lincoln delivered the Gettysburg Address.

ANDREW JOHNSON

---◆---

SEVENTEENTH PRESIDENT

Senator Andrew Johnson of Tennessee, returning from Lincoln's inauguration in March of 1861, came close to losing his life at Lynchburg, Virginia. A mob dragged him from the train by his nose, kicked him, spat upon him, dropped a noose around his neck, and proposed to hang him. According to the story, they let him go when a sporting suggestion was made that Tennessee should be allowed the privilege of hanging their own traitor. The mob was infuriated because of all the twenty-two Southern senators he alone stood out for the Union. The Civil War had already burst into reality and Virginia was about to secede from the Union. Johnson got safely back to his home in the hills of East Tennessee, where he stumped hard against secession, "hell-born and hell-bound," as he called it. This was border country economically and politically, a land of small farms, few slaves, and opinionated men. It voted a good majority for the Union, but the rest of the state went the other way, and on the 24th of June, the governor proclaimed Tennessee part of the Confederacy.

Johnson was a Democrat, but a year later he was a strong Lincoln man and defended him in the Senate more than once. When the Confederate government of Tennessee withdrew from the capital at Nashville in February 1862, Lincoln sent Johnson there as military governor. It was a good choice, for although the military situation in Tennessee remained fluid to a degree, Andy Johnson held on resolutely at Nashville and did his best to adjust Tennessee to Reconstruction and Reconstruction to Tennessee. Tennessee was the first of the Southern states to be reconstructed and the only one to escape military government after the war.

Because of his loyal work in Tennessee and his unique position as a loyal Southern senator it was thought that his nomination for the vice-presidency on the Lincoln ticket in 1864 would help erase sectional lines. The thought has been attributed to Lincoln himself. It was typical of Lincoln that he chose a man of strong character and positive talents. Andrew Johnson's origins were not unlike those of Lincoln, both of them the children of a moving frontier. Johnson's father was a city constable, a sexton, and porter in a bank at Raleigh, North Carolina. Dying when Andrew was four, he left his wife and child in poverty. At ten the boy was apprenticed to a tailor, being at that age totally illiterate. It happened that a charitable man came to read to the boys in the tailoring shop, his book, *The American Speaker*, being a collection of the orations of British statesmen. When he realized how intently the Johnson boy followed his readings, it occurred to him to give Andrew the book, and from it Andrew learned to read and spell. At eighteen he moved to eastern Tennessee and opened a tailor shop in Greeneville. He shortly married a shoemaker's daughter, an educated girl who took his education in hand. Debating came easily to him and this led to politics, first as a town alderman and then, at twenty-two, as mayor.

Because of his own poor circumstances, Johnson felt a kinship with the working people and "poor whites." He naturally thought of himself as their spokesman and on this idea built up great political power in a few years, as a Jackson Democrat. He served in the state legislature, in the United States House of Representatives for five terms, as governor of Tennessee for two terms, and in 1857 became a United States senator. The impression he made on Charles Francis Adams at that time was of "nerve—apparent force and coolness in a position of danger." A different impression was recorded in 1865 when he was sworn in as Vice President of the United States. Feeling ill and tired, he had braced himself with whisky, with the disastrous result that he rose unsteadily to his feet, took the oath, and then for fifteen minutes rambled through a maudlin speech. "A bad slip," Lincoln admitted to a friend, "but Andy ain't a drunkard!"

Andrew Johnson believed that he understood Lincoln's projected plan for reconstruction of the South and he followed it. But the copy is never as subtle or successful as the original. Nor had Johnson Lincoln's incomparable skill in handling willful men. It was part of his tragedy that he was a Democrat in a Republican administration and that, aside from this isolation, he had been a lone fighter all his life and did not know how to gather a party about him. In all his four years in the presidency, he presented the gallant but impractical spectacle of a lone man fighting a well-organized Congress.

While Congress was in recess, Johnson proceeded with his program to re-admit the Southern states to the Union. On May 29, 1865, he issued a general amnesty to former Confederates, except certain classes of military and civil officers and persons having more than $20,000 of taxable property. He then proceeded to extend to all the Southern states the pattern of reorganization set by Lincoln for Tennessee, Arkansas, Louisiana, and Virginia. All whites who received amnesty and took an oath of loyalty to the Union went to the polls and elected a state constitutional convention that met to abolish slavery and annul secession. All but Mississippi ratified the Thirteenth Amendment. They also elected state governments and members of Congress. The vote was not given the Negroes, who at that time were not allowed to vote in the North except in five of the New England states and New York.

Johnson's plan was a well-conceived appeal to moderation. Under articulate, forceful, and tireless leadership it might have succeeded, since the attitude of the North toward the South was generally moderate. In December, Congress met and rejected the members elected from the former Confederate states. The House was dominated by the "radical Republicans," a mixed group of abolitionists and practical politicians. Their leader was Thaddeus Stevens, a fierce old man with a club foot, who seemed to have abandoned human considerations for party and power. By a superbly organized plan, he and his friends destroyed the Johnson Reconstruction with moderation by a series of bills passed over Johnson's veto. The bills, treating rebellion with rough justice, disfranchised rebels and felons, gave the Negroes the vote, and imposed military government. Their objectives were narrow, their severity was self-defeating.

The radicals next attacked the President and the independence of his office. In two bills, they deprived him of the right as Commander-in-Chief of the army to issue direct orders to the army, and in the Tenure of Office Bill, of the right to dismiss an official without the consent of the Senate. Johnson had retained Lincoln's cabinet, and several members, notably Secretary of State Seward, served him loyally and well. But the Secretary of War, Stanton, had been disloyal from the first, acting as a spy in the cabinet for the radicals in Congress. Johnson only gradually came to realize his treachery. Now he decided to dismiss him. The Senate refused its approval, under the Tenure of Office Act. In the meantime Johnson had named General Grant Secretary of War and had asked him to refuse to yield to Stanton should the Senate order Stanton reinstated. In this way the Tenure of Office Act could be taken to the courts for a judgment on its constitutionality. Grant did not want to do this, but Johnson understood that he would resign as Secretary of War before the Senate made a decision, in time for another man who would be willing to stand for a court trial to be named Secretary. Grant and Johnson later quarreled violently over this understanding, or misunderstanding.

With Stanton reinstated and Grant yielding to the order of the Senate, Johnson dismissed the Secretary a second time. For this and other offenses, designated as "high crimes and misdemeanors," the House impeached Johnson. The trial was long and tense, ending in the President's acquittal by one vote. During the trial, faced with the prospect of being thrown out of the presidency, Johnson was clear-headed and even astute. With typical stubbornness, he determined to make a comeback in politics, at the end of his term. Twice he ran unsuccessfully for the Senate, but on the third try, in 1874, succeeded. He died less than five months after taking his seat, in March 1875.

HIGHLIGHTS OF HIS ADMINISTRATION

~§ The strategy of Congressional Reconstruction:

Freedmen's Bureau Bill of January 5, 1866, extending the personnel and powers of the War Department's "bureau of refugees, freedmen and abandoned lands" and giving it authority to protect the Negroes from repressive black codes. Passed. Vetoed and not passed over the presidential veto. A second version was voted on, vetoed, and passed over Johnson's veto, in July 1866.

The Fourteenth Amendment to the Constitution, June 16, 1866. Its provisions include that by which all persons born or naturalized in the United States are citizens, "nor shall any State deprive any person of life, liberty or property without due process of law. . . ." Ratified July 28, 1868.

The Reconstruction Act of March 2, 1867, dividing the South into five military districts, except Tennessee, which had been accepted back into the Union, with a military governor over each district, this government to continue until a constitutional convention elected by all citizens regardless of race or color, except those disfranchised for felony or rebellion, "shall have written a constitution acceptable to Congress, and the legislature shall have ratified the Fourteenth Amendment."

Act of July 19, 1867, giving the registrars of voters the right to determine whether voters should be disfranchised on the basis of having served voluntarily (as distinguished from involuntarily) in the Confederacy.

The Tenure of Office Act, which forbade the President to dismiss officials without the consent of the Senate. Passed over Johnson's veto, March 2, 1867.

The impeachment of the President: on March 4, 1868, seven managers of the House presented eleven charges to the Senate, siting as a court of impeachment, Chief Justice Chase presiding. The "high crimes and misdemeanors" charged were generally: that Johnson's dismissal of Secretary Stanton—though Stanton had resisted dismissal by camping out in his office—violated the Tenure of Office Act; that Johnson had assumed the right to declare certain laws of Congress unconstitutional; that he had maliciously criticized Congress in his "Swing around the Circle" speeches; that he had opposed Congressional Reconstruction. To convict it was necessary to have the votes of 36 out of the 54 Senators. The Senate voted on May sixteenth on the eleventh charge. Johnson was acquitted, 19 to 35. Recessing for ten days, the radicals tried to break down at least one senator voting for acquittal. They failed. A vote on the first and second charges showed the same division as before. They did not request a vote on the rest of the charges.

The French in Mexico: America held that the French imposition of Emperor Maximilian by force of arms on Mexico in 1864 violated the Monroe Doctrine. Secretary Seward induced Napoleon III to withdraw his army from Mexico, on April 5, 1866. Maximilian was too proud to leave with them, was captured, tried, and shot, June 19, 1867.

Ratification, May 28, 1867, of the purchase of Alaska arranged by Secretary of State Seward. Unpopularly known as "Seward's Folly," it cost $7,200,000.

The Fifteenth Amendment to the Constitution, passed by Congress on February 27, 1869, and ratified by the states on March 30, 1870, providing that the right to vote shall not be denied "on account of race, color, or previous condition of servitude."

91

ULYSSES SIMPSON GRANT

EIGHTEENTH PRESIDENT

Like most of the military, General Grant's party affiliation was uncertain. For two years after the end of the Civil War, Andrew Johnson, a Democrat in a Republican administration, courted him, but early in the election year 1868, Johnson quarreled with Grant and threw him into the waiting arms of the Republicans. The Republican convention therefore unanimously nominated him for President, and he was almost as easily elected in the autumn, carrying 26 of the 34 states voting, including five Southern states under the heel of the carpetbaggers.

Grant was an oddly attractive man, like many men of genius a great brain in an unconventional casing: slender and stooped, a little shabby in the plainest of army clothes, mild in manner. Charles A. Dana called him "the most modest, the most disinterested, and the most honest man I ever knew." One of his staff described him as he wrote dispatches to order up his forces for the Battle of Chattanooga: "His work was performed swiftly and uninterruptedly. . . . His thoughts flowed as freely from his mind

93

as the ink from his pen. . . . He sat with his head bent low over the table, and when he had occasion . . . he would glide rapidly across the room without straightening himself and return to his seat with his body still bent over at about the same angle at which he had been sitting. Looking over the dispatches I found that he was ordering up Sherman's entire force from Corinth, and was informing Halleck of the dispositions decided upon for the opening of a line of supplies and assuring him that everything possible would be done for the relief of Burnside in East Tennessee . . . the taking of vigorous and comprehensive steps in every direction throughout his new and extensive command."

So much for Grant on the battlefield. The American people loved him and the whole Grant legend. They felt that he was a great and good and simple man, and probably no power on earth could have kept them from putting him in the White House, so long as he was willing. It was a great reward in a life that had had dismally few rewards. Born in a small settlement on the Ohio 25 miles southeast of Cincinnati, son of a rising young man in the leather-tanning business, his only boyhood aptitude was for handling horses. His father was determined that the boy should make something of himself, and since he could not interest him in the tannery, bethought him of sending him to West Point. When he told Ulysses, the boy was less than enthusiastic. As he said later: "A military life had no charms for me, and I had not the faintest idea of staying in the army even if I should be graduated, which I did not expect." He graduated 21st in a class of 39, in time to take part in the Mexican War, serving both in General Taylor's Rio Grande campaign and General Scott's Mexico City campaign. There followed several years of garrison duty, with slow promotion and low pay. Since he was now married and had children, he worried about the little money he made and he grew more and more discontented with the army duty that kept him away from his family. Shortly after he was promoted to captain at Fort Humboldt, California, his commanding officer accused him of being drunk on duty and threatened to have him court-martialed. It was suggested that he resign, and it suited Grant to do so since he was anxious to get back east.

There followed six poverty-stricken years, as a farmer, in the real estate business at St. Louis, and finally, swallowing his pride, as a clerk in his father's leather store at Galena, Illinois. When the Civil War broke, he offered his services to the War Department and asked for a regiment to command, but was ignored. In the meantime he had been in Springfield, the state capital, training and mustering in militia. One of these outfits, the Twenty-First Illinois, became unhappy about the colonel they had

94

elected and asked the governor if they could have Grant instead. Thus Grant got his first Civil War command.

Serving in the Department of the Missouri, Grant gave the Union armies their first important victories by capturing the Confederate forts Henry and Donelson in western Tennessee—it was at Donelson that he earned his army nickname, "Unconditional Surrender." In spite of these successes, and more importantly, the evidence that Grant had a rare understanding of military strategy, he was set aside and humiliated by his mediocre and jealous department commander, Halleck.

His weakness for drink was well known, but charges in the press that his effectiveness was lessened by it were plainly unjust. With the confidence of Lincoln and a shift in the upper level of command, he was at last able to put into effect his plans to capture the Mississippi Valley and roll back the Confederate armies in the west. Brought east to take command of all the Union forces, he forced the issue with the valiant and enduring Lee in Virginia and brought the war to a successful conclusion. In victory he was a generous and modest man. In the hysteria following Lincoln's assassination, he seemed a tower of strength.

It was generally understood that Grant knew nothing about politics, but there was confidence that his famous common sense would save him from mistakes. He might even make a great President. Nothing was to prove further from the truth. His common sense disappeared in judging people, so that in the world of ambitious politicians he proved an incurable innocent. Regarding his election as purely and simply a personal reward for services, he never applied himself to comprehending the office of President. He gradually yielded to the influence of his most insistent advisers, who inevitably were the clamorous spoilsmen in his own party. The few good men he chose for his cabinet were dismissed, or quit, with one exception. Hamilton Fish remained as Secretary of State, to become one of the most distinguished men ever to hold that office.

Only one President besides Grant has been so tarnished by scandals in his administration. Personally honest, and even touchy about his honor, he was always simple-minded in believing what he was told, and he had a poor boy's admiration for the glitter of wealth. In the scandal that came nearest to him, he had allowed the plausible Jay Gould to persuade him to order the Treasury to stop selling gold to put up the price of the metal. Increase in the value of gold, he was told, would encourage Europeans to buy more western wheat, and this would be a boon to the farmers. When the plot was revealed to him a few days later, with the gold crisis of "Black Friday" on Wall Street, he felt betrayed. But he was criticized for not having understood the plot from the beginning.

It was a time of industrial expansion and speculation, none of which Grant understood. Many politicians were led astray by the money-making fever. Of those around Grant who fell under suspicion, his secretary Babcock was tried, but acquitted in the St. Louis Whisky Ring fraud; his Secretary of the Treasury Richardson resigned after revelation of the Sanborn Contract graft in the Internal Revenue Service; his Secretary of War Belknap resigned under threat of impeachment for accepting a small bribe from an Indian agent.

On leaving office after two terms, Grant made an extended tour of the world, receiving honors and homage wherever he went. Returning late in 1879, he was prepared to accept a third term, but his supporters were not able to get the nomination for him in the Republican National Convention of 1880, and he was deeply humiliated. Faced with the necessity of making money, he entrusted all his capital to one of his sons. Four years later his son's firm failed and Grant was broke and in debt. Writing his *Memoirs* he hoped would alleviate his financial distress. Suffering painfully with cancer of the throat, he kept on with his writing until his death at the age of sixty-three.

HIGHLIGHTS OF HIS ADMINISTRATION

◦§ "Black Friday," September 24, 1869. Jay Gould and Jim Fisk, owning control of the Erie Railroad, schemed to promote the sale of wheat to Europe. If the price of gold were to rise, Europe would buy more American wheat, and more wheat would move from the west on the Erie. Gould met Grant through the President's brother-in-law, Corbin, a New Yorker, and explained to him the relation between the price of gold and wheat. Grant thought it would help the farmers in the west and ordered the Secretary of the Treasury to stop selling gold, as it was necessary to do to keep the price of gold level. Gould and Fisk proceeded to buy gold on the market and bid up the premium from about $132 to $162. Dozens of Wall Street brokers faced ruin. Some of them reached Grant. He understood the trick that had been played on him and at once ordered the government to sell gold, thus breaking the "corner."

◦§ The *Virginius* Affair: In 1868 Cuban patriots began a guerilla war against Spanish rule. Rebel organizations in the United States shipped in men and guns to supply it, one of their vessels being the *Virginius*, sailing under the American flag. In 1873 the Spaniards seized this ship, and summarily tried and executed fifty-three of the crew and passengers, one of them an American citizen. The incident brought Spain and the United States close to war, but Secretary Fish arranged a peaceful settlement. The ship and surviving passengers and crew were released, and an investigation proved that the ship's American registry was fraudulent.

The Ku Klux Klan Act, April 20, 1871, to increase Federal authority to act against the Ku Klux Klan and other secret white men's societies organized to control the freed Negroes, also to investigate the activities of these societies in the South. The Act resulted in the disappearance of the Klan and the substitution of subtler but more effective means of controlling the Negro vote and eliminating the Republican party. The Act gave the President the right to suspend *habeas corpus* writ. This latter provision was declared unconstitutional by the Supreme Court in 1882.

A general amnesty act for former Confederates, May 1872, removing the disabilities from all but about 500.

The *Alabama* Claims. Following the procedure agreed upon in the British-American Treaty of Washington in 1871, American claims against Britain for losses caused by the Confederate cruisers *Alabama* and *Florida* and others that were permitted to escape from British ports and raid Union shipping during the Civil War were submitted to an international tribunal. The tribunal's five members were chosen, one each, by Great Britain, the United States, and the rulers of Italy, Switzerland, and Brazil. In August 1872, the decision was published. It awarded $15,500,000 in damages to the United States, the neutrals having agreed that Britain must accept responsibility for the escape of the raiders.

The Sioux War of 1876. The discovery of gold in the Black Hills of Dakota in 1875 brought prospectors flooding into the Sioux range lands, supposedly guaranteed to them by treaty. The Sioux, some 2,500 strong, went on the warpath under Sitting Bull. In June 1876, they surprised General Custer and 200 men on the Little Big Horn River in southern Montana and killed them to a man. Sitting Bull and some of the warriors were driven into Canada; one of his lieutenants, Crazy Horse, was captured and murdered. Eventually most of the Sioux agreed to stay inside a reservation. Sitting Bull returned to his people and lived on the reservation until he was killed resisting arrest in 1890.

RUTHERFORD BIRCHARD HAYES

In the years after the Civil War, the ferment and the heroics and the real concern of Americans were in industry, railroads, commerce, finance. The great names were businessmen who met their competition in one way or another and monopolized profits by organizing trusts. Their standard of ethics was crude, and sometimes, in order to get their way, they bought legislators and other government officials, having in their full-blown arrogance contempt for all the little people. The politicians also used money for the power grab, though on a smaller scale, and there were such flamboyant phenomena as the Democratic Tweed Ring in New York City and Senator Roscoe Conkling, Republican boss of New York State. It reads like folklore, but it all happened. It has been pointed out that compared to the great empire builders of this "Gilded Age"—or gilded anarchy—the Presidents of the United States from Lincoln to Teddy Roosevelt, except possibly for Grover Cleveland, are the forgotten men of their time. This is true enough. But their personal reputations have worn better.

At the Republican National Convention of 1876, the leading contender for the presidential nomination was James G. Blaine, a skillful orator in Congress and probably the most popular man in the party, but tainted with charges of easy ethics. With the scandals of the Grant administration dinning in their ears, the delegates were inclined to pay unusual attention to the reformers in the party who were determined to defeat Blaine. Nevertheless, when Robert G. Ingersoll, in nominating him, rose to the heights of oratory and pictured him as a "plumed knight" jousting with his adversaries, the delegates might have stampeded to him, had it not been time to go home for dinner.

With the balloting postponed until the next day, there was an opportunity for last-minute vote trading during the night. Rutherford Hayes was the most prominent of the states' favorite sons, a man "of great purity in private life," but a friend of Grant and the party regulars, not by any means a reformer. The reformers hoped to nominate their own man, Benjamin H. Bristow, Grant's Secretary of the Treasury who had recently made a name for himself by exposing the Whisky Ring frauds. When they saw that this was impossible, they combined with regular party factions opposed to Blaine to nominate Hayes on the seventh ballot.

Carl Schurz, the reformer, said that the Republicans had nominated a man without knowing it. Hayes's strength was that he was a steady, commonplace type, a successful businessman's lawyer, a conservative on the tariff and sound money, and a loyal party man. He was an Ohioan, the first of the "Ohio Dynasty" of Presidents. His father had moved his family from Connecticut to the Western Reserve and set up a whisky-distilling business. He died young, before Rutherford was born, but his widow was fortunate in having a rich bachelor brother who stepped in and provided the care that she and her two children required. Uncle Sardis Birchard sent young Rutherford to Kenyon College and Harvard Law School, then gave him the parental subsidy and advice necessary to launch him on his law career. Later he deeded him the comfortable, big estate at Spiegel Grove, near Fremont, Ohio, that became the Hayeses' permanent home.

As a young lawyer, Hayes wasted five years trying to establish a practice at Fremont (then Lower Sandusky), the home of Uncle Sardis. On moving to Cincinnati, his fortunes changed and he was soon successful in his profession and married to an admirable girl. When the Civil War called patriots to the colors, he secured a majority and served all during the war, rising to command a brigade. He was wounded at the Battle of

South Mountain and breveted major general for distinguished services. In the autumn of 1864, while still serving in the army, he was elected to the House of Representatives. After a single term, he was elected governor of Ohio and served two consecutive terms. In 1875 he was again elected governor and was in this auspicious position when the Republican convention met at Cincinnati in 1876.

Rutherford Hayes was of medium height, with deep-set blue eyes, a methodical man who took constitutionals for his health, but also a good-natured man who had a sense of humor and liked to wear comfortable clothes regardless of how badly they fitted him. He and his wife, Lucy, were dedicated temperance people, not a popular position with politicians.

The election of 1876 was the only disputed election in American history, and it defied a fair solution. The Democrats had put up Samuel J. Tilden, a man eminently qualified for the office of President. He won a plurality in the popular vote and lacked only one of a majority in the electoral vote, with 20 votes in dispute. Nineteen of these were in Florida, South Carolina, and Louisiana, the three Southern states where Reconstruction Republican rule was still in effect; one was in Oregon, where the Democratic governor gave a certificate of election to a Democratic elector, displacing a Republican who, as a Federal official, was ineligible under the Constitution. Since Oregon had given a majority to Hayes, this disputed vote could not fairly be denied him. But in the Southern states, Republican election boards had freely thrown out Democratic votes—in Louisiana what at first appeared to be a Democratic majority of 6,300 was converted into a Republican majority of 4,600 votes—and reported all 19 votes for Hayes. The Democratic electors, charging fraud, met and voted for Tilden. Two sets of returns from these states therefore went to the Senate for the official tally of electoral votes. There was no precedent for settling such a dispute. Finally both parties agreed to pass the decision to a commission.

On the commission were five men each from the House, Senate, and Supreme Court. There was one truly nonpartisan associate justice on the Supreme Court and it was assumed that he would be the balance wheel for a fair judgment. At the last moment he was rescued from this difficult responsibility by being elected Democratic Senator from Illinois. The commission, now eight Republicans to seven Democrats, examined the returns and deliberated for a month. It voted, strictly along party lines, that it could not go behind the election-board returns, and that if the boards had been guilty of wrongdoing it was a matter for the states to decide, not

Congress. In this manner Hayes was given all the disputed votes and was declared elected, just three days before the inaugural date, at four o'clock in the morning, by one vote.

It was a way out of a dilemma, rather than a decision, but it was accepted, and though bitterness lingered in the Democratic party, Hayes fulfilled his term without suffering personally from the animosities of the dispute. This was partly due to his wish to conciliate the South. Assurances had been conveyed on his behalf to Democrats in South Carolina and Louisiana, before the election was settled, that he would favor withdrawal of Federal troops from those states. Once inaugurated, he lost no time in meeting this commitment, and brought to an end military Reconstruction in the South. This was shocking to the Old Guard Republicans. He alienated them further by reviving civil-service reform, that had been smothered practically at birth during Grant's administration. Unable to get legislation for a broad program, he resorted to a direct attack on a few fortresses of the spoilsmen.

His most spectacular assault was on the New York Custom House, which supported two hundred ward heelers of the Republican state boss, Senator Roscoe Conkling. When the Collector, Chester A. Arthur, would not go along with a cleansing of the office, he was removed. Hayes proved to be an honest man of independent spirit with the courage to tackle political abuses. By turning on those in his own party, he made enemies of Conkling and other "Stalwarts," or conservatives. These denied him the nomination for a second term. In going out of office, he left behind for his party a good pattern of political virtue. Retiring to his Ohio estate, he led a happy and humdrum existence, managing private charities and modestly enjoying the honors of an ex-President.

HIGHLIGHTS OF HIS ADMINISTRATION

The first great labor strike, 1877. Three million railway workers tied up most of the railroad lines between the eastern seaboard and the Mississippi. The governors of Pennsylvania, Maryland, and West Virginia asked the President for troops to control sporadic rioting. He complied and the strike ended.

102

✑ The Bland-Allison Silver Coinage Act, providing for coinage of silver dollars at a ratio of 15.62 to 1 of gold. Coinage was to be limited to between $2,000,000 and $4,000,000 a month. Vetoed by Hayes and passed over his veto, February 28, 1878.

✑ The resumption of specie payments, January 1, 1879. With ample gold reserve, this was accomplished without incident.

JAMES ABRAM GARFIELD

TWENTIETH PRESIDENT

Of the four presidential assassinations, the most cruel, in a sense, was that of Garfield. Dying six months after his inauguration, untried but promising, he remains a question mark. At the Republican convention of 1880, he was that party handyman, the "available" candidate to break a tie between two candidates of equal strength in the balloting. In this case it was Grant, for a third term, against James G. Blaine. Garfield came to the convention to nominate Senator John Sherman of Ohio, an admirable man but with a cold personality that considerably diminished his popular appeal. The switch to Garfield started on the 35th ballot and he was nominated on the 36th.

Garfield's early life was remarkable. Born of a poor homesteading family, he knew how mean and hungry life on the frontier could be. His father was a canal laborer who saved up enough money over many years to buy fifty acres of forest in the Western Reserve of Ohio. He built a cabin and cleared the land, planted an orchard and raised two or three crops, then suddenly at the age of thirty-three died, leaving a wife and four children, the youngest, James, a baby.

By the time he was sixteen, James had done every kind of labor that would bring in a little extra money: boiling salts, cutting wood, driving on the Ohio canal. Besides all this he got an education. His community thought a good deal of education and the Bible, and evening lyceums were held at the schoolhouse. James earned enough money to go to college, and after making a beginning at the Eclectic Institute, operated by the Church of the Disciples in Hiram, Ohio, was able to borrow five hundred dollars and finish at Williams College in Massachusetts. At the age of twenty-six, Garfield was back at the Eclectic Institute, as principal and professor of Latin, Greek, history, philosophy, mathematics, and English.

While he attended to his academic duties, the industrious Garfield found time to study law and be admitted to the bar, get himself elected to the Ohio Senate, and become a husband and father. The Civil War presented a new challenge, which he promptly accepted. He organized the boys at Hiram College into a regiment and commanded it. In the winter of 1861–62 he commanded a brigade in eastern Kentucky and won a respectable victory at the Battle of Prestonburg. He served for a time as Chief of Staff to General Rosecrans, commanding the Army of the Cumberland. After the Battle of Chickamauga, he was promoted to major general but resigned from the army to take the seat in the House of Representatives to which he had been elected a full year earlier.

Garfield spent seventeen years in the House, becoming noted for his readiness to rise to his feet and speak on a wide range of subjects. Philosophically he belonged to the Ohio school of gold-standard-and-high-tariff conservatives. During the scandalous period of the Grant administration, he had a slight brush with scandal himself. The congressional committee investigating the Crédit Mobilier stock scheme questioned him on charges that he had taken some of it. He denied this and presented an excellent case in his defense. Nothing was produced to prove him guilty and it was presumed that he had not in fact accepted the stock.

Senator Sherman, who felt that Garfield had deserted him at the convention when his own nomination became a possibility, had this to say of Garfield after he won the election: "He was a large, well developed, handsome man, with a pleasing address and a natural gift for oratory. . . . These qualities naturally made him popular. But his will power was not equal to his personal magnetism. He easily changed his mind, and honestly veered from one impulse to another."

106

Between the election and the inauguration, swarms of office seekers plagued Garfield. They stopped his carriage on the street, forced their way into his home, and wrote him thousands of letters. One of the most persistent was a jobless fellow named Charles J. Guiteau, who asked to be made consul at Marseilles. After several rebuffs, he decided to kill the President and trailed him for that purpose for some time. On the morning of July 2, 1881, Garfield arrived at the Baltimore and Potomac Station in Washington to go to New England to deliver the commencement address at Williams College. Guiteau was at the waiting-room door. He fired twice at the President, missed with the first shot but with the second put a bullet through his side and spine. Garfield lived until September nineteenth, when he died of blood poisoning.

CHESTER ALAN ARTHUR

—◄●►—

TWENTY-FIRST PRESIDENT

For two months in the summer of 1881, President Garfield lay critically wounded in the White House, and the office of the President was in a state of suspended activity. There was then no provision by law for an acting President in case the President was unable to fulfill his duties. So, while the country prayed for Garfield's recovery, there were no cabinet meetings, and only one official paper was painfully signed by the President. There was in fact no executive, and Congress was in recess. The prayers for Garfield's recovery were particularly urgent because of a real fear that the country would be in peril if Vice President Arthur succeeded to the presidency.

So reasonable a man as former President Hayes wrote in his diary: "The death of the President at this time would be a national calamity whose consequences we can not now confidently conjecture. Arthur for President! Conkling the power behind the throne, superior to the throne!" In other words, the politicians had tempted fate once too often. They had picked such a bad Vice President that they had finally gotten the country into trouble!

The object of these misgivings kept himself in seclusion at his Lexington Avenue house in New York, receiving only a few old friends and leaving the house in the evenings for a short walk in the sultry summer air. About midnight on September nineteenth, a New York *Sun* reporter brought him the news that Garfield was dead. With tears in his eyes he could only say, "My God, I do hope it is a mistake." When an official telegram confirmed the report a few moments later, there were a few friends with Vice President Arthur in his study and these agreed that he should be sworn in as President immediately. This was done that night by a New York Supreme Court Justice. The ceremony was repeated September twenty-second in the Vice President's room at the Capitol before the cabinet and about thirty other high government officials, Chief Justice Waite administering the oath. By this time the country had mellowed toward Arthur because of his dignified behavior during the summer of suspense. Even the newspapers with an unfriendly slant had kind things to say about him. The *Sun* cheerfully pointed out: "He is a gentleman in his manners. . . . Truth in speech and fidelity to his friends and his engagements form a part of his character."

Of the various types of machine politicians Chester Arthur was certainly one of the most respectable. A man of personal integrity, educated, and a successful lawyer, accepted socially by some of the most fastidious professionals and businessmen in New York, he played the political game for the sake of the power and the satisfaction of winning. He was second man to Roscoe Conkling, long notorious in the public mind as the ruthless boss of the New York State Republican machine. In New York City, Arthur was the boss. Only three years before, he had been removed as Collector of the Port of New York by President Hayes, following an investigation into corruption in the New York Custom House. His nomination for the vice-presidency by the Republicans in 1880 was a sacrifice to expediency, one of those small concessions that party men make to placate somebody else in the party.

Roscoe Conkling had come to the national convention to make Ulysses S. Grant the Republican nominee for the third time, and with him came Arthur. Tall, handsome, and unfailingly courteous, he was one of the most conspicuous and attractive of all the Conkling Stalwarts in the heat and frustration of the endless balloting at the convention. When the delegates stood firm against Grant and nominated Garfield, it was suggested that to choose Arthur for his running mate would help reconcile

110

Conkling to the party's decision. There is a story that, on the contrary, Conkling was furious with Arthur for allowing his name to be submitted, vowing that it was an empty honor anyhow as Garfield would never be elected. Whereupon Arthur replied: "The office of Vice President is a greater honor than I ever dreamed of. A barren nomination would be a great honor."

If not a man of humility, at least Chester Arthur had a modesty born of good sense. His family and early life should have encouraged him in straight thinking and good morals. Born in Vermont, the middle child of nine, to a Baptist preacher who had immigrated from Ulster, he had known the frugal existence of a village parson's family moving from parish to parish. By the time he was fourteen, the family had settled at Schenectady, New York, and he was able to complete his education at Union College. After that he supported himself by teaching school while he studied law. At twenty-three, he was admitted to the bar in New York City, and as junior partner in a law firm began looking for clients. It was to his interest and to his taste to make friends, so he joined the militia and started working for the Republican party. Shortly he fell in love with a Virginia girl of excellent family and married her.

At the advent of the Civil War, Arthur was, thanks to his extracurricular activities, an ornament of the New York governor's military staff. Suddenly, the need for serious work from all with the slightest military pretensions was urgent. Appointed assistant quartermaster general and stationed in New York City, Arthur was required to clothe, equip, feed, house, and transport troops that poured into the city by the thousands. He handled this with efficiency and honesty, so that in the second summer of the war he was commissioned New York State quartermaster general.

The election of a Democratic governor released him from his war work in January 1863, and he returned, somewhat impoverished, to the practice of law. Postwar Republican politics in New York State brought forth an aggressive, radical faction headed by Roscoe Conkling, who undertook to unify all elements of the party in one machine. Arthur attached himself to Conkling and rose rapidly in one of the most efficient political organizations the state had ever seen, an organization nourished by political spoils. In 1871 Arthur received the richest plum of all from the Grant administration, the office of Collector of the Port of New York. This he held for nearly seven years, until under an impulse for reform, President Hayes undertook to destroy the spoils system and removed him from office.

111

When the assassin Guiteau declaimed, after shooting President Garfield, "I am a Stalwart. Arthur is now President," he was engaging in melodramatics, for he had no discoverable connection with the Vice President or his party. Many believed he was insane, though he was hanged for his crime. The shock of his act and the belief that it emanated from the spoils system made the political climate favorable to civil service reform. Nothing could have been more unpopular at this moment than a confirmed spoilsman in the presidency. To the vast relief of the country, Arthur asserted his independence of the Conkling machine and became a determined disciple of honest government. During his administration an effective Civil Service Bill was passed and an effort was made to punish dishonesty in the postal service's Star Route carriers. On the constructive side, Arthur began the rebuilding of the American Navy, long suffering from neglect.

A widower when he became President, Arthur had his married daughter as his official hostess. The White House became more elegant than it had been since Buchanan. Unfortunately, Arthur's love of society and good living, to which he devoted himself after the daily grind of presidential business, seriously affected his health. In spite of this he hoped that his party would renominate him in 1884 and thus confer its approval on his administration. Many of the independent and reform Republicans praised him for rising nobly to the responsibilities of his office. The press was cordial, his popularity was undoubted. It was hard to find any fault with his conduct in the presidency. Yet from the direction where support really counted, the regular Republican politicians, there came petty sniping and criticism. At the convention that summer, the party refused him the honor he felt he deserved, and nominated James G. Blaine.

In New York, where the Conkling machine had fallen apart, some of Arthur's old friends started a movement to elect him to the Senate and reunite the party under his leadership, but the movement was a dismal failure. Feeling that his efforts for the public good had been little appreciated, Arthur retired with the idea of resuming his law practice in New York. But his health began to fail rapidly and it was discovered that he was suffering from Bright's disease and a heart ailment. In the autumn of 1886, at the age of fifty-six, he died of a cerebral hemorrhage.

HIGHLIGHTS OF HIS ADMINISTRATION

◆§ The Star Route Frauds. These were a conspiracy uncovered by Garfield's postmaster general, by which the second assistant postmaster general Brady, Senator Dorsey of Arkansas, and some of the contractors who carried the mail on the "star routes" in the West made thousands of dollars by inflating their charges to the government. Arthur had the most prominent culprits brought to trial, but they escaped conviction for lack of evidence.

The Pendleton Civil Service Act of 1883. This effectively launched civil service reform by providing a classified service to which appointment was made by examination. The President was given the right to add to the classified list as he chose. A three-man commission was to be appointed by the President to administer the law.

STEPHEN GROVER CLEVELAND

---◆---

TWENTY-SECOND and TWENTY-FOURTH PRESIDENT

Grover Cleveland might have drifted into politics as a young man. Instead, after two periods in the lower ranks of public office, he gravitated to the private practice of law. By middle life he was head of a Buffalo, New York, firm with an impressive corporation clientele—a comfortable, respected, massive man, a sleeping lion in the Democratic party. In 1881 he was drafted as a reform mayor of Buffalo and not only delighted that city by squeezing the graft out of its government, but caught the imagination of the press by the forthright, sensible way in which he did it. Upstate Democrats began to follow in their newspapers the doings of this "ugly honest" mayor, and a year later, the upstaters joined with Abram Hewitt's reform County Democracy of New York City to nominate him for governor. The Republicans were fatally split between the Stalwarts, or followers of Roscoe Conkling, and the Half-Breeds, or followers of James G. Blaine, and Cleveland was easily elected. As governor he carried the fight to the shabby political practitioners, much as he had in Buffalo, and inevitably ran afoul of Tammany Hall.

When the Democratic convention met at Chicago in 1884 to nominate a President, the Republicans had already chosen their man, the brilliant, magnetic, controversial James G. Blaine. The reform, or independent Republicans, a small but articulate group including such great names as Carl Schurz, Henry Ward Beecher, Charles Eliot Norton, and President Eliot of Harvard, bolted the party, as did most of the influential eastern newspapers, on the ground that Blaine was morally unfit. It was a great and rare opportunity for the Democrats to attract Republican votes, and the New Yorkers had just the candidate to do it. Except for Tammany Hall, the New York delegation at Chicago was strong and resolute for Cleveland. Tammany Hall, bitter at the defeats he had handed them during his term as governor, was showy in tall, white hats—and loud—but their strength was small. So it turned out were other islands of opposition. Cleveland was nominated in a landslide on the second ballot.

The campaign that followed was a particularly merciless one. The most angry and eloquent attack on Blaine was pressed by the independent Republicans, or mugwumps, as the New York *Sun* called them. The charge was an old one, now refurbished and spread across the newspapers. He was accused of having sold bonds of the Little Rock and Fort Smith Railroad Company to some Maine friends without delivering to them the full package of equities that each purchaser should have received. The land bonds he kept for himself. Later on, when the company got into difficulties and he feared publicity, he bought back all the securities, and disposed of them at more than the market price to several railroads. Since Blaine was then Speaker of the House of Representatives, this sale to the railroads was soon a subject of gossip that boiled up to a full-fledged investigation. The critical evidence was presumed to be contained in Blaine's correspondence with the Boston firm that handled his stock dealings. A clerk named Mulligan brought the correspondence to Washington, but before the investigating committee had a chance to see it, Blaine got it into his possession and refused to give it up. In other words, he behaved very much like a man who had something to hide. During the 1884 campaign, Mulligan produced more of the correspondence, some very damaging, especially one that had "Burn this letter" written on the back. The war song of the Democrats was therefore:

"Blaine, Blaine, James G. Blaine,
  The continental liar from the State of Maine,
  Burn this letter!"

The Republicans, for their part, unearthed an illegitimate child in Cleveland's past, a painful incident that he acknowledged with courage. Therefore the Republican war song was:

"Ma! Ma! Where's my pa?
  Gone to the White House,
  Ha! Ha! Ha!"

Both parties since then have been extraordinarily shy of candidates with the slightest suspicion of moral turpitude. One mugwump, when confronted with the Cleveland scandal, remarked that obviously, since Blaine had been delinquent in office but blameless in private life, and Cleveland officially honest but culpable in his personal relations, the thing to do was "to elect Mr. Cleveland to the public office which he is so well qualified to fill and remand Mr. Blaine to the private station which he is admirably fitted to adorn." The voters did precisely that, though the election was close.

Grover Cleveland was born in a Presbyterian parsonage, in Caldwell, New Jersey, the middle child of nine. His father accepted a call to Fayetteville in central New York when the boy was four, so that most of his childhood was spent in that village or in that part of New York. When he was sixteen, his father died, and it was necessary to support himself and to think about helping his mother and the younger children. He had already clerked in a store for something more than a year, but the pay was low, so he decided to go west. Borrowing twenty-five dollars, he started out with a friend. At Buffalo he paused to visit an uncle, a wealthy businessman and stockman. The uncle promptly took him in hand and set him to work on his Shorthorn herdbook. A few months later, the young man was placed with a law firm where he clerked and started reading law. At twenty-two he was admitted to the bar.

During the Civil War Grover was the chief support of his mother and younger sisters, so that in the draft of 1863 he felt obliged to borrow money and provide the army with a substitute. He was appointed assistant district attorney for two years and later was elected sheriff of Erie County, an office that he sought because of the rich fees that went with it. He was known for his enormous industry, uncompromising honesty, and, in his occasional hours of relaxation, a preference for the lusty companionship of beer-hall society. Long before he emerged in politics he had left his roistering youth behind, and as a respectable, even stodgy "old bachelor" circled a sedate orbit of club and hotel life.

Cleveland's election as the first Democratic President since Buchanan naturally brought a starved party about his heels snapping for jobs. As a champion of civil service reform he was obliged to resist the party, and yet as a party man he was obliged to pay his political debts. In the end he yielded enough to both pressures to disappoint the civil service reformers and antagonize some of the party, although in the course of his two terms he managed to double the number of Federal jobs removed from patronage and put under the merit system. He dragged out of obscurity such abuses as the fraudulent disposal of public lands, recovering 81,000,000 acres, and the Civil War pension grab, vetoing the Blair Bill of 1887 that would have given a handout to every soldier who could plead any disability, including old age. He also presented to Congress a demand for revision of the high tariff schedules that had been in force since the Civil War. By the time he came up for re-election in 1888, he had assaulted enough areas of special interest to have lost much popularity. Although he won a small plurality in the popular vote, he lost the electoral vote, largely through the defection of his old enemy Tammany Hall.

In the second year of his term, Cleveland married the daughter of one of his Buffalo law partners, Frances Folsom, in a small, private White House ceremony. She was very young and pretty, and though she suffered genuine anguish from the unremitting newspaper publicity, she rose nobly to her position and became one of the most popular of the presidential wives.

During the four years of Harrison's administration, Cleveland, practicing law in New York, grew increasingly restless and anxious to get back in the political fight. The Democrats were glad to have him back, nominating him at the 1892 convention on the first ballot. The presidential campaign was one of the dullest on record, yet there were a few rumbles in the calm. The People's party (later the Populist party) rising from the discontented agricultural areas south and west, and demanding free silver coinage, polled a million popular votes and 22 electoral votes. In July, locked-out workers at the Homestead works of Carnegie Steel joined in bloody battle with a small army of Pinkerton guards, a shocking incident in the developing war between labor and management. The election went overwhelmingly for Cleveland.

Two months after Cleveland's inauguration, the panic of 1893 was touched off by the collapse of the National Cordage Company. Within a year four million men were out of work and hundreds of businesses had collapsed. In the same month of the panic, Cleveland developed a serious illness that had to be kept secret. A malignant growth appeared and grew rapidly on the roof of his mouth. It.was necessary to remove the upper left jaw. This was done in complete secrecy aboard a private yacht as it steamed up the East River at New York. He was well enough, with an artificial jaw in place, to address Congress when it met in special session in August.

Cleveland's indifference to public opinion when he thought he was right was monumental. He believed in maintaining the gold standard and the fiscal responsibility of the government; so that, as the gold reserve dwindled under the uncertainties of the depression, he resorted to selling bonds for gold through the New York bankers. At the same time he persuaded Congress to repeal the Sherman Silver Purchase Act of 1890, to halt the increasing volume of silver notes, which could be used to draw off gold. Though successful in defending the gold dollar, he lost the support of the silver Democrats, in the west and south, who denounced him as a tool of the eastern money men. At the same time, he continued his campaign, begun during his first administration, for tariff reform. In his view, protective tariffs were unsound economics, and had in effect seriously reduced government revenues. The Wilson-Gorman Act that resulted from all his effort was such a disappointment that he would not sign it, and let it become law without his approval.

In foreign affairs, Cleveland brought the Monroe Doctrine back to life by intervening in a long-standing boundary dispute between Venezuela and Great Britain. Though his Secretary of State, Olney, was unnecessarily bellicose in his handling of the British, the idea of disinterested help for a small South American country against the British Empire was satisfying to most Americans. Those who cherished thoughts of territorial expansion were disappointed by Cleveland's refusing to accept Harrison's treaty for the annexation of Hawaii. In withdrawing it from the Senate, he recognized that it had been contrived by the American interests there and did not represent the united wishes of the Hawaiians.

Leaving the White House, Cleveland recognized that he had not only lost the leadership of his party but had lost popularity with many other interests. Not the least of these was labor, which resented his sending Federal troops to break the Pullman strike of 1894. But he left behind him, for better or worse, a statement of issues that were to be vital in politics for many years to come. Retiring to New Jersey, he became a kind of unofficial elder statesman of Princeton University.

HIGHLIGHTS OF HIS ADMINISTRATION

⋅§ The Repeal of the Sherman Silver Purchase Law, October 30, 1893.

⋅§ The Wilson-Gorman Tariff Act of 1894, passed after radical revision of tariff rates upward, defeating Cleveland's intention of removing high rates of protection.

⋅§ Coxey's March. Jacob Coxey, a wealthy businessman of Masillon, Ohio, led 20,000 unemployed on Washington, arriving on April 29, 1894.

⋅§ The Pullman Strike, in May 1894. Four thousand workmen of the Pullman Palace Car Company went on strike as a protest against wage reduction. Their union, The American Railway Union, led by Eugene Debs, ordered a boycott of all Pullman cars on the railroads, tying up most of the lines west of Chicago. Without a request from Governor Altgeld of Illinois, Cleveland took the initiative and sent Federal troops to Chicago to break the strike.

⋅§ The Venezuela Boundary Dispute, 1895–99.

119

BENJAMIN HARRISON

TWENTY-THIRD PRESIDENT

The presidential campaign of Benjamin Harrison, grandson of William Henry Harrison, was a sober, colorless, and polite affair. Gone were the torchlight parades, picnics, rustic humor, and carnival spirit of William Henry's day, and in their place the Republican party had a large campaign fund and a management with very little respect for the democratic processes. In a letter preserved for history, the party treasurer instructed one of the Indiana faithful to "divide the floaters into blocks of five and put a trusted man in charge of these five, with the necessary funds." In the Democratic party political standards were just as low. There the New York candidate for governor traded Democratic votes for Harrison in return for Republican votes for himself under banners that read "Harrison and Hill." Harrison won by the narrowest margin in the electoral vote and lost the popular vote by 100,000. It was not a good victory, for in spite of the cynicism of a few politicians, the mass of voters on the whole disapproved of commercializing elections.

Even Harrison's inauguration was inauspicious. A rainstorm drowned out the words of his address, and the outgoing President, Cleveland, kindly held an umbrella over the new President's bare head. The object of this attention was a small man with a big beard and steel-gray eyes, a man of integrity, considerable intellect and a great talent for public speaking. He was to realize almost immediately that the practical politicians in his party required nothing more from him than that he hand out the patronage and content himself with being a figurehead. He came to show a marked dislike for this rôle and such party bosses as Senator Thomas C. Platt of New York and Senator Matthew S. Quay of Pennsylvania, but he was not a fighter and remains in history as one of the less positive Presidents. Congress took the leadership in his administration and rolled up an amazing record of legislation in the years 1889–90, earning for itself the nickname of "the billion dollar Congress."

The Democratic weekly *Puck* cartooned Harrison as a very small man extinguished by a very large "grandfather's hat." He was born and raised under the shadow of the old General, being seven years old when his grandfather died. His father farmed a part of the Harrison land at North Bend, Ohio. Young Benjamin went to Miami University, studied law in Cincinnati, then elected to set up in practice at Indianapolis. He was serving as reporter for the Indiana Supreme Court, when in the second year of the Civil War, he decided that it was his duty to help raise a regiment for the Union Army. He assembled one of the companies and hired a drillmaster to get it into shape. When the regiment was complete, he was appointed its colonel.

From the testimony of his superiors and of his men, who called him "Little Ben," he was a strict disciplinarian and a brave and fiery leader in a charge. He fought the long campaign with Sherman from Chattanooga to Atlanta in the summer of 1864, taking command of a brigade in the field. He was mustered out, breveted a brigadier general, having more than earned that rank. He returned to his law career in Indiana and might have had no further concern with public life had not the Indiana legislature elected him to the United States Senate in 1880. This gave him sufficient stature so that the Republican National Convention in 1888 accepted him as its presidential nominee when its perennial favorite James G. Blaine firmly declined the honor.

Harrison was reputedly warm and genial with his family and old friends but crusty and cold with everybody else, even his political intimates. As one observer put it, "He can make a speech to ten thousand men, and every man of them will go away his friend. Let him meet the same ten thousand men in private, and every one will go away his enemy." Washington was not without colorful and popular statesmen. Among them were the new Secretary of State, James G. Blaine, who believed in a spirited foreign policy, a Pan-American customs union, and a "strong" attitude toward Great Britain. Then there was the Commissioner of Pensions, Corporal James Tanner, who believed every Civil War veteran who needed a handout should get it, and when Congress passed the Dependent Pension Act of 1890, had the pleasure of seeing this accomplished. In Congress, where there was a small Republican majority in both houses, the most conspicuous figures were the Speaker of the House, "Czar" Thomas B. Reed, and the Chairman of the Ways and Means Committee, William McKinley.

The 51st Congress made a name for itself by the remarkable quantity of bills passed, some useful, some useful only to special interests, and many extravagant. There was the McKinley Tariff, answering the demand of eastern manufacturers for high protective duties. In order to get sufficient votes for passing this bill, pro-silver western congressmen were mollified by the Sherman Silver Purchase Act. In response to popular agitation against the rising power of trusts and monopolies, the Sherman Anti-Trust Law was passed—to remain a feeble gesture for many years. Neither Harrison nor Congress had a broad enough comprehension of the country's needs, neglecting particularly the growing dissatisfaction of the agricultural interests in the west and south. This factor, plus the unpopularity of the McKinley Tariff and uneasiness over the general extravagance of Congress, produced a party upset at the 1890 congressional elections, with an overwhelming Democratic majority returned to the House of Representatives. Two years later, in the presidential election, Cleveland was elected President in another decisive Democratic victory.

Harrison retired to his law business, from which he emerged twice during the McKinley administration, as counsel for Venezuela in the British-Venezuelan Arbitration Commission of 1899, and as a member of The Hague Peace Conference that same year.

HIGHLIGHTS OF HIS ADMINISTRATION

✍ The opening of the Oklahoma District to settlement, April 22, 1889.

✍ The Dependent Pension Act of 1890, giving pensions to all needy Civil War veterans, with 90 days' or more service, and also to their widows and children if in need. Though only 450,000 veterans were on the rolls, the pension rolls were increased to 966,000, and by 1899 annual pension costs had risen from $89,000,000 before the bill to $157,000,000.

❧ The McKinley Tariff of 1890, providing a complicated schedule of specific and *ad valorem* duties on all manufactured goods from abroad that competed with those made in the United States, some duties being so high as to exclude imports. Raw sugar was put on the free list, but refined sugar was dutiable. Revenue from import duties was so reduced by this act as to have serious effect on government income.

❧ The Sherman Silver Act of 1890, providing for the purchase by the Treasury of 4,500,000 ounces of silver a month, paid for in notes redeemable in gold or silver, at the Treasury's option. The law was interpreted during Cleveland's administration to mean that the Treasury would pay gold for silver notes, and this interpretation was essential for the maintenance of the gold standard. The silver notes were consequently a drain on the gold reserves.

❧ The Samoan crisis. The United States had a coaling station at Pago-Pago in the Samoan Islands and an agreement with their king to protect him from other foreign governments. Germany and Great Britain made similar Samoan agreements. In 1887 the German consul proceeded to depose the king and put his own man in control, throwing the islanders into a state of war and threatening to involve the United States and Great Britain. On March 16, 1889, American, British, and German warships were looking down their guns at each other in Apia Harbor when a hurricane struck, sinking all the ships except a British vessel. The three powers reached an agreement by which the islands should be independent under a joint protectorate. This was modified in 1900, Great Britain withdrawing, the United States taking Tutuila, with the harbor at Pago-Pago, and Germany taking the rest of the Islands.

❧ Secretary of State Blaine's decision to assert American control of the sealing business in the Bering Sea, by ordering, in March 1889, the seizure of foreign sealers caught in those waters. The British protested the seizing of her ships and forced the American claim to arbitration in 1892. The decision was a severe reprimand of Blaine's impetuosity. It was decided that the Bering Sea was not a *mare clausum* in which Americans had proprietary rights and that the United States should pay damages for all ships seized there beyond the three-mile limit.

◄§ Relations with Chile. In the revolution of Chileans against the dictator Balmeceda in 1891, the American minister Patrick Eagan was notably friendly with the dictator. The revolutionists, who successfully took over the country, were angry at two incidents: the detention of their supply ship *Itata* at San Diego, later held by an American court to have been unjustified; and a leak to the Balmecedists of their plans for the capture of Santiago through an officer of the American naval squadron off the coast. With anti-American feeling running high, some of the crew of the U.S.S. *Baltimore* got into a street row in Valparaiso, and two were killed, October 16, 1891. The Chilean foreign office was sluggish and rude in acknowledging American protests, and Eagan was ordered to suspend intercourse. In a few weeks the Chileans were more amenable, met U.S. demands, and appropriated $75,000 for the victims of the riot.

◄§ Trouble in Hawaii. On January 16, 1891, Queen Liliuokalani was forced to abdicate under pressure from a coalition of wealthy whites and Hawaiians. These set up a government and moved to secure American annexation. A counter-revolutionary movement by British and some native interests seemed in the making, when the American minister ran up the American flag and American Marines were landed to patrol Honolulu. Harrison had a treaty of annexation drawn up and sent to the Senate, where it was stalled until after Cleveland became President.

WILLIAM MCKINLEY

The Republican party looked forward to the presidential campaign of 1896, almost certain of victory. The times were in its favor, since the Democratic Cleveland administration would carry the stigma of economic depression, now beginning to show signs of disappearing. More important, the Republicans had an almost perfect candidate, a man who could unite the whole party, perhaps inspire it. Governor McKinley of Ohio was that man. None could forget him in the years when he was in the House of Representatives, a powerful leader, a noble Roman in looks, and according to report, a man of personal purity. Moreover, he came from Ohio, the state of Presidents—Hayes, Garfield, Harrison (not to mention Grant, who was born there)—and of the new industrial age.

Another of William McKinley's assets was Marcus Alonzo Hanna, an unusual millionaire in the coal and iron business, who had put business aside to concern himself with politics. More specifically, he was concerned with making McKinley President, because he sincerely believed that McKinley, as a champion of protective tariffs, was best for the American economy, and consequently, for the American people. There was no question of Hanna's honesty in politics. Like Richard the Lion-Hearted, he might be opinionated but his heart was pure. He wanted nothing for himself, except perhaps, some day, the honor of sitting in that exclusive club, the United States Senate.

The Republican nominating convention in June, 1896, accepted McKinley as its presidential candidate on the first ballot. There was some debate over the live and burning issue of the day, the unlimited coinage of silver, but the "sound money" men won, and the party platform included a clear demand for the preservation of the gold standard. McKinley and Hanna were personally in favor of bimetallism, or silver and gold maintained at parity, although they placed their faith in maintaining it in an illusory international agreement. But they decided to go along with the party statement.

The Democratic convention, meeting in Chicago in July, refused to endorse the conservative administration of the Democratic incumbent, President Cleveland, and turned to the young, aggressive radicals and free-silver men of the west and south. It came out with a platform demanding the free and unlimited coinage of silver and gold, at the ratio of 16 to 1. Having been spellbound by young William Jennings Bryan of Nebraska's famous speech, in which he enunciated the lines "You shall not press down upon the brow of labor this crown of thorns, you shall not crucify mankind upon a cross of gold," the Democrats nominated him for President.

The presidential campaign of 1896 aroused more loves and hates, more loyalties and fears than any since the North and South divided over the slavery question. Bryan, without much of a campaign fund, but with youth, the power of words, and a rich, carrying voice, stumped the country, bringing his arguments directly to some five million people. He talked not only about silver but about the rights of the common people, the farmers, workingmen, and small businessmen. His followers had to some degree absorbed their understanding of economics from a remarkable book, William H. Harvey's *Coin's Financial School*, published in 1894 and sold in the millions of copies. Appealing to the unsophisticated, it offered arguments against the orthodox ideas of the "gold standard," and whipped up their prejudices with crude illustrations. It was the handbook of the silver movement.

Hanna, who became McKinley's campaign manager, realized that fighting Bryan was like fighting a great natural force. It was necessary to oppose him with a vigorous and broad attack. He did this by plastering the country from end to end with copies of McKinley's speeches and those of prominent men who supported him. With the spreading of the written word went squads of men to explain the sound and sensible arguments of

Republican economics. The cost of this "educational" campaign was met by collecting a huge fund, largely from scared businessmen who shuddered to think of what would happen if the crazy radical Bryan took over the country.

McKinley stayed at home in Canton, Ohio, receiving delegations and speaking to them from his front porch. His speeches were carefully prepared ahead of time, and so, often, were the remarks of the spokesmen for the delegations. Neither candidate indulged in any personalities, but their partisans released their feelings in such impassioned abuse that any unbiased observer—if there was such an animal in the United States that summer—must have feared lasting scars on the public morale. Bryan was attacked in editorials, cartoons, and even from the pulpit as not only an anarchist but the embodiment of evil, while the abuse flowing the other way was apt to focus on Mark Hanna, represented as an ugly, cynical money man. In November McKinley was elected by a handsome majority, and the New York *Tribune* relieved itself of the opinion that the malicious conspiracy of Bryanism had been defeated "because right is right and God is God." Mark Hanna was made happy with a seat in the Senate, displacing venerable John Sherman, who was elevated to the cabinet, where as Secretary of State his age and dwindling mental powers made his tenure short.

William McKinley, who was now represented as the savior of his country, had his beginnings in a village beside the Mahoning River in eastern Ohio. His father was an iron founder who made a scant living for his family of eight children. Since young William was eighteen at the outbreak of the Civil War, he readily gave up the hope of going to college and enlisted as a private in the army, serving in Rutherford Hayes's Ohio regiment. He was a commissary sergeant at the Battle of Antietam but was promoted immediately afterward to officer rank and rose steadily until, at the end of the war, he was breveted major for gallant service. Returning home, Major McKinley, now twenty-two, began the study of law. Two years later he was admitted to practice and selected Canton, Ohio, as his home. He immediately began to make friends in political circles.

When McKinley was elected to the House of Representatives as a young man of thirty-three, he understood the needs of his constituents and intended to take care of them as best he could. Since Ohio desired tariffs to protect its manufacturers, he made himself an expert on the tariff. Finally, as chairman of the House Ways and Means Committee, he had the satisfaction of sponsoring in 1890 a tariff bill that gave his constituents all they wanted. He was personally popular in Washington. Some thought him overserious, but all admired his temperate and reasonable attitude in debate. There was a great deal of sympathy too for the personal tragedies he had suffered, the loss of both his children and the invalidism of his wife.

129

As McKinley tried to adapt his thinking to the broader constituency of the American people, he was faced with the possibility of war with Spain over Cuba. Cuban revolt against Spanish rule, long chronic in the island, had broken out once more in 1895. The rebels, fighting a guerilla war in the hills and back-country villages, made 200,000 Spanish troops look ridiculous. Finally, in desperation, the Spanish governor rounded up many of the rural population and put them in concentration camps, where they suffered all the miseries of hunger and disease. A natural sympathy among Americans for the oppressed Cubans was inflamed by the Hearst press and other sensational newspapers until there was a popular demand for American intervention. Cleveland had resisted this demand and attempted to halt the filibustering expeditions that set forth from American shores to help the rebels. McKinley was opposed to war and during the first year of his presidency made a patient and creditable attempt through the American minister in Madrid to persuade Spain to set Cuba free.

At the same time, McKinley was inclined to be responsive to the wishes of the American people. The blowing up of the American battleship *Maine* in Havana Harbor on February 15, 1898, by an explosion never explained but evidently from outside the ship's hull, made the demand for war with Spain irresistible. Therefore, at the point where Spain seemed ready to yield to diplomacy and grant autonomy to Cuba, McKinley yielded to the demand for war. Arguing that not autonomy but total freedom was the American goal in Cuba, he sent a war message to Congress on April 11, 1898. The war, fought against a weak enemy, lasted only four months. It proved that the American Navy was an efficient fighting force and the War Department, on the contrary, needed drastic overhauling—though the regular army fought well. It gave the nation several glorious heroes, including Theodore Roosevelt. It launched the United States into an era of territorial expansion and placed it at the beginning of its rise to power in world politics.

When McKinley ran for re-election in 1900, he was at the top of his popularity, and the country seemed to be enjoying a golden age, at least in material prosperity. Running again opposed to the unquenchable William Jennings Bryan, he won by a handsomer majority of electoral votes than before. The attack on him by an assassin the following September thus plunged the entire country into a state of shock. Leon F. Czolgosz, an anarchist, had approached the President in a reception line at the Pan-American Exposition in Buffalo, with a handkerchief concealing a pistol, and shot him twice point-blank. This was on September sixth. McKinley clung to life for several days, until September fourteenth. The assassin was tried, judged sane and found guilty, and executed on October twenty-ninth.

HIGHLIGHTS OF HIS ADMINISTRATION

~§ The Dingley Tariff of 1897, restoring most of the rates in the McKinley Tariff of 1890. Better written, this bill provided sufficient revenue, which had been lacking in the McKinley bill.

~§ The War with Spain: Congress declared war on April 25, 1898, at the same time pledging that the United States would withdraw from Cuba once its independence was established.

Commodore George Dewey destroyed the Spanish fleet in Manila Bay on May 1, 1898.

The American Army landed near Santiago, Cuba, June 22, 1898. It was made up mostly of regular troops, but included a regiment of volunteer cavalry, commanded by Colonel Leonard Wood, later, on Wood's promotion, commanded by Colonel Roosevelt. Santiago surrendered on July 17th.

The second Spanish fleet, under Admiral Cervera, was destroyed off Santiago by the American fleet of Admiral Sampson, on July 3rd, and the fighting stopped with an armistice on August 12th.

Peace with Spain, signed December 10, 1898, gave the United States Puerto Rico and Guam as indemnity, and the Philippines, for which the United States paid $20,000,000. Cuba was to be independent and turned over to the Cuban people by the American forces when they had restored it to order.

~§ Annexation of Hawaii by joint resolution of Congress, July 7, 1898. It was made a territory in 1900.

~§ "The Open Door" in China. Secretary of State John Hay sent a protest to the governments of Great Britain, Germany, and Russia, September 6, 1899, in regard to their evident intention to partition China, suggesting instead an "open door" to all nations who desired to trade with her. Chinese patriots, recognizing also the intentions of the great powers, organized a secret society of "Boxers," armed themselves, and seized the government. On June 19, 1900, they ordered all the foreign ministers out of the country. The ministers feared that they could not get to the coast from Peking safely, and therefore barricaded themselves in the British Embassy.

An international expedition, including Americans, was sent to rescue them, which was accomplished on August 14th. In the aftermath, China agreed to pay each power a large indemnity. The United States secured public support from the big powers for the open-door policy, and thus won a diplomatic victory.

THEODORE ROOSEVELT

———◀◉▶———

TWENTY-SIXTH PRESIDENT

In 1900 Theodore Roosevelt was Governor of New York, a position that held a great deal of interest for him and that he wished to retain. Arriving as a delegate to the Republican National Convention at Philadelphia in June, he was aware that there was a movement to nominate him for the vice-presidency, to fill the vacancy left by the death of Vice President Hobart. This movement had the hearty support of the Republican regular organization in New York, controlled by Thomas C. Platt, but it was opposed by Mark Hanna and also, quietly, by President McKinley. These men mistrusted Roosevelt's attitude toward business, suspecting that at heart he was a reformer, as indeed he was.

Neither they nor Roosevelt himself were to have any say in the matter. As Roosevelt put it candidly in his autobiography: "Senator Hanna was anxious that I should not be nominated as Vice President. Senator Platt was anxious that I should be nominated as Vice President in order to get me out of the New York Governorship. . . . My supporters in New York State did not wish me nominated for Vice President because they wished

133

me to continue as Governor; but in every state all the people who admired me were bound that I should be nominated as Vice President." His admirers at the convention started a Roosevelt boom that no one dared resist, and he was nominated for the vice-presidency by the vote of every delegate except his own.

Roosevelt had been Vice President for six months when McKinley was shot. He came to Buffalo immediately, but as the President seemed to be recovering from his wounds, he joined his family in the Adirondacks. It was necessary to fetch him down from a mountain, where he had gone on a tramp, when McKinley took a turn for the worse. By wagon and special train, Roosevelt reached Buffalo shortly after McKinley's death and was sworn in as President, on September fourteenth. On the train bringing McKinley's body back to Washington, Hanna warned him sourly, "Theodore, do not think anything about a second term."

Few things were less profitable than telling Theodore what he could not do. Ever since his sickly boyhood he had been challenged to do the things he could not do. Born of a prominent and wealthy family in New York City, he suffered so badly from asthma that he was tutored at home, when his health would permit. At about fourteen he decided to overcome his physical frailty and timidity by taking up boxing. Thus began his cult of the vigorous life, which improved his health and made him a devotee of exercise and the great outdoors. With this, he quite consciously cultivated the quality of physical courage, probably a less intricate form of the moral courage with which he was liberally supplied. While he was an undergraduate at Harvard, his father died, leaving him enough money to free him from the necessity of making a living.

As a brainy and high-minded young man, he decided that public service was the most attractive career, and so eased himself into politics. His first step was to get accepted by the Republican Club in his district, his next to be elected to the New York State Assembly. The two years between 1882 and 1884 educated him in political methods, good and bad, and in the social and economic injustices of the New York slums. His fight against the wrongs he discovered gave him the label of a reformer, as did his efforts to defeat the nomination of James G. Blaine for President in 1884. The death of his young wife and his mother on the same day this year caused him to leave politics abruptly and go west.

For two years he was a rancher on the Little Missouri River in the Dakota country, taking satisfaction in working with his wranglers and becoming a passable cowhand. Returning to New York, he found it not so easy to pick up his political career, losing in a race for the mayoralty of the city. He accepted an appointment to the Civil Service Commission by President Harrison and stayed on in that office during Cleveland's administration until 1895, when he became New York Police Commissioner in a reform city government. As the talk of war with Spain began dividing public opinion into those for and those against, Roosevelt was delighted to be appointed assistant Secretary of the Navy in the new McKinley administration, and to have the task of preparing his favorite branch of the service for a war that he considered necessary and inevitable. The moment war was declared, however, he could no longer abide a desk job and joined his old friend Army Surgeon Leonard Wood in raising the First United States Volunteer Cavalry for service in Cuba.

Roosevelt's enormous enjoyment of life made almost everything he did a Great Adventure. Of all the soldiers who took part in the capture of Santiago in the Cuban war, he, leading his dismounted "Rough Riders" up that part of the defenses known as San Juan Hill, became the greatest hero. Returning to New York, he was elected governor of the state, with the grudging consent of the practical politician Senator Platt. As governor he troubled businessmen by initiating taxes on certain businesses and so antagonized the party organization that Platt was glad to kick him upstairs into the vice-presidency. He nevertheless remained a loyal Republican and an asset to the party.

In succeeding to the presidency, Roosevelt made a politic statement that he would continue the McKinley policies. This meant no more than that he would not tamper with the protective tariff. He retained all the McKinley cabinet, as well he might, for McKinley was an excellent judge of men and had brought into it such first-class statesmen as Elihu Root and John Hay. Aside from this, the entire sense and purpose of the Roosevelt administration was to reverse the trend of government under the McKinley-Hanna doctrine. From a narrowing down of Federal interests on the theory that the less government interference there was, the better off the country would be, Roosevelt started the government on a movement to widen its interests and controls. He popularized the idea that business should be restrained from creating monopolies, that industry should be made to respect the rights of the consumer, and above all, that the wasting of the country's natural resources by greedy or careless interests should be stopped.

In concrete accomplishments he inaugurated a Department of Commerce and Labor, with facilities to look into the trusts; he revived the Sherman Anti-Trust Law and in the Northern Securities Case won a Supreme Court decision that broke up the holding company that bound James J. Hill's railroad empire together. Congress gave him a bill to empower the Interstate Commerce Commission to fix railroad rates, a pure food and drug act, and a meat-packing act. It also gave him the Newlands Reclamation Act, by which the great storage dams, such as Roosevelt, Hoover, and Grand Coulee, were built. Conservation was perhaps one of Roosevelt's most original and important contributions to the public welfare. He set up a Forest Service under the most prominent of the conservationists, Gifford Pinchot, set up a commission to investigate the use and misuse of natural resources, and assembled a great meeting of conservationists in Washington.

Besides these matters of domestic importance, he was a frank imperialist. The Panama Canal, a powerful navy, and a constant concern with world politics solidified the United States' position as a Great Power. Though the United States had no fight with any nation during his regime, it was glad to clean up the last disagreement outstanding with Great Britain by settling the Alaska–British Columbia boundary. Under the Monroe Doctrine, Roosevelt intervened in a dispute between Germany and Great Britain with Venezuela, over claims Venezuela refused to pay. In a similar financial difficulty, the bankrupt government of Santo Domingo accepted Roosevelt's treaty by which a receiver paid European and other creditors out of revenues. This idea of guardianship in Latin America was the "Roosevelt Corollary" to the Monroe Doctrine. Roosevelt's skill with people and ability to grasp intricate problems quickly made him a first-rate diplomat. It led him into the practice of personal diplomacy abroad, notably in negotiating the treaty that ended the war between Russia and Japan.

Perhaps Roosevelt's greatest effect on Americans was in his propaganda for reform in its industrial and financial institutions. He will always be remembered as a "trust buster" and opponent of "malefactors of great wealth." However, he resisted being classified with the many sociologists and writers who were then exposing "crimes against society." He insisted that he was not a reformer and added to the popular vocabulary the word "muckraker," giving it a contemptuous meaning. As a person he was bright, engaging, and unique, the beloved "Teddy" of the American masses. His re-election in 1904 was a triumph.

The White House was never so full of exciting doings. Besides attracting to his official entourage some of the most brilliant men ever to serve a President, he charmed Americans in more homely ways by presiding as a jolly and tireless genius over a lively White House family. And, as if this were not enough, he drew about him a group of cronies, whom he called his "tennis cabinet," and with whom he not only played tennis but went on horseback rides and point-to-point hikes in Rock Creek Park and swam the Potomac.

To retire such a man as Roosevelt from public life was almost a crime. But he was opposed to a third term, and so, choosing his great friend William Howard Taft to carry on his policies, he left Washington at the end of his term in 1909, resolved to quit politics. Then he went off on a great hunt in Africa. Returning through Europe, where he was admired as the most fascinating American of the age, he met Rudyard Kipling, who wrote an American friend: "I saw him for a hectic half hour in London and a little at Oxford. Take care of him. He is scarce and valuable." At home again, he was disturbed by the way Taft was handling the presidency. Finally, in spite of his promise to Taft that he would not run for President, he announced, in February 1912, that he was a candidate for the Republican nomination.

In a bitter contest at the national convention that summer, the Old Guard leaders took control and made Taft the nominee. Roosevelt was now angry and took his followers out of the Republican party to form the Progressive, or "Bull Moose" party. Running as its candidate, he in effect split the Republican vote in the presidential election, but the Democrat Woodrow Wilson won such an overwhelming majority of the electoral vote that the Republicans' split could not be said to have lost them the election.

During the campaign, an assassin made an attempt to kill Roosevelt, shooting him in the chest. He survived, to lead an expedition to Brazil the next year, where he contracted a fever from which he nearly died. In World War I he was desperately anxious to be of service, but President Wilson refused to have him in the army. Through his later years, Roosevelt continued to write and make speeches voluminously. During his life he published an astonishing number of readable books, including his *Winning of the West*, his *Autobiography*, *African Game Trails*, and *Through the Brazilian Wilderness*. He died, comparatively young, of a heart embolism.

HIGHLIGHTS OF HIS ADMINISTRATION

& showed The Panama Canal: The Second Hay-Pauncefote Treaty with Great Britain was signed on November 18, 1901, superseding the Clayton-Bulwer Treaty of 1850 that stood in the way of the canal's being built by the United States. On January 22, 1903, the Hay-Herran Treaty with Colombia, providing terms for construction of a canal across the Isthmus of Panama, was signed in Washington. Colombia failed to ratify this.

The Panama Department of Colombia declared itself an independent republic, November 4, 1903. The United States lost no time in recognizing the Republic of Panama and in concluding with it the Hay–Bunau-Varilla Convention. By this the United States obtained a strip of land ten miles wide across the Isthmus of Panama for construction of a canal, and agreed to pay $10,000,000 in cash for it plus $250,000 a year beginning in 1913. (The annuity was increased to $430,000 in 1922 and then to $1,930,000 in 1955.) The Canal opened on August 15, 1914. It cost $350,000,000.

⋑ The strike in the anthracite mines, shutting them down on May 15, 1902. The operators refused to negotiate. Finally, by infinite patience and through the influence of Mark Hanna and the financial interests behind the operators, Roosevelt in the following October persuaded the operators and the miners to accept arbitration. Immediately the miners went back to work. The arbitration commission handed down a decision five months later, giving the miners an increase in pay and union recognition.

⋑ The Newlands Reclamation Act, providing for irrigation dams, signed by Roosevelt, June 17, 1902.

⋑ Seizure by Germany and Great Britain of the gunboats and blockade of the ports of Venezuela, in December 1902. Roosevelt intervened to protect Venezuela, and persuade the European powers to submit their financial claims, which Venezuela had refused to pay, to The Hague Tribunal. The Hague Tribunal made an award on February 22, 1904.

⋑ Settlement of the American-British dispute over the boundary between Alaska and British Columbia, by negotiation, October 20, 1903.

⋑ Creation of the Department of Commerce and Labor by Congress, February 14, 1903.

⋑ The decision rendered, March 14, 1904, by the Supreme Court that the Northern Securities Company violated the Sherman Anti-Trust Act. Northern Securities, a holding company for James J. Hill's Northern Pacific, Great Northern and Chicago, Burlington and Quincy railroads, was forced to dissolve.

⋑ Negotiation of a treaty of peace between Japan and Russia completed by Roosevelt at Portsmouth, New Hampshire, September 5, 1905.

◢§ Roosevelt's signing of the Hepburn Bill, June 29, 1906, giving the Interstate Commerce Commission the right to fix railroad rates.

◢§ A trip around the world by the United States Navy, including 16 battleships, all new since the Spanish War, starting out from Hampton Roads, Virginia, on December 16, 1907. On its return, the fleet was reviewed by Roosevelt, February 22, 1909.

WILLIAM HOWARD TAFT

———◆◇◆———

TWENTY-SEVENTH PRESIDENT

Rarely has an American President enough political power to deliver his office to the man of his choice. Theodore Roosevelt did this in 1908, and his choice was William Howard Taft, a faithful follower whom he placed in one responsible position after another, and whom he loved like a brother. Taft was lukewarm on the presidency. As he wrote Roosevelt in 1906, "I would much prefer to go on the Supreme Bench for life than to run for the Presidency . . . in twenty years of judicial service I could make myself more useful to the country than as President." This was as a candid and just appraisal of his abilities. Nevertheless, he was propelled toward the presidency. At the Republican National Convention of 1908, he was nominated on the first ballot and was elected triumphantly, losing only the South and four western states.

Taft was the son of a distinguished lawyer of Cincinnati, Ohio, an active Republican, later United States attorney general, and a diplomat. In one generation the Tafts developed a family pattern of politics, civic interest, and legal careers. William Howard, following it, went to Yale, where he enjoyed playing campus politics and graduated with honors. Back in Cincinnati, he studied law, and on being admitted to the bar, was almost immediately recognized as one preordained for public service. A massive young man, "Big Bill," Taft had both wit and humor, and a balanced attitude toward private ambition and public duty. Appointments were his without the asking: assistant prosecuting attorney in Cincinnati; collector of internal revenue; then at twenty-nine one that was really welcome, superior court judge in Cincinnati, to fill an unexpired term. He ran for re-election to this office and won, but before this term was over, President Harrison invited him to Washington as United States solicitor general.

In Washington Taft struck up a friendship with a young Civil Service commissioner, Theodore Roosevelt, whose own career for the moment was moving on a dead level. Two years later, in 1892, Taft left Roosevelt behind, when he was elevated to the Federal judiciary. At thirty-four he became judge of the Sixth Circuit Court and moved back to Cincinnati, remaining eight years—until President McKinley needed someone to bring civil order to the newly acquired Philippines. As head of the Second Philippine Commission, Taft put into effect the code of government for the Philippines conceived by Secretary of War Elihu Root, and he became their first American governor in 1901, remaining in Manila until he succeeded Root.

During his four years in the cabinet, Taft became a high-level trouble shooter. In 1906 Cuba was in turmoil following a general election, and Roosevelt felt that, under the Platt Amendment of the Cuban Constitution, the United States should intervene. He sent Taft and a small staff aboard a cruiser. In what Taft later called "those awful twenty days," he experienced the frustration of trying to reason with a revolution, in the end imposing a provisional American government. The supervision of the building of the Panama Canal, with its many problems of labor, local politics, and techniques, became his responsibility. It would be hard to name anyone in the United States who seemed better qualified than he for the presidency.

The country had no reason to be particularly disappointed in Taft's administration. He put some good legislation on the books: a postal-savings-banks law; a law providing that campaign expenses of candidates for Congress be made public; two Amendments to the Constitution, one making an income tax permissible and the other providing for the election of senators by popular vote rather than by state legislatures; a bill offering trade reciprocity to Canada, which unfortunately was refused by Canada. However, most of this legislation was generated in Congress itself.

As soon as Taft was inaugurated, Roosevelt went to Africa for a big-game hunt. During his absence, the progressives in the Republican party, dedicated Roosevelt men, became alienated from Taft. An open quarrel developed when the Secretary of the Interior, Ballinger, released for sale part of the land reserved by Roosevelt to the public domain and, further, favored the claims of a private corporation on certain mineral lands in Alaska. Taft supported Ballinger against the progressives, and when Roosevelt returned, his relations with Taft became more and more formal. Rumors sprang up that he would seek the Republican nomination for President in 1912. He assured Taft that this he would not do, but the Roosevelt movement gathered impetus, and by February 1912 he was of a different mind. He announced he would run.

His announcement had the effect of rallying most of the Republican party to Taft. The convention, a stormy one, made it plain that the party organization was intact and that it considered the progressives a minor, dissident element. Taft was placed in nomination by a rising Republican, Warren G. Harding of Ohio, and nominated on the first ballot. Roosevelt immediately withdrew from the Republican party and organized the Progressive, or "Bull Moose" party, becoming its candidate for President. In the election Taft and Roosevelt had 1,300,000 more popular votes between them than the Democratic candidate, but in the electoral vote Woodrow Wilson had a sweeping victory.

Convinced that it would be improper for him to practice law again, since he would sooner or later have to argue cases before judges whom he had placed over Federal courts during his presidency, Taft became professor of law at Yale. During the first year of the First World War he gave much of his time to the peace movement, becoming president of the League to Enforce Peace. In 1921 he had his great reward, when President Harding named him Chief Justice of the Supreme Court, an eminence that he nervously hoped he could occupy worthily. This he did until his last illness nine years later.

HIGHLIGHTS OF HIS ADMINISTRATION

⋙ The Sixteenth Amendment to the Constitution passed by Congress, July 12, 1909, providing for authority of the Federal government to levy income taxes: ratified by the states, February 25, 1913.

⋙ The Payne-Aldrich Tariff Bill, passed in special session, August 5, 1909. As the Payne Bill in the House, it gave a moderate reduction of rates; rewritten in the Senate, it became a high-tariff bill.

⋙ Decisions rendered in 1911 by the Supreme Court against the Standard Oil and American Tobacco Companies, under the Sherman Anti-Trust Law.

⋙ The Seventeenth Amendment to the Constitution, passed by Congress, May 16, 1912, providing for popular election of senators, ratified May 31, 1913.

THOMAS WOODROW WILSON

---◆◉◆---

TWENTY-EIGHTH PRESIDENT

Just as the regular Republicans were confronted with the rise of the progressives, the regular Democrats in the east were realizing with dismay
that the new man they had brought forth in New Jersey politics was
another independent, quite as progressive as Teddy Roosevelt. Governor
Woodrow Wilson, college professor, former president of Princeton, the
exclusive college for rich men's sons, protégé of Colonel George Harvey,
the ultra-conservative editor of *Harper's Weekly,* elected to his office by
the New Jersey Democratic machine, was setting himself up as a leader
of the young Democratic liberals. He had dismissed Harvey and broken
with the New Jersey bosses. What was more, he had been extremely
successful as governor in putting reform bills through the New Jersey
legislature. In the meantime he had attracted attention in the country at
large by speeches in which he demanded better morals in government.
Thus he had activated many liberal western Democrats, most important
of them Colonel Edward M. House of Texas. House was instantly and

permanently drawn to Wilson and proceeded to convert William Jennings Bryan. It was Bryan's support that made Wilson a serious contender for the presidency.

The Democratic National Convention met in Baltimore in 1912. The conservatives, bitter over Wilson's turnabout, dug in their heels, determined that he should not be nominated. Their candidate was Champ Clark, an average "regular" politician. There was, oddly enough, no Wilson organization at the convention. The candidate himself was resting with his family at Seagirt on the New Jersey shore, and Colonel House had gone to Europe. The galleries were full of noisy Wilson supporters, but practically speaking, Wilson's future lay in Bryan's hands. It was a long, slow process, but inching upward through ballot after ballot, Wilson took the nomination on the 47th roll call.

Woodrow Wilson's turn to politics was not unexpected. Preoccupied with American history and government as a teacher and writer, he was simply late in finding a political opening. Born in Staunton, Virginia, the son of a distinguished Presbyterian churchman, he had grown up with the idea that there is no finer life for a man than that of public service. With an active intellect in a frail body, he was brought up in a precious atmosphere of high thinking and personal superiority. Like John Adams, he worried a great deal about himself, his virtues and his failings, but thanks perhaps to the influence of his hearty Irish father, he was able to enjoy many of the ordinary pleasures, such as good company of both sexes and lifting his tenor voice in a glee club. His father's ministry required the family to move about occasionally. Tommy Wilson, as he was known until he dropped his first name as an author, spent most of his young life in Augusta, Georgia. A few years after Dr. Wilson moved his pastorate to Columbia, South Carolina, Tommy entered Princeton. Here he developed gradually into a social being, finding plenty of congenial young intellects and taking to college life with a tender feeling for its privileges and its friendships. His chief talent was the art of persuasive talking, which he did so well that he decided to take up law and go into politics.

At the University of Virginia law school he decided that routine law work was boring, but he ground away at it. He also began his literary career by publishing in magazines essays on American government and British statesmen. In the middle of his second year, he fell ill with a chronic digestive trouble and had to drop out of school, but he finished his law reading at home and was duly admitted to the bar in Atlanta, where he had elected to practice. After a year of trying to get a practice going, he decided that scholarship offered a better life and a steadier income. He quit the law and went up to Johns Hopkins University in Baltimore for a graduate course in history and political science, to prepare himself for teaching.

146

While there he finished and published his book, *Congressional Government*. This, offered as his thesis for a Ph.D. at Johns Hopkins, brought him a reputation as a scholar and an offer to teach at Bryn Mawr College. He was now able to marry the girl he had been in love with for two years. A man never at rest, he enlarged his academic life at Bryn Mawr, Wesleyan University, and Princeton, by writing voluminously essays, popular history, and government theory. In 1902 the trustees of Princeton elected Wilson president of the college that was in the process of becoming a university.

As an educator Wilson had progressive ideas, which were acceptable to Princeton so long as he dealt only with scholarship. When he tried to make life more democratic by abolishing the social clubs and when he engaged in a dispute with the dean of the new graduate school over the school's location, many of the alumni turned against him. He was stubborn enough to campaign for his convictions. Stepping into politics, in a sense, was a release from a difficult position. Two years later, on the night of his election to the presidency, the Princeton boys marched to his house by torchlight and serenaded him, the second Princeton-bred President.

Wilson explained during the campaign that his "New Freedom" meant "a body of laws which will look after the men who are on the make rather than the men who are already made." As President he took the leadership of Congress and addressed it personally. It enacted almost the complete body of laws he wanted: a revision of the banking and loan system; a credit system for the farmers; a strengthening of the anti-trust law; a mechanism to control illegal competition; tariff revision downward and an income tax; and laws cleaning up certain types of labor exploitation, especially child labor, though the latter was voided by the Supreme Court. Personally Wilson refused to handle patronage or even mix socially with politicians. He had no particular concern for organized labor, but he rudely and finally rebuffed the bankers, or "money trust" as he called them.

With all his legislative success, Wilson began to worry about his isolation and loneliness in the White House, a loneliness that became plain misery when his wife died in 1914. Except for the indispensable Colonel House and his secretary, Joseph Tumulty, whom he had attached during his governorship of New Jersey, few men were on terms of firm friendship with him or even liked him very much. Members of his administration criticized him as cold and aloof, and members of his own party in Congress were stung by what seemed his deliberate rudeness. In this he forfeited the personal leadership he needed, for both himself and his party. Still, his leadership was magnificent for its high purpose and courage. If he thought the cause just, he ignored the enemies who rose up against him. In 1913, American businessmen, with fat concessions in Mexico and about

$1,500,000,000 invested, were outraged when he refused to recognize the pro-American President Huerta. Wilson objected to Huerta because he had seized the government and assassinated the elected president. Unfortunately no one, not even the Mexican people, wanted Wilson to interfere. At this point some American sailors landed in a forbidden area at Tampico, Mexico, to buy gasoline and were arrested. Admiral Mayo, commanding the naval forces in Tampico Harbor, secured the release of the men and an apology, but he wanted more. He demanded that the Mexicans hoist the Stars and Stripes and salute it. Wilson backed up his admiral and when the Mexicans refused to salute the flag, occupied Vera Cruz. At this point the "A, B, C Powers" (Argentina, Brazil, and Chile) saved face for both sides by mediating a settlement that eliminated Huerta and gave Mexico a new president.

By the time of the presidential election in 1916, the only campaign issue of any importance was American neutrality in the European war. This had broken out on August 1, 1914, between the Allied Entente—Russia, France, and Great Britain—and the Central Powers—Germany and Austria. Wilson declared American neutrality on August 4, 1914, but the course of neutrality on the high seas was a perilous one. Great Britain blockaded Germany with a cordon of ships and mines in the North Sea, and Germany retaliated by sending submarines to sink ships en route to England and France. The German policy was the more devastating because of the nature of the submarine as a weapon. It sank a ship without warning and left its crew and passengers to drown. On May 7, 1915, the big *Lusitania* was sunk with the loss of 1153 men, women, and children, including a number of Americans. On May thirteenth, Wilson sent a note to Germany demanding disavowal of the attack and reparation. When this did not bring a satisfactory answer, he sent a sterner note, one that the pacific Secretary of State Bryan thought so close to a war ultimatum that he resigned. Germany yielded a little, agreeing to give passengers time to escape in boats, and in the spring of 1916 suspended submarine warfare.

Some of Wilson's supporters in the 1916 presidential campaign coined the phrase "He kept us out of war." He deplored the boast, but it was too catchy a slogan to suppress. Actually he was uncertain that he could keep out of the war and had begun to prepare to fight, Congress authorizing additions to the Army, the Navy, and the Merchant Marine. The close election, in which Wilson carried California by only 4,000 votes and with it the electoral vote, reflected uncertainty on his war policy. While he hoped to keep out of the war, he unmistakably sympathized with the Allies.

Americans were responding to Allied propaganda and much of American business was by now involved in the munitions and supply trade with the Allies. Germany could easily tip the scale, and this she proceeded to do in January of 1917, when she notified Washington of a resumption of submarine warfare. Wilson's answer to this was to suspend diplomatic relations with Germany and ask Congress for the authority to arm merchant ships. A filibuster in Congress by "a little group of willful men" refused this, yet it was plain to Wilson that war was ahead. Ambassador Walter Page in Britain warned him that resumption of submarine war would mean the collapse of England. He delayed for nearly a month, praying for another way out, during which time the Bolshevik revolution began in Russia, foreshadowing the release of German armies from the eastern front to reinforce the western front. On April 2, 1917, Wilson read his war message to Congress and on the sixth Congress passed a resolution declaring war on Germany.

For nineteen months all the country's resources were efficiently organized for war, its manpower, communications, food, industry. Even its private thoughts and opinions were brought under more complete control than ever before in war by propaganda and harsh espionage laws. Long before peace was in sight Wilson made public his Fourteen Points, his charter for the peace. Based on a forgiveness of the vanquished, it called for open and free political and commercial relations between countries, respect for national minorities, an independent Poland, but otherwise a restoration of pre-war nations, disarmament, and a league of nations. Three weeks after an armistice ended the war, November 11, 1918, he sailed for France to put forth his plans for peace. He left behind him a Republican Congress and he ignored the suggestion that taking with him some Republican statesmen, such as Taft and Elihu Root, would give his mission broader national support.

At the Versailles Peace Conference Wilson had to deal with the Prime Ministers of France, Britain, and Italy (Clemenceau, Lloyd-George, and Orlando), all tough-minded statesmen who respected his idealism. They were willing to accept the League of Nations Covenant, but they insisted on imposing the harshest terms on Germany, who was not even represented at the conference. Each victor nation claimed some special spoils or security. Ray Stannard Baker, the press director of the conference, described the completed treaty as having "all the unimaginative greeds and fears, the vanities, the petty interests of the nations." Wilson had stood alone in opposing much of the treaty, but in the end he had to place his confidence in the League of Nations as a possible means of correcting mistakes at some future time. This first attempt at a permanent peace organization provided for a council, assembly, secretariat, and court of international justice. It was to arbitrate disagreements, guarantee members against aggression, and discuss disarmament. At the last moment Wilson had taken the precaution to consult some of the leading Republicans on the Covenant and incorporated changes which they had suggested. On July 10, 1919, he sent the Treaty, with the League in it, to the Senate.

The Senate, in an ugly mood, partly because it had not been consulted in the making of the Treaty, rejected it, both with and without reservations. During the Senate's long consideration of the League, Wilson had taken the issue to the people in a western speaking tour. On the trip he collapsed physically, and, rushed to Washington on his train, suffered a paralytic stroke. For many months, while he was critically ill, the League was thrashed out in the Senate and he could do no more for it than to reject the reservations. The Republican leaders were content to leave it at that, for they believed it would give them a great party issue for the 1920 presidential campaign.

Wilson made a partial recovery from his stroke and was able to get about in a wheelchair. For political purposes, his illness was greatly exaggerated by the opposition. He rode with his successor to the inauguration in 1921, and then, with his second wife, moved into a Washington house. His last speech was on Armistice Day in 1923. Speaking to a crowd in front of his house, he stood on the steps leaning on a cane, a frail old man in formal black, holding a high silk hat in his right hand.

HIGHLIGHTS OF HIS ADMINISTRATION

❧ The Underwood Tariff, October 3, 1913, reducing tariffs on an average of 27 per cent to 37 per cent, and including a graduated income tax.

❧ The Federal Reserve Act, December 23, 1913.

❧ An act creating the Federal Trade Commission, September 26, 1914.

❧ The Clayton Anti-trust Act, October 15, 1914.

❧ An act creating the Federal Farm Loan Board and Banks, July 17, 1916.

❧ The Adamson Act, providing for an eight-hour day on interstate railways, passed September 3, 1916.

❧ Relations with Mexico: On April 10, 1914, American sailors were arrested for illegal landing at Tampico, Mexico, but were released with an apology two hours later. Admiral Mayo, commanding the American force in Tampico Harbor, because similar acts of petty annoyance had been common, demanded that Mexicans salute the American flag. They refused. American marines seized Vera Cruz, April 21st. On the 27th, troops under General Funston replaced them. Under settlement effected by Argentina, Brazil, and Chile, President Huerta resigned, July 15th, and left Mexico. Venustiano Carranza became president, and on September 15th, Wilson ordered the withdrawal of American troops from Vera Cruz.

Francisco Villa rebelled against Carranza and became leader of a bandit gang in the northwest, raiding American towns across the border. General Pershing and a small army, ordered to the border, pursued Villa into Mexico in March 1916, and clashed with Mexican regulars. To avoid war, Mexico and the United States agreed on a mixed commission to fix a method for peaceful relations. It failed to get agreement and disbanded, January 15, 1917. Wilson withdrew U.S. troops, January 28.

⊷ Establishment of an American trusteeship in Haiti: With Haiti in turmoil following a revolution, United States Marines landed there, July 28, 1915, forced an election for president, and established American trusteeship under a treaty imposed on the new government.

⊷ Purchase, Danish West Indies, renamed Virgin Islands, from Denmark at $25,000,000, March 3, 1917.

⊷ Amendments to the Constitution:

The 18th, or Prohibition Amendment, passed December 18, 1917. Ratified, January 16, 1920.

The 19th Amendment, giving women the vote, passed June 4, 1919. Ratified, August 26, 1920.

⊷ The United States role in the World War:

The position of neutrality, declared on August 4, 1914, was jeopardized by the sinking of the *Lusitania*, May 7, 1915. As a result of Wilson's protests, Germany suspended submarine warfare in the spring of 1916.

January 31, 1917: Germany issued an announcement that she would resume submarine warfare.

March: Five American merchantmen sunk.

April 2: Wilson appeared before Congress and asked for a declaration of war on Germany.

April 6: Congressional resolution declaring war.

May 18: The Selective Service Act was passed by Congress. Under this an army of 4,000,000 was trained, 1,300,000 saw action, and 126,000 died.

January 8, 1918: Wilson released his "14 points" program for peace.

November 11, 1918: An Armistice was proclaimed, Germany accepting Wilson's 14 points.

January 18, 1919: Peace Conference opened.

June 28, 1919: Treaty of Versailles signed.

WARREN GAMALIEL HARDING

───◆◉◆───

TWENTY-NINTH PRESIDENT

As the high aspirations of the War for Democracy unwound with a tired rattle, it looked as though Americans generally were ready for a change in Washington. The Republicans, out of office for eight years, might well have the Presidency within their grasp, which meant that the Republican nomination for president in 1920 would be a great prize. The party had a variety of men who were ready to try for it, the earliest and most ready being a general with a notable war record, Leonard Wood. Next was a range of politicians, most prominently Governor Frank Lowden of Illinois, to the left the progressive Hiram Johnson of California, and a jumble of possibles and favorite sons in between, including, far down in the ratings, Senator Warren Harding of Ohio.

During the year before the Republican convention met to choose a candidate, General Wood appeared to be the favorite, but his lavish financing by and through a soap manufacturer named Procter raised charges that he was trying to buy the Presidency, and a Senate sub-committee on investigation proved that he had spent the horrendous sum of $1,773,303, possibly a lot more. When the convention came to order in June 1920, at the Chicago Coliseum, the delegates were not solidly lined up, as is the Republican custom, and this showed at once on the balloting. At the end of the fourth ballot Wood and Lowden were in the lead, deadlocked, with the bulk of the votes scattered. The delegates, sweating and impatient in the Coliseum's temperature of nearly 100 degrees, were at this point astounded and rebellious when the convention chairman, elderly Senator Henry Cabot Lodge, calling for a vote on adjournment until the following morning, declared the "ayes" had it in spite of an uproarious volume of "no's" and left the podium.

That night Lodge, with his senatorial clique and some others, in a suite at the Blackstone Hotel, for six hours thrashed at the problem of selecting a candidate to break the deadlock, finally arriving at the conclusion that Warren Harding was the man who aroused the fewest objections. Around two o'clock he was summoned and told that he was to be given a chance for the next few ballots. When he emerged from the smoke-filled room looking pleased, and those who had supported him inside came out full of good tips for the reporters wandering about in the Blackstone corridors, the word spread rapidly that Harding "was the man." When the balloting resumed that morning, Harding's manager, skilled bluffer and manipulator Harry Daugherty, was the busiest man on the floor, weaving and darting about among the delegates, gathering votes. By the eighth ballot he had a creaky Harding bandwagon moving and on the tenth Harding was nominated. The convention then spontaneously nominated Calvin Coolidge of Massachusetts for Vice President.

Warren Harding had the classical look of a statesman and something of the classical family background of American presidents. He was born on a farm in the hamlet of Blooming Grove, Ohio, his father successively a teacher, a farmer, and a homeopathic doctor, never quite earning a living, his mother turning to midwifery to help out. Warren went to rural schools and got along well, except that now and then a boy would tease him by calling him "nigger," the result of an untraceable legend that somewhere among the Harding ancestors there had been a Negro. The legend plagued Harding most of his life until, in his days of political prominence, a racist college professor brought out a book of such rabid, irrational obsession that it virtually laid the story to rest. At sixteen Harding graduated from Iberia College, then no more than a small rural academy, and his family moved to Marion, a quiet small town not yet on the way to becoming an important railroad and industrial small city. At eighteen, after trying and discarding several jobs, he became the editor and part owner of a little newspaper, hardly more than a flyer, called *The Star*. Gradually he turned it into a conveyor of news, and as Marion grew, so grew *The Star*. At twenty-five, with wealth still ahead of him, but

154

handsome, graceful and conspicuously virile, he attracted the attention of Florence Kling De Wolfe, plain but lively daughter of the richest man in town, and a recent divorcee. She fell in love with Harding and, in spite of her father's objections, married him.

Harding drifted into Ohio politics inevitably because of his flair for handling people and pleasing them with silver-voiced oratory, though of a strange corkscrew English in which subjects and verbs collided nonchalantly around the curves. Two terms in the State Senate, one as lieutenant governor, and a term in the United States Senate appeared to be his sole qualifications for the high office of President, but he had in fact, perhaps unfortunately, learned much in Ohio, especially a tolerance of how practical politics is practiced. And he had attracted as his own personal booster one Harry Daugherty, lawyer-lobbyist, a venal and shrewd operator. In his campaign for President, though he was obliged to tour the country and make speeches, he achieved most publicity with his "front porch" electioneering in Marion, where he was at his best, shaking hands with thousands who came in a kind of pilgrimage of the people. While his opponent, Governor James M. Cox of Ohio, spoke to the Democratic doctrine of Wilson's League of Nations, Harding came out for a great national return to "normalcy." In the election "normalcy" won by a wide margin.

In preparing for the Presidency Harding chose his Cabinet partly for political reasons but largely for prestige, and only one crony was rewarded. He felt a great obligation to Harry Daugherty and was determined to make him Attorney General. For Secretary of the Interior he selected Senator Albert B. Fall, well recommended but distrusted by the ardent conservationists. The most prestigious choices were Andrew Mellon, the aluminum magnate, as Secretary of the Treasury, Herbert Hoover as Secretary of Commerce, and Charles Evans Hughes as Secretary of State. To Hughes he gave the management of what he considered his most important effort as President, the Washington Disarmament Conference. Opening with impressive ceremony November 12, 1921, attended by representatives of nine governments, the purpose of the conference was to promote peace by limitation of naval power and by stabilizing the relationship of all the powers interested in the Pacific islands and China. Out of it came three treaties, but long before World War II these had been repudiated or forgotten.

The Harding presidency has to be remembered for the irresponsibility of the Executive, which let corruption grow like fungi in certain places. Least likely to be forgotten was the "Teapot Dome," a case in which Secretary of the Interior Fall sought and received compensation for diverting to private interests the naval oil reserves at Teapot Dome in Wyoming and Elk Hills, California. The first step in this devious operation

155

was to have the oil reserves transferred from the Navy to the Interior Department. Secretary of the Navy Denby could see nothing wrong with that, and the President himself approved. Fall, who was perennially in need of cash to keep up his ranch in New Mexico, then proceeded to negotiate secretly the lease of Teapot Dome to Harry F. Sinclair's oil company and the lease of Elk Hills to the oil interests of his old friend Edward L. Doheny, receiving a total of $404,000 from the two men. As soon as both transactions were completed, in January 1923, he resigned from the Cabinet and retired to his ranch. The following October, the Senate Committee on Public Lands began an investigation of the leases. With Democrat Thomas J. Walsh of Montana taking charge of it, with persistence and brilliance rare in congressional investigations, the whole story was eventually set down in the records. The oil reserves were recovered; Fall, tried for accepting a bribe, was convicted and sentenced to one year in jail and a $100,000 fine.

The Department of Justice under Daugherty sheltered various forms of graft. Its Prohibition Bureau was reputedly the most corrupt, not only selling protection to bootleggers, but operating its own bootleg racket, including the genteel delivery of good bonded liquor to the White House. Its Bureau of Investigation, under the free-wheeling former private detective William J. Burns, believed it had the right to tap telephones and raid offices even when the object of its interest happened to be members of Congress. Daugherty himself was charged with selling favors and putting pressure on Federal judges when such favors were involved. Daugherty was never proved guilty of anything either by a congressional investigation or later in the courts, but his factotum, Jess Smith, who did business as influence peddler at "the little green house on K Street," suffered an emotional collapse and committed suicide in the spring of 1923. The only case of graft that the President ever had to confront was that of his Director of the Veterans Bureau, Charles R. Forbes, who disposed of war-surplus goods to his own advantage and got kickbacks from contractors on veterans' hospitals. Harding's action in that case was to send Forbes out of the country and force him to resign. All of these men were among those Harding called his "poker cabinet," the group who played poker once or twice a week at the White House. Since the President believed he should honor Prohibition in the public rooms downstairs, the poker parties were held upstairs in his study, where liquor could be served. The First Lady, or the Duchess, as Harding liked to call her, filled the glasses and kept them filled until the party broke up, usually about midnight.

Early in 1923, though looking and feeling unwell, Harding decided to run for re-election in 1924, and therefore set in motion plans for a speaking tour of the states with a sight-seeing trip by boat to Alaska. On June 29 the

Presidential train started west on an ambitious schedule of speeches and personal contact with the people. It was on his way back from Alaska, at Seattle, that Harding was taken ill. His personal physician, "Doc" Sawyer, pronounced it ptomaine poisoning from seafood, but his Naval Aide Lieut. Commander Joel T. Boone, also a doctor, discovered on examination an enlargement of the heart. He took this information to Secretary of Commerce Hoover, who had joined the train when it reached California, and he immediately wired Dr. Ray Lyman Wilbur, President of the American Medical Association, requesting that he meet the train at the end of its run from Seattle to San Francisco. Dr. Wilbur did so, accompanied by a heart specialist. Harding was taken to the Palace Hotel, where his condition worsened with an attack of pneumonia, then improved so that he could sit up in bed and receive a few visitors. On the evening of August 2, with no warning and only his nurse in the room, he died.

No other President has left so much debris, political and personal, on dying. Besides the cases of graft that had to be investigated interminably and resolved in the courts, his love affairs were discovered. Nan Britton, who had been his mistress for many years and had a daughter by him, published a book, *The President's Daughter*, which instantly became a best seller. Harding's love letters to another mistress turned up in Ohio, but were not released to the public. A former operative in the Bureau of Investigation produced a book called *The Strange Death of President Harding*, which became another best seller. Proved eventually to be utter fabrication, it popularized the theory that Harding had not died a natural death, but had been poisoned by his wife to save him from dishonor. The ultimate slander in American history, it has been impossible to entirely eradicate this from American legend.

HIGHLIGHTS OF HIS ADMINISTRATION

⋅§ The Fordney-McCumber Tariff Act of 1922.

⋅§ The Washington Disarmament Conference, opening on November 12, 1921. By a treaty of March 29, 1922, the United States, Great Britain, France, Italy, and Japan agreed on a Naval Limitations Treaty to run until 1936, fixing the ratio of strength among the leading powers. The Conference also, with nine nations represented, negotiated a treaty to maintain the open door in China, and among other agreements relating to the Far East, persuaded Japan to agree to withdraw from Shantung in China and from Siberia.

JOHN CALVIN COOLIDGE

——◦◦◦◦◉◦◦◦——

THIRTIETH PRESIDENT

In the middle of a summer night, a telegraph operator drove up to the darkened Coolidge farmhouse in Plymouth Notch, Vermont, and delivered to Vice President Calvin Coolidge the message announcing the death of President Harding a continent away in San Francisco. Shortly before three o'clock on the morning of August 3, 1923, in the threadbare dining room of the old house, by the light of kerosene lamps, Coolidge was sworn in as President by his father, a notary public. Both men had shaved and dressed carefully. Mrs. Coolidge stood beside her husband and in the background were his stenographer, his chauffeur, a Congressman, and a few lucky reporters. Newspaper descriptions of this scene introduced Coolidge to the American people in a way they could never forget. From the day he was born, one Fourth of July, he was a man of good luck, as well as one gifted with an instinct for politics.

Another case in point was the combination of circumstances that lifted him from the modest position of Republican governor of Massachusetts to the vice-presidency in 1921. In September 1919, Boston was thrown into confusion by its police, who went on strike in an attempt to organize a union affiliated with the American Federation of Labor. For two nights and a day, the city was terrified by disorders and the fear of disorders, as every newspaper reader in the country knew. Although, as governor, Coolidge took no direct part in bringing order back to Boston, afterwards he was drawn into the debate on the right of policemen to strike. The Boston police commissioner maintained that they had no right, and when the men tried to return to their jobs he refused to take them back. Samuel Gompers, president of the A. F. of L., backed up their right to organize and act as members of any ordinary union. He addressed this argument to the police commissioner and to Governor Coolidge, who, by a quirk of Massachusetts law, was the commissioner's immediate superior. Without the slightest desire to antagonize labor, nevertheless Coolidge decided to take a firm stand against the policemen. In a telegram to Gompers he summed up in crisp, eloquent words the stand for law and order. The sentence that rang most true in American ears all across the land was: "There is no right to strike against the public safety by anybody, anywhere, any time."

Amid the enthusiasm for Coolidge in Massachusetts that autumn, powerful Senator Henry Cabot Lodge held out to Coolidge hope of the presidential nomination the next year. Before then Lodge had changed his mind, so that at the 1920 Republican National Convention the hopes of Coolidge interested only a small following, devotedly led by the rich Boston department store owner Frank W. Stearns, an amateur in politics. In their "smoke-filled room," Lodge and his senatorial cabal chose another favorite son for the nomination, Warren Harding of Ohio. For the second place on the ticket they again ignored Coolidge and picked Senator Irving L. Lenroot of Wisconsin.

It was early evening of a Saturday when the convention took up the vice-presidential nomination. Many of the delegates were angry with the leadership for forcing Harding's nomination, and all were tired. As soon as Lenroot was placed before the delegates as vice-presidential nominee, Senator Lodge, chairman of the convention, turned over the gavel to Frank Willis of Ohio and went outside for a breath of air. At this point some of the Oregon delegates put their heads together. One of them, Wallace McCamant, had read the volume of collected Coolidge speeches and messages called *Have Faith in Massachusetts* and was greatly impressed by them. Why not Coolidge for Vice President? he asked. In a few minutes the Oregon delegates agreed. Climbing on a chair, he raised his voice above the hubbub and demanded the Chair recognize him. Then in one of the shortest nominating speeches on record he gave the convention Coolidge for Vice President. The idea caught like a prairie fire. Lenroot was eliminated, as were a few other entries, and Coolidge was the convention's choice.

He satisfied the popular notions about Yankees. He was a spare man with reddish sandy hair and a face that never changed expression. He was reputed to be thrifty, upright, and sensible, and little was ever known to belie that reputation. Born in the green hills of Vermont, he grew up a painfully shy boy in the isolated farm hamlet of Plymouth. His father kept a store there and did his stint in community politics as selectman, road commissioner, school commissioner, and even as representative to the state legislature. When the time came for college, young Calvin went to Amherst in Massachusetts, where, after a long, lonely time, he eventually established a reputation as an odd but clever boy. The college associations filled a great need in him for sentimental attachments and he never forgot them. He decided to become a lawyer, electing to serve an apprenticeship and study law at the same time in a legal firm. The first offer came from a firm in Northampton, Massachusetts, close to Amherst. A county seat and trading center, it was a good place to practice law, so he accepted the offer without delay.

Coolidge's rise in politics is a study in the deliberate, cautious but sure method of moving up one rung at a time. Restrained and correct, he left nothing to chance or the opposition. He started by being elected to the Northampton common council, was then chosen as the council's solicitor, went to the state legislature, and at thirty-eight was mayor of his town. At the same time he looked after a small, stable law practice. Personally he was retiring and parsimonious, though he had a fancy for seeing his pretty young wife elegantly dressed. After a term as mayor he went back to Boston as state senator and president of the senate, and was then elected lieutenant governor, and finally, governor. This might well have been the top of his ladder. In all these years he enjoyed an unblemished reputation as a conservative and regular Republican. Home was Northampton, where he rented half of a two-family house, and for vacations he took his family to his father's house in Plymouth, Vermont.

Catapulted from this mossy existence into Washington society as the Vice President, his eccentricities made him a legend, an enigma, and the unruffled butt of dozens of funny stories about his vast silences, his thrift, and the dry humor that was mined from his few comments. He admitted that he was bored with the outward show and emptiness of his office, but he dutifully walked through the paces that were set for him. At least, for

161

the first time, the Vice President was invited to cabinet meetings, and these he regularly attended. When he moved to the head of the table on Harding's death, it was with a sense of getting down to work and doing a proper job.

The Coolidge philosophy was the simple one of leaving things alone as much as possible. Conditions on the whole were good while he was in office. He had some trouble with the farm bloc in Congress, who proposed a radical and expensive bill to relieve agriculture of its surpluses and low prices, but he knocked this down twice with vetoes. The World War veterans were more difficult. He vetoed their multi-billion-dollar Bonus Bill, but Congress passed it over his veto. In the matter of taxation Congress again resisted him, voting down Secretary of Treasury Mellon's proposal to reduce the wartime surtax on high incomes, though later yielding partial reduction. However, he was better attuned to the mood of the American people than Congress. His election in 1924 was an emphatic vote of confidence.

While prosperity continued at home under its own power, Coolidge raised American prestige abroad by the Kellogg-Briand Pact of 1928, a gesture in which fifteen nations agreed to substitute arbitration for war. For bringing it about Secretary of State Frank B. Kellogg was awarded the Nobel Peace Prize. A more enduring accomplishment was the introduction of peace and reason into relations with Mexico, after many years of blundering and misunderstanding over the rights of American businessmen in that country. Coolidge sent his Amherst classmate, Dwight W. Morrow, a partner in the New York banking house of Morgan, as ambassador to Mexico. By patience and tact Morrow not only settled the dispute over oil concessions that at the moment made one more clash at arms seem imminent, but he put Mexican-American relations on a healthy, friendly basis for many years to come.

Four years to the day after he became President, while vacationing in the Black Hills of South Dakota, Coolidge announced his retirement from public office. In his quotable words, he did not "choose to run in 1928." And so, at the peak of his popularity, when re-election seemed more than probable, he made one of the wisest decisions of his life. As he said in his homely way, "It's a pretty good idea to get out when they still want you." He could look back on a good administration, so far as he could tell. On March 4, 1929, he returned to Northampton. There for the first time he bought a home of his own, with lawns and trees, a retreat from public stares. Of his two sons, one had died in the White House and the other was about to be married. He published his *Autobiography* and wrote articles for the newspapers, lucky to be out of politics when economic disaster struck the nation and the Republican party. Just two months before Franklin Roosevelt and the Democrats took over the government in 1933, he died suddenly of a coronary thrombosis.

HIGHLIGHTS OF HIS ADMINISTRATION

Soldiers' Bonus. The Adjusted Compensation Act of May 19, 1924, gave veterans of the World War endowment and insurance policies at the rate of $1.25 for each day of overseas service and $1.00 for each day of service at home. The total cost to the nation: about $3,500,000,000.

The Kellogg-Briand Peace Pact, signed at Paris, August 27, 1928, by the United States and 14 other nations, renounced war "as an instrument of national policy." Forty-eight other nations were invited to sign, and many did. No method of enforcement was provided.

HERBERT CLARK HOOVER

THIRTY-FIRST PRESIDENT

Not being trained in the candid manners of the politician, Herbert Hoover hesitated to declare himself a candidate for the presidency in 1920, although as America's chief civilian war hero, he could well turn out to be the people's choice, if he were nominated. His name to most people meant the man who fed starving Belgians under the heel of German occupation, the man who told American housewives how to conserve food once the United States got into the war, and the superman who straightened out and fed Europe once the war was over. It was not certain whether he was a Democrat or a Republican, but both parties would be glad to have him. At first he announced that he was not a candidate for public office. Then, reflecting perhaps that seeking the presidency was not out of line with his ideals of public service, he announced that he would accept the Republican nomination on a liberal platform, including the League of Nations with reservations. His announcement fell coldly on the ears of the Republican leadership. Ultraconservative and strongly opposed to the League of Nations, they managed the nomination of one of their own kind, Warren Harding.

Hoover accepted the minor cabinet post of Secretary of Commerce in President Harding's administration, turning down the offer of a partnership in the Guggenheim mining company at a princely salary to do so. This indicated that he continued under the spell of the presidential idea and was prepared to do yeoman's work for it. He was one of the handful of distinguished Republicans who stood by the party and served in the dubious Harding regime. Characteristically, he plunged into the work of making his department fulfill its maximum possibilities. With imagination and drive, he extended its functions and personnel until it became an important source of information and help to business. In 1921 this productive effort was interrupted by an appeal for help from an unexpected direction. Russia was in the midst of famine as the result of failure of the wheat crop, and Maxim Gorki, her famous novelist, thought to appeal to America. Hoover rose to the occasion in spite of the unfriendly relations between the Bolshevik government and the United States. The Bolsheviks, trusting in Hoover and his Quaker integrity, agreed to his conditions. A month later American food was arriving in the famine areas.

In 1927 the Mississippi Valley had its worst flood in the memory of man, and obviously the man to undertake the job of moving a million and a half people to safety was Hoover. It was the first chance Americans had had to watch him operate among them and they were filled with admiration. He became such a byword as a saver of lives that the humorist Will Rogers took occasion to observe, when a Near East earthquake failed to start him off in that direction, that "Bert was only resting between calamities." So it was that when President Coolidge announced that he would not run for re-election in 1928, the Republican leaders were ready to accept Hoover. At the national convention that year, he was nominated decisively on the first ballot. Pitted against the Democrats' great soul, Alfred E. Smith, a Catholic and a "wet," or anti-prohibitionist, he ran away with the election in November, even carrying several normally Democratic Southern states.

There were three men in Herbert Hoover's career, the mining engineer, the humanitarian, and the politician. By far the best story lies in the mining engineer, or the first forty years of his life, unsurpassed by any boy's adventure fiction. He was born of Quaker parents in West Branch, Iowa. The family cottage, next door to his father's blacksmith shop, was small and mean, but his childhood was both cheerful and disciplined in the Quaker tradition of rising above poverty, with faith in the dignity of man and the duty of good works. His father died of typhoid fever when Herbert was six, and his mother supported her three children by taking in sewing, while she also answered frequent calls to speak in Friends' meetings. She

166

too died young, when Herbert was ten, and her children were divided among relatives. Herbert went to live with his uncle, Dr. Henry J. Minthorn, head of the Friends Pacific Academy at Newberg, on the Willamette River in Oregon.

At seventeen, with two hundred dollars in his pocket, Herbert set off to acquire a college education at Leland Stanford University, the bright, new institution of David Starr Jordan at Palo Alto, California. He worked his way through college by office work and a laundry delivery service, and in the summers as a member of geological surveying teams.

His spirits were dashed when, graduated and ready to launch himself into a mining engineer's career in the year 1895, a year of depression, he discovered that the world was full of unemployed engineers. For a time he was grateful for miner's wages in the Sierra diggings, but he finally managed to wedge himself into the office of the most distinguished mining engineer in San Francisco as a copyist. Louis Janin soon discovered that his young typist, though shy on the outside, was a superb mental mechanism in the details of mine management and an indomitable boss of men. He advanced him rapidly in the work of his office, and after two years, generously recommended him to the London firm of Bewick, Moreing and Company as the manager of a string of gold mines that they had under development in central west Australia. This was the first of his mining responsibilities, at the age of twenty-three. As autocrat of the mining camps, superintendent of the mine superintendents, and representative of the investors' interests, he had a phenomenal success in Australia. In the camps they called him "Boy" Hoover or "Hail Columbia" Hoover, though to his face, respectfully, "Chief."

Since mines are usually in remote, even exotic places, Hoover's travels to his work were often adventures. For fifteen years he crisscrossed the world by steamer and train, by cart and by caravan, a matter-of-fact, busy engineer, whose mind was not however closed to the various cultures that he had an opportunity to observe at close range. When he was married in 1899 to a girl he had fallen in love with at Stanford, he took his bride off to China, where he was to be director of the Imperial Bureau of Mines, enjoying the rare experience of prospecting for gold in the Gobi Desert, escorted by a retinue in full medieval panoply. He and his wife were also to withstand the hazards of the Boxer Rebellion in 1900, besieged in Tientsin. In Burma, Hoover investigated an abandoned silver mine in the remote jungles and turned it into one of the most profitable mining properties in the world. In Russia, he reorganized a private iron and steel industrial principality in the Ural Mountains into a profitable concern with which the Russian Tsar was so impressed that he engaged the brilliant young American to survey the Imperial family's mines.

167

By the outbreak of the European war in 1914, the Hoovers, with their two little boys, were anchored in a comfortable London home, wealthy enough though not super-millionaires. In the first distressing weeks of the war, thousands of Americans were stranded abroad, and Hoover was their Good Samaritan in London, finding money and ships to take them home. While he lingered over this, preparing for his own return, the tragic plight of Belgium, occupied by the German army and facing starvation, was brought to his attention. He undertook to organize relief. Aware of the political, financial, and administrative difficulties of the undertaking, he closed out his private business and devoted himself entirely to it. Under the unfriendly eyes of the Germans and the Allies, eventually ten million people were fed and clothed at a cost of nearly a billion dollars. As Hoover described the operation, "It was like trying to feed a hungry kitten by means of a forty-foot bamboo pole, said kitten confined in a barred cage occupied by two hungry lions."

Once the United States declared war on Germany, Wilson required Hoover in Washington as wartime Food Administrator. After the war, as head of the Supreme Economic Council, he fed and clothed war sufferers and restored order to the chaotic communications systems of the belligerents. With this large administrative experience and his seven years as Secretary of Commerce, Hoover was well prepared for the presidency. However, personally he was strange to the fellowship of politicians. Undoubtedly strong-minded and warmhearted, he was apt to be brusque in human relations, which was a distinct handicap in the art of politics.

Inaugurated in March 1929, at the peak of Coolidge prosperity, Hoover had his head full of plans to improve government efficiency, economic processes such as the banking and bankruptcy laws, the condition of children, and education, with a vision of "the final triumph over poverty" for Americans. Seven months later came the stock-market crash of October 1929, and the crumbling of American business. Hoover met the emergency energetically, calling on the states and private relief agencies to spread their resources among the men thrown out of work, and requesting industry to keep up their payrolls. He hoped that with a great united, voluntary effort the country could pull itself out of trouble. To keep the people's spirits up, he incautiously assured them that it would all be over in a few months, a promise that someone with a talent for slogans interpreted as "prosperity just around the corner." Nothing was further from reality. The depression continued to grow worse. Bread lines appeared, hundreds of thousands of jobless took to the roads, others put up tin shacks in city parks, businessmen sold apples on street corners. People mistook the

168

forced cheerfulness of the administration in Washington for indifference and called their shack-towns "Hoovervilles."

Like other Presidents before, Hoover was blamed for not knowing how to cure a depression. He had hoped the Agricultural Marketing Act, passed shortly before the crash and designed to peg farm prices and help in marketing crops, would be an aid to the farmers, but its effect was invisible. Farms in the Midwest and South suffered a serious drought in 1930. The banking community took its turn in disaster when the Austrian bank Kredit Anstalt failed in May that year, forcing most of the European currencies, including that of Great Britain, off the gold standard and threatening the entire structure of international loans. Hoover was obliged to meet the situation with a moratorium on European debt payments.

At the beginning of 1932, he endorsed a series of measures to feed money into the American economy, the most important being the Reconstruction Finance Corporation. These were to do an important job in the process of economic recovery, but they were slow in dribbling their benefits down to the workingman. Hoover was urged to approve of direct relief on a large scale, but he opposed this as an insult to American pride and also on the ground that "we can't spend ourselves into prosperity." Proposals that the government put up funds to rehabilitate industry on a broad scale he also opposed with a deep moral conviction that this would lead to statism and fascism.

By the autumn of 1932, 12,000,000 people were unemployed and there were fears that the banks would close. Running for re-election, Hoover was opposed by an immensely popular Democrat, Franklin Roosevelt, a man who was exactly his opposite in training, personality, and political philosophy. There was no doubt that, in the tradition of depression-cursed Presidents, Hoover would be voted out of office. He was, most emphatically, carrying only six states.

The slurs and injustices of politics were particularly wounding to a man of Hoover's humanitarian philosophy. But his appetite for good works was not seriously impaired. In private life he gave freely of his time to such organizations as the Boys Club of America, the United Nations Children's Emergency Fund, and CARE. He set for himself an ambitious program of writing and public speaking, in which he enjoyed the privilege of an elder statesman in offering advice to both Republicans and Democrats. His most distinguished public service in the years following World War II were the two "Hoover Plans" for reorganizing the executive branch of the government. In each case, he had charge of a large staff of experts known as the Commission on Organization of the Executive Branch of the Government, the first appointed by President Truman, the second by President Eisenhower. These plans, resulting from intensive study, made recommendations—more than half of which were adopted—for economy, efficiency, and fairness to free enterprise.

A Chicken *for* Every Pot

THE Republican Party isn't a *"Poor Man's Party."* Republican prosperity has erased that degrading phrase from our political vocabulary.

The Republican Party is *equality's* party—*opportunity's* party—*democracy's* party, the party of *national* development, not *sectional* interests—the *impartial* servant of every State and condition in the Union.

Under higher tariff and lower taxation, America has stabilized output, employment and dividend rates.

Republican efficiency has filled the workingman's dinner pail—and his gasoline tank *besides*—made telephone, radio and sanitary plumbing *standard* household equipment. And placed the whole nation in the *silk stocking class.*

During eight years of Republican management, we have built more and better homes, erected more skyscrapers, passed more benefactory laws, and more laws to regulate and purify immigration, inaugurated more conservation measures, more measures to standardize and increase production, expand export markets, and reduce industrial and human junk piles, than in any previous quarter century.

Republican prosperity is written on *fuller wage* envelops, written in factory chimney smoke, written on the walls of new construction, written in savings bank books, written in mercantile balances, and written in the peak value of stocks and bonds.

Republican prosperity has *reduced* hours and *increased* earning capacity, silenced *discontent*, put the proverbial "chicken in every pot." And a car in every backyard, to boot.

It has *raised* living standards and *lowered* living costs.

It has restored financial confidence and enthusiasm, changed *credit* from a *rich* man's privilege to a *common* utility, *generalized* the use of time-saving devices and released women from the thrall of *domestic drudgery.*

It has provided every county in the country with its concrete road and knitted the highways of the nation into a *unified* traffic system.

Thanks to Republican administration, farmer, dairyman and merchant can make deliveries in *less* time and at *less* expense, can borrow *cheap* money to re-fund exorbitant mortgages, and stock their pastures, ranges and shelves.

Democratic management *impoverished* and *demoralized* the *railroads*, led packing plants and tire factories into *receivership*, squandered billions on *impractical* programs.

Democratic mal-administration issued *further* billions on mere "scraps of paper," then encouraged foreign debtors to believe that their loans would never be called, and bequeathed to the Republican Party the job of *mopping up the mess.*

Republican administration has *restored* to the railroads solvency, efficiency and par securities.

It has brought the rubber trades through panic and chaos, brought down the prices of crude rubber by smashing *monopolistic rings*, put the tanner's books in the *black* and secured from the European powers formal acknowledgment of their obligations.

The Republican Party rests its case on a record of stewardship and performance.

Its Presidential and Congressional candidates stand for election on a platform of sound practice, Federal vigilance, high tariff, Constitutional integrity, the conservation of natural resources, *honest* and *constructive* measures for agricultural relief, sincere enforcement of the laws, and the right of *all* citizens, regardless of *faith* or *origin*, to share the benefits of opportunity and justice.

Wages, dividends, progress and prosperity say,

"Vote *for* Hoover"

HIGHLIGHTS OF HIS ADMINISTRATION

◦§ The Agricultural Marketing Act, signed into law on June 15, 1929, in an attempt to bolster farm prices by controlling and subsidizing marketing.

◦§ The stock-market crash, which began October 21, 1929, and had its blackest day on October 29, 1929.

◦§ The Hawley-Smoot Tariff, signed June 17, 1930, increasing tariffs across the board. It produced retaliatory tariffs by 25 countries.

◦§ The Reconstruction Finance Corporation, set up by Act of Congress, January 1932, to "prime the pump" of industry. It was authorized to lend money to railroads, banks, agricultural agencies, and later to local government agencies. During its existence its commitments came to $11 billion.

◦§ The Bonus Army march to Washington, which arrived in June 1932, to demand payment of full face value on the veterans' endowment policies. The veterans built and occupied a shacktown on the Anacostia Flats in Washington, until they were evicted by the National Guard.

◦§ Twentieth Amendment to the Constitution, fixing the presidential and congressional terms to commence and end in January, ratified February 6, 1933.

FRANKLIN DELANO ROOSEVELT

THIRTY-SECOND PRESIDENT

For some years after the death of Woodrow Wilson, the Democratic party was not only the minority party, it was a fragmented minority. There was a young man in New York, however, named Franklin Roosevelt, who was trying to foster a national feeling in the party and to conciliate the various factions. Most of the Democratic leaders, from state down to municipal levels, received letters from him. Nothing much came of his efforts, but when the time came to think of a candidate for President in 1932, he was probably better known to the party's rank and file than any other man. He was also well known to the bosses. They admitted that he was an irresistibly charming man, a magnificent vote getter. But he was just too independent! The classic story about Roosevelt and the bosses goes back to 1910, when he was a freshman in the New York State Senate. Charles F. Murphy, leader of Tammany Hall, the New York City Democratic organization, was told about the young man's election in a Republican district and commented: "Well, if we've caught a Roosevelt, we'd better take him down and drop him off the dock. The Roosevelts run true to form and this

173

kid is likely to do for us what the Colonel is going to do for the Republican party, split it wide open." True to Murphy's prophecy, the first thing Roosevelt did in the legislature was to prevent the election to the United States Senate of Murphy's candidate, a machine politician called "Blue-Eyed Billy" Sheehan.

In 1932 Roosevelt's presidential candidacy went before the Democratic National Convention with a few of the party regulars on his side. Among them was his campaign manager James A. Farley, a big, pleasant, astute politician with the poise of a bishop. At the convention he went foraging for Roosevelt votes. The anti-Roosevelt bloc held the votes of New York that he needed; they were all for Tammany's idol, once the state's great governor, Al Smith. Roosevelt had done many things for Smith in the past, and helped him in 1928 when he ran for President unsuccessfully against Herbert Hoover. But now his own star was rising. Farley's foraging finally brought in the Texas and California votes, and with these Roosevelet was nominated on the fourth ballot. John Nance Garner of Texas was then nominated for Vice President. Before the convention adjourned, Roosevelt flew to Chicago and accepted the nomination with a speech in which he gave the campaign to come its watchword, the New Deal.

Franklin Roosevelt was born into a family of the Hudson River gentry, descended from Dutch settlers, wealthy and traditionally Democratic. Theodore Roosevelt, a Republican, was a fifth cousin. Franklin, the only child of his father's second marriage to a beautiful and imperious woman, grew up handsome, kind and charming, went to Groton and Harvard, and studied enough law at Columbia University to pass his bar examinations. Before the end of his freshman year at college, his father died and he became the young squire of a handsome estate at Hyde Park in Dutchess County. On Saint Patrick's Day in 1905, he married a lovely young distant cousin by the name of Anna Eleanor Roosevelt; though the star of that occasion was President Theodore Roosevelt, who gave the bride away, since she was his favorite niece. Roosevelt was taken into the office of one of New York City's best law firms and settled into what appeared to be a promising legal career. Weekends he was gregarious, almost perfectly good-humored, an energetic sportsman but with a turn for serious interests. With his temperament and his money, he was certain to be interesting to politicians.

Before long some of the Democrats in Dutchess County suggested he run for the state senate. Since it appeared that only one Democrat had been elected to the senate from his district in fifty-four years, Roosevelt accepted the suggestion as a sporting proposition. He campaigned intensively in an automobile, penetrating rural areas and talking to farmers who had never seen a candidate for senator before, and storing away in his capacious mind useful information on agriculture. He won, to his surprise. Two years later, in 1912, he won again in another novel campaign.

Taken ill with typhoid fever, he was not able to stump the district, so he persuaded a newspaperman named Louis McHenry Howe to come to his aid. Howe ran a campaign of newspaper advertising. Thus began one of the most valuable relationships of Roosevelt's life. Louis Howe was for some twenty years his closest and most constant adviser.

Roosevelt became a Woodrow Wilson progressive in 1912, and in the Wilson administration was assistant Secretary of the Navy. The Navy had been his hobby since boyhood, so he performed every duty, even the routines of procurement, with rare enthusiasm. He launched himself into the campaign that took on the aspect of "preparedness" when the European war began in 1914. Once the United States was in the war, he tried to get into uniform but was turned down on the ground that he was more useful in the Department. His name is always linked with one of the celebrated naval exploits of the war, the North Sea Mine Barrage, a subsurface curtain of mines, 240 miles long, that stretched from Scotland to Norway and blocked German submarines exiting from their home bases to attack Allied shipping.

During his seven years in Washington, Roosevelt was not idle politically. He handled some of the New York patronage for Wilson, and in 1914 was a candidate for the Democratic nomination for United States Senator in New York. He lost, his only defeat at the polls, except for 1920. In that year he accepted the vice-presidential nomination on the Cox ticket as a representative of the Wilsonian wing of the party. In the spirit of rendering to a great leader, then ill and discredited, the respect due him, he campaigned hard for the League of Nations. When the losing fight was finally lost at the polls, he was delighted to pick up his old life in New York, his law practice, and a well-salaried insurance business. He was then still a young man but with practically everything he could desire, in his family, friends, income, a feeling of success, possibly a career in politics. Less than a year later he was lying gravely ill with poliomyelitis at his isolated summer home on Campobello Island in the Bay of Fundy. He survived, but with paralyzed legs.

Once out of the doctors' hands, Roosevelt proceeded to adapt himself to his handicap. It was difficult for a man of bounding, athletic vigor to be anchored in a wheelchair. He not only overcame the difficulty, he censored it out of his life, to some degree. Later, as a public figure he refused to present the image of a cripple, and photographers were on their honor not to photograph him in his wheelchair. Most Americans had a mental picture of him as a whole man. In the meantime, for seven years after his illness, he was definitely in private life. His wife, Eleanor, began to take part in women's civic activities to keep him in touch with politics.

In 1924 Roosevelt discovered Warm Springs, the Georgia summer resort where a pool of naturally warm water seemed to help paralytics to regain the use of their limbs. He began taking the treatment and was so pleased with it that he developed the Warm Springs Foundation for infantile paralysis victims. He was able to discard his crutches for leg braces, and for the first time hoped to walk again. This hope, such as it was, had to be abandoned in 1928, when Al Smith dragooned him into running for governor of New York. Smith, nominated for the presidency, believed that without Roosevelt on the ticket he would not be able to carry that state. In the election Roosevelt won, while Smith lost both the state and the presidency.

In two terms as governor, Roosevelt foreshadowed some of his style as President. He defeated a power lobby and established the principle of public power control. To meet the needs of the jobless during the depression following the 1929 stock-market crash, he introduced the radical concept of unemployment relief—the first governor to do so. He also acquired some of the personal advisers whom he took to Washington—the social worker Harry Hopkins, the labor expert Frances Perkins, who was to become the first woman cabinet minister, and the group of Columbia University professors whom Louis Howe nicknamed the "brain trust." During the latter part of his tenure, while he was looking for support in his pre-convention campaign for the Democratic presidential nomination, municipal scandal erupted in New York City. Over the weeks the corruption of officials became so evident that many of the decent citizens demanded that Governor Roosevelt remove the mayor, Tammany's Jimmy Walker. Reluctant to offend Tammany or the forces of decency, he finally decided he must stand with the latter. Summoning the mayor, he questioned him in a public hearing and allowed him to resign.

In his campaign for the presidency Roosevelt outlined his program for the New Deal. It offered hope to "the forgotten man," equality of opportunity, and the benevolence of the state to those in want. The people were tired of Hoover and his crusade for "rugged individualism," and at the polls they voted as much against Hoover as for Roosevelt. The result: nearly 90 per cent of the electoral vote for Roosevelt. Between the election and the inauguration in March 1933, there were four months of ever deepening depression. Bread lines, shack-towns of the homeless in city parks, stark, smokeless factory chimneys, were commonplaces of the American scene, and the unemployment figures were variously estimated from twelve to seventeen million. In the middle of February, hysteria was added to gloom when the Detroit banks closed, starting a country-wide bank panic. The following day in Miami, an assassin tried to kill the President-elect, taking instead the life of Mayor Anton Cermak of Chicago.

Roosevelt's inaugural address on March fourth, broadcast to the nation by radio, was a master stroke in the art of leadership. Full of reassurance, hope and valor, its message was largely in this short paragraph: "So first of all let me assert my firm belief that the only thing we have to fear is fear itself—nameless, unreasoning, unjustified terror which paralyzes needed efforts to convert retreat into advance."

Of Roosevelt's three terms and three months, the first two terms embraced the New Deal, the rest the World War. The New Deal included measures for economic recovery, and for reform based on the presumption that cataclysmic depressions could be prevented. Immediately after his inauguration the President began sending bills to a willing Congress called in special session. He declared a bank holiday and secured legislation under which the solvent banks were able to reopen in a few days, and many of the rest somewhat later. In the "hundred days" session of Congress, a Civilian Conservation Corps was authorized, to absorb unemployed youths; the Agricultural Adjustment Administration was created to raise the level of farm prices; the dollar was taken off the gold standard; agencies were established and given money to funnel relief money to the states and into public works; other agencies were created to relieve small debtors; and the National Industrial Recovery Act was passed, hopefully designed for the self-regulation of industry.

Much of this legislation was invalidated by the Supreme Court, some of it thereafter rewritten in improved form. Woven into the early efforts of Congress and continuing to emerge from time to time were the more durable New Deal reforms: the Tennessee Valley rehabilitation program; a long list of conservation measures; social security for the unemployed, elderly and dependent; fair labor standards; the abolition of child labor; reform of the stock market; reciprocal trade agreements; supervision of labor relations; and, not the least, the end of Prohibition.

These laws, by which government penetrated further than ever before into the lives of Americans, suggested to the conservatives that Socialism was its guiding philosophy. In fear and bitterness, and in partisanship, they loosed a violent attack on "that man in the White House" that was one of the strange phenomena of the Roosevelt era. Roosevelt sometimes struck back at his "economic royalist" critics. His ill-considered and unsuccessful attempt to "pack" the Supreme Court by adding new justices was a rare case of his losing temper with the opposition. In many mannerisms he was open to criticism, particularly as an administrator. He operated in a confusion of boards and alphabetical agencies, casual and even facetious about the conflicts he created. Yet the essentials were always straight in his own mind. He kept his campaign promises to add public welfare to the state's responsibilities, to reform and stabilize the economy, and failed only in delivering the country from depression. Recovery was heartbreakingly slow with all the relief dollars, made work, and pump priming. It reversed sharply in 1937–38, became certain only with the boom in war industries at the end of the decade.

Four elections showed that Roosevelt held his popularity well for twelve years, regardless of the conservative minority. The Republicans he defeated, with never less than 80 per cent of the electoral vote, were widely different men. The least successful was Alfred M. Landon of Kansas in 1936; the most successful Thomas E. Dewey of New York in 1944; and the most interesting, Wendell Willkie of Indiana in 1940.

Roosevelt rose to his full stature as a leader with the coming of World War II. He perceived Hitler's importance in world politics during the thirties, earlier than most of his countrymen. In 1939, when the German army invaded Poland and thus began the war, the United States was strongly isolationist, with an army long denied the congressional appropriations to give it modern weapons. Within a year a new era had started, appropriations ballooned, weapons development was underway, and Roosevelt had reached into the Republican party for two particularly able men, Henry L. Stimson and Frank Knox, to head the War and Navy departments. He had called for 50,000 new airplanes, an astonishing number compared to those few then in the air forces. Hitler's blitzkrieg in western Europe in the spring and summer of 1940 stepped up the pace of rearming and in the autumn prompted Congress to authorize the first peacetime draft. In June Roosevelt turned over to Dr. Vannevar Bush's National Research Council the extremely secret and extremely experimental clue to nuclear fission that led to the atomic bomb.

Regardless of official neutrality, and in the interest of American defense, Roosevelt traded fifty over-age American destroyers in the summer of 1940 to Great Britain for air and naval bases in the West Indies, thus also preparing to defend the Atlantic sea lanes against German submarines. In December he broadcast a "fireside chat" to the American people in which he explained his "arsenal of democracy" policy. The voices that were raised against it were many. There was a strong minority in favor of staying out of the war, either because of a moral objection to war as such, or as a matter of prudence, or in the faith that the United States was safe behind the Atlantic. Nevertheless, he continued in the direction that he believed was the only way to security, and gradually public opinion fell in behind him.

Early in 1941 he addressed Congress in his "Four Freedoms" speech, inspirational in tone, but blunt in its statement of his war aims: all-out self-defense and increasing armament production to supply "all those resolute people everywhere who are resisting aggression and are thereby keeping war away from our hemisphere." He followed it immediately with the "Lend-Lease" Bill which enabled Great Britain to secure the munitions she needed without loans or cash payments. When Russia was invaded by Germany, lend-lease was immediately extended to her. Without resorting to such propaganda mills as were thought necessary in the First World

War, Roosevelt, and Churchill too, knew how to make an effective gesture. In August these two met on a ship off the coast of Newfoundland and released their eight-point statement of war aims, which, with a mutual taste for eloquence, they called "The Atlantic Charter."

In the meantime, in May 1941, an American freighter was sunk by a German submarine. Roosevelt declared a "limited national emergency" and proceeded to freeze German credits and shut down German consulates. In September the United States and Germany were virtually at war in the Atlantic following a skirmish between a U-boat and an American naval vessel. At this time, the United States, with Great Britain and the Netherlands, in order to curb Japan's announced plans to extend her empire over the Asiatic mainland and the western Pacific, had put into effect an embargo on Japanese imports of strategic materials such as scrap iron and oil. Roosevelt, realizing that this drastic action would be met by drastic counteraction as Japan's need for these materials became acute, took the Philippine army into the United States armed forces in July and prepared to bulid up Philippine defenses. He feared Japan would strike either at the Philippines or to the southward, and hoping to win time to put the Philippines in a state of readiness, he continued to dicker with Japan at the diplomatic level. That Japan would break out of this situation with an attack on Pearl Harbor, December 7, 1941, came as a crashing surprise.

The war placed Roosevelt in command of more power than any one man had ever before known. As commander-in-chief, he had the over-all responsibility for army, navy, and air forces totaling 15,000,000, with a staggering amount of ships, airplanes, guns, and other necessities of war. He also had at his disposal the money and resources of the most productive industrial country in the world. That he was equal to such enormous power was due to many talents, including an understanding of military strategy, but particularly to his patience and courage. He mapped out certain areas of responsibility and respected them. For instance, unlike Hitler, he trusted the generals to do their job and backed them up. The mobilization of industry he placed in the hands of a bureaucracy that had some of the conflict and confusion of the New Deal agencies, but it got things done. His own area of responsibility was in deciding policy, composing differences, and acting as the diplomat in military decisions with America's allies.

Roosevelt and Churchill worked well as a team, and Roosevelt, following every move of the war in his map room at the White House, served to co-ordinate the American Joint Chiefs of Staff with the British high command. Hating red tape, he favored expediting decisions informally. The first decision faced after war was formally declared was whether to shift attention to the Philippines and the Pacific islands, or to "beat the Axis" in Europe first. The latter course was taken since the Axis was the greater menace. Roosevelt's relations with Stalin were never good, and Russia was consistently a difficult and unco-operative ally. He met Stalin twice, at the Teheran Conference in November 1943, and at Yalta in the Crimea, in February 1945. In the first meeting, Roosevelt and Churchill confirmed plans for the invasion of France, which would give the Russians a "second front" against the Germans. Roosevelt also secured from Stalin the promise to open a second front against Japan as soon as Germany was defeated.

In the Yalta meeting, near the end of the war in Europe, Stalin signed an agreement with Churchill and Roosevelt fixing the time of his attack on Japan. Agreement was also reached on the occupation of enemy territory after the war. Roosevelt, who was preoccupied with his plans for a world organization similar to the League of Nations, secured, as he thought, Stalin's participation. He also secured his promise of free elections in Russian-occupied territory in Europe, a promise that Stalin broke within the month. A great optimist, Roosevelt returned to Washington confident that Stalin could be counted on for a good peace.

The matter of Roosevelt's health was now of serious concern. From a robust man with a massive head, he had shrunk and aged to the point of gauntness. Although during the presidential campaign the previous autumn, when rumors of his ill-health were circulating, his personal physician had asserted that he was perfectly fit, the fact was that a battery of doctors, including a heart expert, had ordered him to take a long period of total rest. He apparently did not take their opinion seriously, or at any rate chose to ignore it. In April 1945, while relaxing at Warm Springs, he suffered a massive cerebral hemorrhage, lapsing into coma and death. For a man of sixty-three, he seemed to have had an incredibly long life.

HIGHLIGHTS OF HIS ADMINISTRATION

∼§ Bank holiday declared, March 5 to 13, 1933.

∼§ The "Hundred Days" of congressional action requested by President Roosevelt to produce economic recovery (March 9 to June 16, 1933) included:

An act to create the Civilian Conservation Corps, March 31, 1933, designed to make employment for youths.

An act to set up the Agricultural Adjustment Administration, May 12, 1933, designed to subsidize farmers to cut production.

The Federal Emergency Relief Act, May 12, 1933, designed to make work for the unemployed by grants and loans to states and localities for public works.

The Tennessee Valley Authority Act, May 18, 1933, designed to rehabilitate a 40,000-square-mile area in the Tennessee basin by public power, navigation, flood control, farm reform, and industrial development.

The Gold Repeal Joint Resolution, June 5, 1933, that took the United States off the gold standard by making debts payable in legal tender.

An act creating the Home Owners Loan Corporation, June 13, 1933, designed to finance small mortgages.

The Glass-Steagall Act, June 16, 1933, creating the Federal Deposit Insurance Corporation, designed to separate investment from commercial banking, restrict the use of bank credit for speculation, extend the Federal Reserve System, and guarantee bank deposits.

The Farm Credit Administration Act, June 16, 1933, designed to reduce interest rates on farm loans, refund old loans, and make new ones.

The National Industrial Recovery Act, June 16, 1933, creating the National Recovery Administration to supervise the drawing up of fair-practice codes for industries, and the Public Works Administration to make work for the unemployed in a variety of construction projects.

A National Labor Board, set up in August 1933, to supervise section 7 (a) of the NIRA, which protected labor in free collective bargaining; replaced in June 1934 by the National Labor Relations Board.

United States recognition of the U.S.S.R., November 16, 1933.

The 21st Amendment to the Constitution, repealing the Prohibition Amendment; ratified by the states, December 5, 1933.

The Gold Reserve Act, January 30, 1934, nationalizing gold and enabling the President to devalue the dollar.

The Tydings-McDuffie Act, March 24, 1934, providing for Philippine Independence in 1946.

The Treaty with Cuba, May 31, 1934, repealing the Platt Amendment.

The Securities Act, June 6, 1934, creating the Securities & Exchange Commission.

A Trade Agreements Act, June 12, 1934, enabling the Secretary of State to negotiate most-favored-nation trade treaties with foreign countries.

The Federal Housing Administration Act, June 28, 1934.

The Works Progress Administration authorized, April 8, 1935, to prime the pump of industry with loans for non-Federal projects.

ی Invalidation by the Supreme Court of the National Industrial Recovery Act in its decision in the Schechter Poultry Corp. case, May 27, 1935.

ی The Wagner Labor Relations Act, July 5, 1935.

ی The Social Security Act, August 14, 1935, providing for unemployment insurance, old-age retirement insurance, assistance to the needy, the aged, and to dependent mothers and children.

ی The Wheeler-Rayburn Act, August 26, 1935, authorizing the Federal Power Commission, designed to regulate electric power in all aspects in interstate commerce. It also authorized the Federal Trade Commission to regulate the gas industry in interstate commerce.

ی Invalidation by the Supreme Court of the Agricultural Adjustment Administration, January 6, 1936.

ی The Inter-American Conference, Buenos Aires, December 1936, which produced agreements among the Western Hemisphere nations to consult with each other for self-defense.

ی The second Agricultural Adjustment Act, February 16, 1938, providing that the Secretary of Agriculture could, with the approval of two-thirds of farmers involved, fix the acreage to be planted to crops; set up parity payments to farmers who limited their crops; make conservation payments to farmers who observed acreage allotments; make commodity loans and create storage for surplus crops.

ی The Fair Labor Standards Act, June 25, 1938, providing for maximum hours and minimum wages, and banning child labor, in producing goods that moved in interstate commerce.

ی The Neutrality Act of September 5, 1939, requiring belligerents purchasing American goods to pay cash and carry them, and forbidding American citizens to travel on belligerents' ships or enter danger zones.

ی Roosevelt's announcement, September 3, 1940, of exchange of 50 over-age American destroyers to Great Britain for 99-year leases on air and naval bases in the British West Indies.

ی The Burke-Wadsworth Conscription Act, the first conscription in peacetime, signed into law on September 16, 1940, calling for registration of all men between 20 and 35 and drafting 800,000 men into the armed services.

ی Roosevelt's speech to Congress, January 6, 1941, appealing for support of the nations fighting for the "four freedoms"—of speech and religion and from want and fear.

❧ The Lend-Lease Act, passed by Congress, March 11, 1941.

❧ Roosevelt's acceptance of the Philippine army into the armed forces of the United States, July 26, 1941, and appointment of General Douglas MacArthur to command all the U.S. armed forces in the Far East. Japanese credits frozen in the U.S.

❧ Meeting aboard a ship in Argentia Bay, Newfoundland, August 14, 1941, of Roosevelt and Winston Churchill, to assert their common war aims: "The Atlantic Charter." It included the four freedoms, renunciation of territorial ambitions, restoration of independence to nations, equal trade opportunities.

❧ The Japanese attack on Pearl Harbor, December 7, 1941. Six battleships wrecked, sunk, or run aground (later all but two were salvaged); 2,403 American sailors, soldiers, marines, and civilians killed. Same day, the American air force grounded on fields in the Philippines was wiped out by Japanese bombers, and Guam was bombed (both on December 8, local time).

❧ The United States declaration, December 8, 1941, that a state of war existed with Japan.

❧ Capture of Guam by the Japanese, December 10, 1941.

❧ Declaration of war on the U.S., December 11, 1941, by Germany and Italy, in accordance with their pact with Japan.

❧ Surrender of Corregidor, the final surrender in the Philippines, May 6, 1942.

❧ Casablanca conference between Roosevelt and Churchill and the Combined Chiefs of Staff, January 14–24, 1943. It was announced that the war would end only with unconditional surrender of the enemies.

❧ Conference at Teheran, Iran, between Roosevelt, Churchill, and Stalin, November 28–December 1, 1943. Invasion of Europe via Normandy settled on; Churchill's proposal for a second thrust into central Europe from the Mediterranean turned down by Roosevelt and Stalin. Stalin agreed on invasion of Japan after the surrender of Germany.

❧ Dumbarton Oaks Conference, Washington, D.C., August–October 1944, to formulate the principles of the United Nations charter.

❧ Meeting of Roosevelt, Churchill, and Stalin at Yalta, the Crimea, February 4–11, 1945, for discussion of occupation of Axis territory after the war and creation of an international peace organization.

HARRY S. TRUMAN

———◆———

THIRTY-THIRD PRESIDENT

In the spring and summer of 1944, with public attention absorbed in the battle for the beachheads of Normandy, there still were a few men who had to keep house for the Democratic party and decide on the candidate for Vice President in that year's election. President Roosevelt was not only preoccupied with the war, he was a tired and ailing man whose interest in another term for himself and for the game of politics in general was dulled to the point of boredom. It was almost impossible to persuade him to designate his choice for Vice President. The top contenders were the incumbent Vice President Henry Wallace and the Director of War Mobilization James F. Byrnes. The politicians and the labor leaders wanted neither, an opinion that would ordinarily have great influence on Roosevelt. But as a man who found it impossible to be unkind, he would not deflate the hopes of either Wallace or Byrnes, so they both arrived at the Democratic National Convention in Chicago that July believing they had the President's favor.

Chairman of the National Committee Robert Hannegan and some of the top party leaders had agreed on a vice-presidential candidate some

185

months before and had exhausted their ingenuity in trying to persuade Roosevelt to settle the thing with that one potent sentence, "I'm for Harry Truman." He seemed to agree with them, yet would not give them the flat, plain statement. As an intuitive politician, he probably saw that Senator Harry S. Truman was a good choice, partly because of the prestige of Truman's special committee investigating war contracts, partly because he belonged to the regular, grass-roots element in the party. At the convention, rivalry among the candidates was intense, particularly as there was an informed opinion among those closest to the President that his health was precarious and he might not survive a fourth term, or that he might even resign once the war and the peace were settled. The situation was so uncertain that Truman had agreed to support Byrnes and place him in nomination. At the last moment the Hannegan forces secured a message from Roosevelt approving Truman and he was nominated, though the Wallace following went down fighting to the end.

Roosevelt died in the afternoon of April 12, 1945, not quite three months after he began his fourth term. Truman was summoned from the Capitol to the White House, and there, a little after seven in the evening, he was sworn in as President. It was a sombre ceremony in the Cabinet Room, witnessed by Truman's wife and daughter, a few of his Senate cronies, and a phalanx of New Dealers mourning their lost leader.

There was enormous curiosity and not a little anxiety about the man who had succeeded to Roosevelt's unprecedented power. He was born on a farm in Jackson County, Missouri, not far from Kansas City. His father wandered away from the farm and traded in farm animals. Most of Truman's boyhood was spent in Independence. He grew up more a town boy than a farmer, learned to play the piano, developed an affection for the neighborliness of town life, and selected the girl he intended to marry. When he found he could not afford college, he went to work in Kansas City, but after several unpromising jobs returned to the land and managed his mother's farm for many years. The World War caught him up immediately, since he was a member of the National Guard, took him to France, and after the battles were over, returned him to Missouri as a major. He now married his boyhood sweetheart in Independence and decided to venture once more into the business world. With a partner he opened a haberdashery in Kansas City, but the postwar depression ruined the business in short order, and it was then, in the extremity of no income and a large debt, that he entered on the career of a public officeholder. With the support of the Pendergast political machine in Kansas City, he was elected a judge in Jackson County—an administrative, not judicial, office. His record in this position and later as presiding judge was so distinguished that he was selected by Boss Pendergast to run for the United States Senate.

Such was the background of the successor to the Squire of Hyde Park. In the next eight years his responsibilities were even more global than those of Roosevelt. Immediately, in the first year, he had to face the Communist cold war; the fact of the atomic bomb; demobilization of the American armed forces distributed around the world; reconversion of American industry; occupation and reconstruction of Germany and Japan; restoration of order to the economic and human chaos of Europe; the Communist problem in China. Starting this period as a novice being briefed intensively on the background of all these problems, by summer he was able to make executive decisions with confidence, and in the autumn sent to Congress with a flourish a 21-part "Fair Deal" program of domestic reforms that fairly rocked the Capitol. It was obvious that he had a great capacity for hard work and a zest for combat, and though he entered on his duties in a humble spirit, he was not by any means rattled by their complexities. In expressing himself, his language was likely to be blunt and earthy. There was a reassuring feeling that he was competent, a President with character and common sense.

In the first summer, Truman assessed the Russian postwar state of mind at the Potsdam Conference, when he met with Stalin and Clement Atlee (replacing Winston Churchill for the British) to lay the groundwork for peace. While Roosevelt's great legacy, the charter of the United Nations, was being ratified by the United States Senate, Truman was grasping the fact in Potsdam that the other part of the Roosevelt dream, a peace of justice and understanding, had gone down the drain. Stalin categorically refused to honor his promises to Roosevelt at Yalta of free elections in Russian-occupied Europe. On the contrary, he demanded that the Western Allies recognize the Soviet puppet governments already set up in that area. In a sense, Stalin's "pigheadedness," as Truman called it, did the West a service, for it gave fair warning that Russian policy would be separatist and aggressive. The warning was certainly not lost on Truman. He became convinced that the Free World would have to defend itself.

Before he left Potsdam, Truman made another vital decision. The first intimation of a dire weapon in American hands was an ultimatum prepared by Truman, Churchill, and the Combined Chiefs of Staff and sent to Japan on July twenty-sixth. Surrender in safety, it demanded, or face "utter destruction." The Japanese government rejected this with scorn, and on August second, Truman, on the best advice of his military and civilian officials competent in the matter, gave the order to drop the atomic bomb on a Japanese target. On August sixth the first bomb fell on Hiroshima; the second on Nagasaki, August ninth. Truman had no doubt about the wisdom of using the bomb to bring the Pacific war to an end, as it did on August fourteenth, when Emperor Hirohito agreed to surrender unconditionally. The following September second, in an impressive

187

ceremony on the deck of the battleship *Missouri*, the Japanese foreign minister, General Umezu, signed the terms of surrender. General MacArthur signed for the United States, and representatives of all the other Allies, including Russia, also signed. On August ninth, Russia had finally kept her word and declared war on Japan. By surrendering, Japan escaped a joint Russo-American invasion, such as occurred in Germany. Occupation and reconstruction became the responsibility of the United States alone, and in the hands of MacArthur was accomplished with admirable smoothness.

The full force of Truman as President was best shown by his leadership of the Free World in resisting the spread of Russian Communism. Accepting the fact that the United States was the only nation able to take action immediately after the war, he went to Cngress in the spring of 1947 and asked for $400,000,000 to secure Turkey and Greece against Communist penetration. In his address he then stated what became known as The Truman Doctrine: "I believe that it must be the policy of the United States to support free peoples who are resisting attempted subjugation by armed minorities or by outside pressures. I believe that we must assist free peoples to work out their own destinies in their own way. I believe that our help should be primarily through economic and financial aid, which is essential to economic stability and orderly political processes. . . ."

Congress appropriated the funds requested, and later raised them to $700,000,000.

Meantime, Secretary of State George Marshall had set up a staff to consider means of rescuing the West European economy, then foundering in postwar problems. The resulting proposals were first made public by Dean Acheson in May 1947 and by Secretary Marshall the following month at Hárvard commencement. These took shape as the "Marshall Plan," probably the most successful economic revival plan ever attempted. Truman sent it to Congress in December 1947, suggesting an appropriation of $17 billion, spread out over four years.

The following April Russia threw a blockade around the zones in Berlin occupied by the Western Allies, to protest their reconstruction plans for West Germany. Truman had no intention of abandoning the Allied position in Berlin. With the British, the American Air Force supplied West Berlin by air until December 1949, when the blockade was relaxed. The Berlin Airlift forced Russia to respect the skill and will of the Allies.

In 1948 Truman began negotiations with eleven countries for collective security, following the passage of a resolution presented to Congress by Republican Senator Vandenberg guaranteeing support for his action. This developed into NATO, which in 1950 was given authority and arms to protect the West from Russian aggression, its forces placed under command of General Dwight Eisenhower, with headquarters in Paris. In the same year Truman launched his "Point Four Program" to extend help to under-developed countries.

The success of Truman's grand strategy *vis à vis* Russia depended on bipartisan support in Congress, and this was forthcoming because of the fear of Russian aggression. His domestic policies were received, by contrast, with vivid Republican criticism. His "Fair Deal" was mostly snubbed. His attempt to have a Civil Rights bill passed so aroused the southern Democrats that a "Dixiecrat party" split off and ran its own candidate for President in 1948, attracting over a million votes. Industry experienced a period of turbulence after the war, for labor, fearing cutbacks in the conversion to a peace-time basis, took a militant course, and an epidemic of strikes began in the fall of 1945. Truman's answer was an executive order setting up fact-finding boards, by which many were settled. But the following year he resorted to more drastic measures. In order to halt a railway strike he prepared the Army to seize and operate the railroads. When the redoubtable John L. Lewis shut down the bituminous coal mines, Truman had the Department of the Interior take them over and try to open them up; and when Lewis called a strike against the Department, he was slapped with an injunction and taken to court, and both he and the union were fined. In the end the miners went back to work. Denying the military men control of the atomic bomb, which they badly wanted, Truman handed it over to a civilian Atomic Energy Commission, authorized by Congress in July 1948. He had already endorsed the reorganization of the armed services into one department, with a Secretary of National Defense. All in all, Truman faced re-election in 1948 with a formidable array of antagonistic interests. The Republicans naturally took full advantage of their opportunities and were delighted that he was sometimes quick-tempered and indiscreet with the press. However, he confounded his critics by making a rousing 22,000-mile whistle-stop campaign through the country and winning the election by a comfortable majority.

The second Truman administration was marked by a pervasive fear of Communist infiltration, aggravated by the smear tactics of Republican Senator Joseph R. McCarthy. It was also accentuated by the sensational trial and conviction of a minor State Department employee, Alger Hiss, for perjury in denying that he had passed on secret documents to the Russians. The main factor, however, was the real menace of Communism in Korea, irrupting into the Korean War. The background of this was the triumph of Russian Communism in China, which in itself was grievous to many Americans with warm feelings of attachment to that land. The United States had continued to support Chiang Kai-shek and his Nationalist Government (at a cost of $2 billion) in the hope that he would hold against the massive Communist forces. In 1949 his army crumbled and he fled to

189

Formosa. Communism thereafter possessed the Asiatic mainland northward except for the peninsula of South Korea.

In June 1950, Communist North Korea decided to gather in this last anti-Communist fragment. Truman was of the opinion that this could not be permitted. He announced that he would send American forces to help the South Koreans, and the United Nations Security Council called for an international force from its members, which was put in charge of General MacArthur, then in Japan. By winter, the U.N. army had driven the North Koreans back behind their frontier, the 38th Parallel. Massive reinforcements of Chinese Communists for the North Koreans reversed the U.N. victory, prolonged the war, and cost both sides heavy casualties in rugged winter fighting. The battle line was stabilized near the 38th Parallel for two years while the Communists and U.N. disagreed on the terms of an armistice. The Communists wished repatriation of all North Koreans and Chinese in South Korean hands, but since many of these informed the U.N. that they did not wish to leave South Korea, the U.N. insisted that their return be on a voluntary basis. The truce was not signed until June 1953, when Eisenhower was President and Stalin dead, the Communists finally accepting voluntary repatriation.

A political incident of the war created a furor in the United States. General MacArthur provoked a quarrel with Chief of Staff Omar Bradley and Truman by releasing his own views on the conduct of the war, which, briefly, called for a large-scale attack on China. Aside from the fact that MacArthur spoke at a time when Truman had decided that the moment for making peace had arrived, he had already been given an emphatic no on his proposals, by General Bradley, who ordered him to keep his peace. Instead, he wrote a letter to the Republican Minority Leader in the House of Representatives, Joseph Martin, challenging the President's policy and repeating his demands for total victory. With the advice of General Bradley and General Marshall, Commander-in-Chief Truman then dismissed MacArthur. Later, Congress censured the General for disobeying instructions, but in the meantime he was hailed as a hero, given an ovation in Congress, and cheered wildly on a speaking tour of the country.

Returning home to Independence, Missouri, Truman lived for nearly twenty years, with the dignity and discretion of a man already committed to history, even through the controversial 1960's, until his death, the day after Christmas, in 1972.

HIGHLIGHTS OF HIS ADMINISTRATION

◄§ Victory in Europe, May 7, 1945.

◄§ Signing of the United Nations charter at San Francisco, June 26, 1945.

&cs; Potsdam Conference, July 17–August 2, 1945.

&cs; First atomic bomb dropped, August 6, 1945.

&cs; Formal signing of Japanese surrender, September 2, 1945.

&cs; End of hostilities in World War II proclaimed, December 31, 1946.

&cs; Aid to Greece and Turkey approved by Congress, May 15, 1947.

&cs; Taft-Hartley Labor Management Act passed by Congress, vetoed and passed over Truman's veto, May–June, 1947.

&cs; Peace treaties with Bulgaria, Hungary, Italy, and Rumania ratified, June 14, 1947, by the U.S. Senate.

&cs; Act revising presidential succession passed by Congress, July 18, 1947.

&cs; Defense Department set up by Congress, July 26, 1947.

&cs; Berlin Blockade, April 1, 1948, to September 30, 1949, frustrated by British-American Air Lift.

&cs; The European Recovery Program (Marshall Plan) passed by Congress, April 2, 1948.

&cs; North Atlantic Treaty Organization (NATO) approved in Washington, April 4, 1949.

&cs; Beginning of war in Korea, June 25, 1950.

&cs; Attempted assassination of President Truman, November 1, 1950, by two Puerto Rican nationalists who tried to storm the front door of Blair House, where the Trumans were living during the renovation of the White House.

&cs; Ratification of the Twenty-second Amendment, February 26, 1951, limiting presidential terms to two. The amendment specifically provides that no person who has held the office of President or acted as President for more than two years of a term to which some other person was elected shall be elected more than once.

&cs; Opening of the Supreme Headquarters, Allied Powers, Europe (SHAPE) in Paris, April 2, 1951, by General Dwight Eisenhower.

&cs; Dismissal of General Douglas MacArthur, April 11, 1951, for failure to clear his public statements with his superiors, as instructed.

&cs; Seizure of steel mills ordered by Truman to prevent a strike, April 8, 1952.

&cs; Invalidation of steel-mill seizure, June 2, 1952, by the Supreme Court.

&cs; Puerto Rican commonwealth status achieved, July 3, 1952.

DWIGHT DAVID EISENHOWER

———◆———

THIRTY-FOURTH PRESIDENT

In suggesting to General Dwight Eisenhower, in 1948, that he would help him to get any honor he might want, including the presidency, President Truman was merely bowing to history. He knew that any man who leads his country to victory in war may have the country's highest honor, and he would have done his party a favor by hitching it to the chariot of the General who had beaten the Axis in Europe. Eisenhower declined the offer, both because he had no taste for politics and because he had a positive horror of the New Deal, the Fair Deal, and the whole "soft" philosophy of the welfare state. The Republicans, who suited his political philosophy better, also would have liked him for the presidency. Finally he composed a letter to the publisher of the Manchester, New Hampshire, *Leader* which for that year quieted the presidential talk. In part, he wrote: "Politics is a profession; a serious, complicated and in its true sense a noble one. . . . Nothing in the international or domestic situation especially qualifies for the most important office in the world a man whose adult years have been spent in the country's military forces."

Eisenhower then spent two years as president of Columbia University, without pay, trying to come to grips with the strange and elusive apparatus of education. He published an account of his command in the European war, *Crusade in Europe*, which made him better than independent financially. And in 1950 he accepted a responsibility for which he was admirably fitted, command of the NATO forces, the Supreme Headquarters, Allied Powers in Europe (SHAPE). Hardly had he settled in Paris before some of the most persuasive men in the Republican party were nagging him again about the presidency. They found that the crack in his defense was public service, and they finally convinced him that the party and the country needed his counsels of moderation. Once he had agreed to run in 1952, he entered into the plan wholeheartedly. The Republican convention nominated him on the first ballot. As running mate it gave him a young party wheelhorse, Senator Richard M. Nixon, who agreed to take on much of the dusty, dirty work of campaigning.

Dwight Eisenhower captured the American public at once. It was not only his boyish grin, it was an impression of something more substantial, a homespun honesty. The "common touch," for which he was famous, was not only gracefully applied, it was sincere. The dirtiness of the election campaign that year was not of his making, nor to his taste. He defeated the Democratic candidate, the wise and witty Adlai Stevenson, handily. In fact his popularity then, in his re-election in 1956, and in the off-year congressional elections, far exceeded that of his party.

Eisenhower's background was interesting. His father, a failure at making a living, came of a God-fearing Pennsylvania Dutch family that migrated to Abilene, Kansas, only a few years after that town ceased to be the railhead of the Texas cattle trails. They were of the River Brethren, a sect of the Mennonite religion, severe, moral, and superb farmers. Because his father worked for small wages as a mechanic, young Dwight grew up in poverty, but his mother, a strong-minded, religious woman, accepted struggle as a moral way of life. She brought up six sons, all of whom worked to put meat and potatoes in the family pot and all of whom became successful business or professional men. Dwight Eisenhower solved the problem of a college education by securing an appointment to the United States Military Academy. His record there was better than average, at his graduation sixty-first in a class of 168. On his first post, Fort Sam Houston, Texas, as a freshly-minted second lieutenant, he met and married a pretty, dark-haired girl from Denver, Mamie Dowd.

The years were long and the promotions slow for a peacetime army officer. Eisenhower was patient, but also alert to grasp any opportunity for improving himself. Assigned to the War Department as a major, he became useful in writing reports and speeches, putting into play a talent for the written word. He was attached to the Chief of Staff, General MacArthur, who liked him so well that on retiring as Chief of Staff and accepting the position of military consultant to the Philippine Common-wealth, he asked Eisenhower to accompany him. Eisenhower went and stayed until, in 1940, with war preparedness underway and renewed vitality in the army, he decided it was time to get back into the main stream. From the moment of his return, his career began to move ahead. A brilliant tactical showing on maneuvers and assignment to the War Plans Division in the War Department brought him within range of the searching eyes of the Chief of Staff, General George Marshall, who tested him on a plan for an operational command in Europe. Eisenhower went to London briefly, and on his return, submitted the plan in thirty tightly written pages. He was entirely unprepared for his own appointment to that command.

From the middle of 1942 until the end of 1945, he was Commanding General in the European Theatre, and directed the Allied armies in all their campaigns, from the landings in Africa, capture of Sicily, occupation of Italy, to the invasion of France and the destruction of the German armies there and beyond the Rhine. As a general he was not, of course, the General-Grant type of intuitive genius. He was a well-trained executive, with the sensitive perception to know what went well and where things went wrong, and the spring-steel nerves to make decisions. He had a high regard for morale, and it was said of him that his own buoyancy was a reliable factor in promoting that in his command. And yet, before the invasion of France, he prepared a memorandum to be published in case the landings on the Normandy beaches failed. The people who worked for him during the war often came to idolize him. The British top brass, the French, Canadian, and Australian officers, and the officers of the smaller national elements collected in the Allied effort, respected and got on with him, which was the essential fact that made him a success in his command.

Eisenhower liked to say he was a middle-of-the-roader—that kind of a conservative. The record of his administration in social and economic legislation is not unlike that of Truman, in spite of his disapproval of the welfare state. During his terms of office, ten million people were added to the social security rolls, a new Department of Health, Education and Welfare was created, legislation was passed to protect labor unions from corruption, a Civil Rights Commission was set up to investigate racial discrimination, and a National Defense Education Act was passed to make loans available to students. There were many other constructive measures of importance, so that the public business moved forward as it should, and as fast as it should. The Air Force Academy was inaugurated; the St. Lawrence Seaway was built; the National Aeronautics and Space Administration was put in business and began launching satellites into orbit without mishap; in the arsenal of defense intercontinental missiles and nuclear

195

submarines became realities; in foreign commerce, reciprocal trade treaties were extended; and Alaska and Hawaii were added to the states.

The political temper of the country was improved early in Eisenhower's administration, for the pungent vapors of McCarthyism (false charges of Communism to destroy character) were somewhat dissipated when Senator Joseph R. McCarthy of Wisconsin was "condemned" by the Senate for insulting and contemptuous behavior toward that august body. In a hearing initiated by the Department of the Army, which had been outrageously bullied by the slanderous McCarthy, millions of Americans saw televised a demagogue in action, and had as well the rare treat of seeing a demagogue put out of action.

The real irritants of Communism showed no sign of abating. The death of Stalin made no change in Russian foreign policy, although a more moderate spirit was evident toward the United Nations' terms for an armistice in Korea. Eisenhower flew to Korea, as he had promised before the election, and with the Communists yielding on forcible repatriation of their people held as prisoners in South Korea, brought the war to an end with an armistice. But there were other explosive situations in Asia. One of these was Formosa, or Taiwan, where Chiang Kai-shek and his Nationalist army had taken refuge in 1949. The United States was committed to the defense of Chiang. In the summer of 1954, the Chinese Communists began shelling the small islands of Quemoy and Matsu between Formosa and the mainland, which were occupied by Chiang. The question arose as to how far this defense should go. Congress passed a resolution giving the President authority to use force, if he thought it necessary, in this region. With the end of the bombardment, the emergency passed, but not the tension and debate on government policy toward China.

Indo-China presented another crisis this same year, with the break-up of the French colony and the advance of Communist forces in the province of Vietnam. Before international agreement stabilized the Communist area in Vietnam, the United States had sent aid to the French fighting the Vietnamese Communists. Later, Secretary of State John Foster Dulles said that he had come close to committing American troops as well: "Of course we were brought to the verge of war. The ability to get to the verge of war without getting into the war is the necessary art. . . . If you are scared to go to the brink, you are lost. We've had to look it square in the face—on the question of enlarging the Korean War, on the question of getting into the Indo-China war, on the question of Formosa. We walked to the brink and we looked it in the face." Dulles then turned his attention to negotiating a defensive alliance, the Southeast Asia Treaty Organization (SEATO) with Pakistan, Thailand, the Philippines, Britain, Australia, New Zealand, and France. It was patterned after NATO, but had no army.

Meanwhile danger signals were flying in the Middle East, where a strong man, Gamal Abdel Nasser, had ousted King Farouk in Egypt and made himself dictator. He set out to organize an Arab Federation, obtained arms from Communist Czechoslovakia, menaced Israel, and seized the British-operated Suez Canal. Israeli troops invaded the Sinai Peninsula, defeating an Egyptian army, and camped on the banks of the Canal, while British and French airplanes attacked the Egyptian air force. At this point the United Nations pronounced the British, French, and Israelis guilty of aggression, and President Eisenhower supported it with a statement against the use of force to settle international disputes. This ended the incipient war. Recognizing that the situation in the Middle East was now wide open to Communist influence, Eisenhower sent to Congress a message embodying what came to be called "the Eisenhower Doctrine." It proposed to give financial and direct military help to any country in the Middle East menaced by any other country "controlled by international communism." Congress complied and authorized appropriation of the necessary funds. Russia indicated that she refused to become involved by withdrawing troops and military support from the Middle East. Nevertheless, Nasser continued to subvert governments, adding Syria, Saudi Arabia, and Iraq to his bloc. In 1958, when Lebanon was threatened with similar penetration, its president appealed to the United States for help, and Eisenhower sent it in the form of the Seventh Fleet and 9,000 Marines. This action produced a victory for the West in rescuing Lebanon, but it settled nothing permanently in the still smoldering Middle East.

Obviously the largest continuing problem of the Eisenhower administration was in its commitment to meet the challenge of Communism, often in nationalist form, all around the globe. In Latin America Communism took various forms, none more shocking than the stoning of Vice President Nixon on a good-will tour of South America in 1958, nor more aggravating than the full-blown Communist dictatorship of Fidel Castro that began to emerge in Cuba in 1959. Eisenhower became more and more concerned with foreign affairs in his second term, especially after the death of Secretary of State Dulles in April 1959. In an effort at personal diplomacy, he invited the Soviet Premier Nikita Khrushchev to the United States and arranged a coast-to-coast tour for him in addition to an official Washington reception. In a spirit of Russian-American good will, a summit conference was arranged for May 1960, at which the perennial disagreements over Berlin and disarmament would be discussed. On May 5, Khrushchev wrecked the conference as it was assembling in Paris by charging that an American U-2 plane engaged in aerial espionage had been brought down in Russia and its pilot captured. Russia then proceeded to turn the trial of the pilot, Francis Powers, into a forum for attacking the United States. Convicted and sentenced, Powers was later exchanged for a Russian spy held in the United States.

During eight years in the White House, Eisenhower worked his way prudently into the political duties of his job. At first he left most of these to his special assistant Sherman Adams. A serious heart attack in 1955 incapacitated him for several months, and a slight stroke followed two years later, so that he was justified in delegating as much administrative work as possible to his staff. The services of Adams were lost in 1958 when evidence of petty indiscretions in accepting gifts from a businessman forced him to resign.

From then on, Eisenhower became more fully and successfully the President. Besides foreign affairs, his concern was more and more with the slow-rising struggle of Negroes for their civil rights. The Supreme Court in 1954 pronounced segregation of Negroes and whites in public schools unconstitutional, and in 1955 demanded desegregation with "all deliberate speed." In the South resistance to this demand took many ingenious forms, with emphasis on intimidation and legal procrastination. In 1957 more direct action was taken by the Governor of Arkansas in calling out the National Guard to prevent nine Negro children from entering the Central High School in Little Rock. When a Federal court ordered the troops withdrawn, mob rule took over. The President promptly sent in Federal troops with the statement that mob rule "cannot be allowed to override the decisions of our courts." On this principle the Federal government was forced to rest.

A man of military method, Eisenhower lived long enough in retirement to see the "brinkmanship" of his policy in Indo-China go over the brink into a war of unique ineptitude. At his farm-estate near Gettysburg, Pennsylvania, he could watch without influencing the course of events, nursing his failing health until his death, after long hospitalization, in March 1969.

HIGHLIGHTS OF HIS ADMINISTRATION

⋖§ The Submerged Lands Act, signed into law on April 22, 1953, giving to the states the right to oil off shore up to 10½ miles out in the Gulf of Mexico and up to 3 miles out off the Pacific and Atlantic coasts.

⋖§ End, Korean War, by an armistice, July 27, 1953.

⋖§ Opening, new Air Force Academy, April 1, 1954.

⋖§ Authorization by Congress, May 13, 1954, of the St. Lawrence Seaway, to be built jointly by the United States and Canada.

⋖§ A decision handed down, May 17, 1954, by the Supreme Court, that racial segregation in public schools is unconstitutional.

◦§ The Southeast Asia Treaty Organization (SEATO), created September 8, 1954, in Manila. Nations signing were Pakistan, Thailand, the Philippines, the United States, Britain, France, Australia, New Zealand.

◦§ Senate condemnation, December 2, 1954, of Senator Joseph R. McCarthy for contempt and for abuse of its members, as a result of the sensational, televised hearings in which the Department of the Army charged the Senator with undue pressure to secure favors for an aide in the Army, and McCarthy brought countercharges.

◦§ Bill signed, March 9, 1957, stating the Eisenhower Doctrine, by which the United States would give economic aid and defend any Middle East country asking for help against an aggressor controlled by international Communism.

◦§ Authorization by Congress, September 9, 1957, of a Civil Rights Commission to investigate denial of civil rights.

◦§ Resistance to school integration at Little Rock, begun September 4, 1957.

◦§ Launching, January 31, 1958, of the first American satellite in space, following two launched by Russia the previous autumn.

◦§ President's signing, July 29, 1958, of the bill authorizing the National Aeronautics and Space Administration to direct space exploration.

◦§ Journey of the Sixth Fleet and some 9,000 Marines to Lebanon, July 1958, ordered by the President in response to the request of pro-Western President Chamoun, whose government was threatened by Egypt and Syria. Troops withdrawn in October.

◦§ Statehood for Alaska, January 3, 1959.

◦§ Statehood for Hawaii, August 21, 1959.

◦§ Dedication by Queen Elizabeth II and President Eisenhower of the St. Lawrence Seaway, June 26, 1959.

◦§ The shooting down of a U-2 reconnaissance plane over the Soviet Union, May 1, 1960, and consequent refusal by Premier Khrushchev at Paris to take part in the Summit Conference set for May 16 unless President Eisenhower apologized for the overflight. The conference was cancelled. The pilot Francis Gary Powers was convicted of espionage, August 19, 1960, and sentenced to ten years in prison. He was released, February 10, 1962, in an exchange for a Soviet agent imprisoned in the U.S.

◦§ Diplomatic relations broken off by the U.S., January 3, 1961, with the government of Fidel Castro in Cuba.

JOHN FITZGERALD KENNEDY

—◆—

THIRTY-FIFTH PRESIDENT

During the fifteen presidential elections since Mark Hanna elected McKinley by blanketing the United States with persuasive literature, no one had improved on the method before John F. Kennedy. Faced with the problem of moving a political mass far larger than existed in 1896, Kennedy substituted personal persuasion for the printed word and was breathtakingly successful. His success established a pattern for practicing politicians, as did his modification of the taboo against Roman Catholics in the presidency for the people at large. In 1959, the Kennedy art of personal politics was brought to bear on the Democratic National Convention, set for July the following year. To win the nomination he set up an organization under his younger brother Robert that in the eight months preceding the convention reached every influential Democrat in the country. In the spring he became a virtuoso at winning primaries. So that by the time the convention assembled in the Sports Arena at Los Angeles, the Democratic city bosses, the party regulars, and the elder statesmen of the party, such as former President Truman, realized that it was almost solidly committed to Kennedy.

Adlai Stevenson, twice the nominee and twice defeated, still had an enormous and affectionate following, as was proved by the thousands who chanted his name and waved his banners outside the Arena and in the galleries. He was eloquently placed in nomination and received an impressive demonstration by the delegates. Had he wished to take hold of his popularity, a surge to him might have started. But the surge did not happen, the Kennedy commitments held, and as the first ballot progressed, the Kennedy votes mounted until they neatly topped the majority needed for nomination. The runner-up was Lyndon Baines Johnson, the powerful Texan, Majority Leader in the United States Senate. Johnson, against the advice of his friends, decided to accept the second place on the ticket, much to Kennedy's satisfaction, and was duly nominated for Vice President.

The young man who had come so far as a shrewd politician was one of a family accustomed to politics and publicity. The Kennedys were handsome, compulsively energetic, rich in the upper megaton range, ambitious, Boston Irish in origin, and faithful Catholics. Jack Kennedy's mother was the daughter of "Honey" Fitzgerald, once mayor of Boston and the very pattern of a sentimental Irish politician. His father, Joseph Patrick Kennedy, leaving Boston behind, had become a formidable figure in Wall Street, supported Franklin D. Roosevelt in the 30's, and served as head of the Maritime Commission and of the Securities and Exchange Commission and as Ambassador to Great Britain. When the World War began, he turned isolationist, resigned his post at the Court of St. James's, and broke with Roosevelt, evolving thereafter into one of the most rock-ribbed of the conservative Democrats. Sidelined in public life, he nevertheless was passionately interested in it and cherished the hope that his eldest son, Joe, would take it up as a profession. When Joe was killed in the war, he transferred his hope to young Jack, as did the rest of the family.

Jack was born in Brookline, when the family fortune was modest. As it began to soar and Joseph Kennedy's business centered in New York, he moved his family to the New York suburb of Bronxville for a few years. But the Kennedys shifted around; probably their nearest equivalent to a family homestead was the group of summer cottages, the "Kennedy Compound" at Hyannisport on Cape Cod. Jack went to several schools, finishing his college preparation at Choate. A case of jaundice cut short his freshman year at Princeton, and when he was fit for college again, he entered Harvard. A tour of Europe and visits to his father's embassy in London during his undergraduate days produced a college paper on pre-war British politics, which, polished up, was published as his first book, *Why England Slept*.

In the year between graduation from Harvard and American entry into the war, Jack Kennedy explored the possibilities for a career. He decided against law school, tried Stanford University's business school for six months, and left that for a trip to South America. Returning home, he decided to join the army, but a football injury to his spine in college disqualified him. Five months later, after strengthening his back with exercises, he was able to get into the navy. Early in 1943 he was a lieutenant, junior grade, commander of a motor torpedo boat, on his way to the Solomon Islands. On a night in the following August, with his boat creeping along quietly on one engine, his craft was sighted by a Japanese destroyer that instantly turned and slashed it in two. Kennedy and his crew of twelve were either hurled to the deck or scattered over the water in the midst of flaming gasoline. Two men were killed or drowned, but by swimming and searching for hours Kennedy managed to help six men back to the wreck, where the rest hung on. When the wreck turned over and sank, the eleven survivors swam to an island, Kennedy towing an injured man by a life-jacket strap clenched in his teeth—a five-hour swim. There followed days of looking for help, swimming from island to island, and a long night swim with a ship's lantern into a ship channel to try to intercept another PT boat. On the fourth day Kennedy found two natives and got a message out by them, scratched on a coconut shell. His success in bringing his crew through with heroic effort and tenacity was suitably rewarded with the Navy and Marine Corps Medal for "courage, endurance and excellent leadership."

When, after the war, Jack Kennedy finally decided to make a run for the House of Representatives from the 11th Massachusetts district, the entire Kennedy family that was free and available pitched in to help him campaign. In spite of his forebears, he was not of Boston politics, but a "carpetbagger" living in a hotel, and obviously a long-shot to win. Nevertheless, win he did, in the primary, against a large and miscellaneous field. Since the district was safely Democratic, winning the primary was tantamount to election. So in the autumn of 1946, the voters duly certified him for Congress. After three terms in the House, he defeated the entrenched Republican Henry Cabot Lodge for the Senate, in 1952, the year of Eisenhower's first election to the presidency. Kennedy was re-elected for a second term by the largest margin ever given a candidate for office in Massachusetts. In Congress he was scrupulous in representing the interests of his home area and responding to the requests of his constituents. A cool, unemotional thinker, he was detached from party leaders and unimpressed by pressure groups. In economic and social legislation he could be counted on as a liberal, but he did not yield to the group spirit of the liberals either.

He was inclined to disperse his interests rather than make himself an expert on one subject.

In 1953 he married Jacqueline Lee Bouvier, a girl of gentler tastes than the politically minded Kennedys. The following year, while recuperating from a spinal operation for six months, he wrote *Profiles in Courage*, a series of biographies that won him the Pulitzer Prize. Once off his crutches, he set his sights on the vice-presidential nomination in 1956. Though he lost it, the campaign was a good practice run for 1960, and the impression he made as a good loser, particularly when he turned to and campaigned hard for the national ticket, raised his popularity with the party by several notches. Four years later, while campaigning for the presidency, his popularity rose visibly with passing weeks. Plugging the catch phrase "the New Frontier" and a New-Dealish welfare program, he was actually campaigning on himself, his competence, and his attitudes. Proposing to the Republican candidate Richard Nixon a series of four televised joint debates, he easily took the lead in the first debate and held on to it for the rest of the campaign. Nixon, dogged by illness, poor judgment, and a flagging spirit, disappointed his followers. And yet Kennedy won by an extremely narrow margin in the popular vote.

The Kennedy administration, only two years and ten months up to the tragedy of his assassination in Dallas, was packed with decisions on which hung American relations with Communism, the space program, prestige in the Free World, and, at home, the separatist influences that periodically threaten to disunite the country. Selecting a cabinet for competence, and bringing to Washington a large and well-seasoned personal staff, Kennedy set up an efficient system of hammering out decisions face-to-face with his experts. He paced himself and his staff unmercifully, but his retentive mind and capacity for long hours of effort made the system succeed. It broke down once, at the beginning of his term, in his decision to let loose on Castro's Cuba an ill-prepared, inadequate expedition of Cuban exiles trained and equipped in the United States.

Kennedy later characterized the "Bay of Pigs" invasion as so blundering that he did not see how all the people who planned it could have ever thought it would succeed. The handful of Cubans who landed in Cuba, expecting the populace to rally to their banner, were met by the efficient soldiers of Fidel Castro, rounded up, and taken to prison camps with hardly a ripple in the peace of the countryside. Assuming responsibility, Kennedy grimly set about the business of identifying the failures in his administration responsible for the fiasco, gradually removing them without fanfare. In this delicate matter, he relied on the advice of his younger brother Robert, now the Attorney General, but more importantly Jack Kennedy's most trusted aide.

In this same month, April 1961, Russia triumphantly launched the first man into space. Kennedy's answer was to send to Congress a request for $7–9 billion for acceleration of the American space program. In May the successful flight of Commander Alan Shepard into space and return lifted national morale considerably. From then on, the Mercury Project proceeded successfully, with increasing orbits of the earth, until it was completed two years later with a 22-orbit flight. Another space success was the launching of the first communications satellite in July 1962, American Telephone and Telegraph's Telstar I.

For the uneasy and shifting world outside the Communist domain, Kennedy fought hard and with partial success to maintain the costly American foreign aid program. He also initiated experimentally the Peace Corps, to carry the benevolence of American education, technology, and welfare to under-developed countries. A small program, it was well-managed and slowly expanded as its success seemed assured. The major areas of concern in foreign affairs were Southeast Asia, Castro's Cuba, and the intentions of Nikita Khrushchev. In order to make a personal judgment on Khrushchev, and to gauge French President de Gaulle's position in West European unity, Kennedy flew to Europe during his first summer. Stopping in Paris for a glittering four days of official receptions, during which both he and his wife scored a personal success, he flew on to Vienna for two days with the Soviet premier, returning by way of London.

The conference with Khrushchev was bleak and disturbing. At no point was there any meeting of minds, the Russian expressing truculence on Berlin and the continued development of nuclear bombs. Back home, Kennedy considered it advisable to reassert America's firmness on the defense of West Berlin and also to look to its own defenses. He directed an American battle group in West Germany to march into Berlin, thus testing access to the city by road and making a show of strength. And he sent to Congress additional requests for national defense in increased personnel and conventional weapons, to cost $3,454 million. The aggressive temper of the Russians was clearly demonstrated that summer, when they resumed nuclear testing in the atmosphere, releasing in the Arctic a 58-megaton bomb, the largest ever.

Of more immediate concern was the appearance of Russian nuclear weapons in Cuba in 1962. Rumors of these were presented to Congress by Senator Keating of New York, but the State Department confidently belittled them, and the President accepted its judgment. Aerial photographs in October, however, furnished proof beyond question that medium-range missile sites were being built and equipped, Russian planes designed to carry nuclear bombs were being uncrated on the island. There was also intelligence of some 22,000 Russian troops and technicians in Cuba. This was a major crisis, permitting of no mistakes. A hapless war in Cuba, involving Russian troops, might well be that one small incident that would set off the world's last war. The Kennedy system now worked well, deliberately, and with the utmost secrecy. When his plans were all laid, the Navy ready, and ground forces ordered to Florida, the President released the news of the nuclear missiles in Cuba, forwarded his case to the United Nations, demanded that Russia withdraw the missiles, and clapped a naval "quarantine" or blockade on Castro's island. His timing and strategy were excellent. The tightness of his case before the U.N. cut short Russian denials and quibbling. Premier Khrushchev had two choices—to back down or risk war. He chose the former, and under the monitoring watch of American planes, the Soviet missiles, nuclear bombers, and a considerable number of Russian troops were loaded on ships and sent on their way back to Russia.

When Kennedy took office, the established American policy of contesting the spread of Communism was under challenge in Indo-China, where the revolutionary spirit that had ousted the French persisted. In Laos, the communist Pathet Lao were armed and marching to capture the government, but the President, by personal diplomacy with the Soviet Union, achieved a cease-fire there. In Vietnam, the North had a strong communist government, while South Vietnam was in the hands of a weak one, contrived and supported by the U.S., headed by an inept autocrat, Ngo Dinh Diem, an ideal target for a nationalistic, communist rebellion. By 1961, a rebel fighting force, the Viet Cong (supplied from North Vietnam, China, and the Soviet Union) was waging a guerilla war against Diem with some success. Kennedy's military advisors and advocates of the "bastion against Communism" theory urged him to send in American forces to support Diem. He yielded to some extent, so that the American military presence in South Vietnam grew from a handful of advisers under Eisenhower to nearly 17,000 men in late 1963. But Kennedy remained undecided, forewarned that the Diem regime might be overthrown. On November 1, 1963, a coup deposed Diem, who, with his brother, was murdered, and a military government took over.

The Kennedy prestige abroad was strong in 1963. During a ten-day trip to Europe in June that included Italy, Great Britain, West Germany and Ireland, he was given an impressive ovation in West Berlin. Shortly

206

after his return, it was announced that the Soviet Union, Great Britain, and the United States had finally agreed on a treaty banning nuclear testing. This treaty had been five years in the making and its achievement was taken as a sign of a moderating of Russia's attitude toward the non-Communist world. A few weeks later an amiable plan to install direct telephone communication between the White House and the Kremlin, the "hot line" for use in an emergency, was put into effect.

At home the Kennedy prestige had moved none of his major "New Frontier" programs through Congress. His fight to keep the big steel companies from raising their prices after he had persuaded steel labor to forego wage increases succeeded, but still made businessmen grumble. The farmers turned on the hand that fed them and voted down the government plan for wheat crop control. Meanwhile the push of the Negroes to gain some part of their constitutional rights gained in force, as the resistance of whites North and South gained in stubbornness. Kennedy had been obliged to send troops into Oxford, Mississippi, to subdue a riot when the first Negro matriculated at the University of Mississippi in 1962. His policy, however, continued to be one of non-interference, for he was firmly convinced that racial justice must be induced at the base of the nation's social structure, in the towns, counties, and states.

Jack Kennedy's personal popularity was unquestioned, as was his probable re-election for a second term in 1964. He had brought a sparkle to Washington official life, as his wife had brought elegance and the charm of little children to the constantly fascinating personal side of the White House. The administration was just as brainy but more functional and less theoretic than that of Roosevelt and the New Deal. As the President turned his thoughts to election-year politics, he decided to make a short speaking trip to Texas. Arriving in Dallas by plane on the morning of November twenty-second, he drove in an open car into town, headed for a luncheon meeting at the Merchandise Mart. His wife was beside him, and in front, on the jump seats, were Governor John Connally of Texas and his wife. As the short motorcade, including Vice President Johnson's car, Secret Service and newspapermen's cars, crawled past a high warehouse, the Texas School Book Depository, a rifleman at a window on its sixth floor fired three shots. Two hit President Kennedy, one in the throat, the other fatally in the back of the head. One also severely wounded Governor Connally. A half hour later in Parkland Hospital young Jack Kennedy was pronounced dead.

The suspected assassin proved to be a Marxist who had lived in Russia and married a Russian girl. Hard on the heels of Lee Oswald's arrest, he was gunned down by one Jack Ruby, a Dallas night club operator who claimed he was settling his own personal score with the man who had killed his President. While millions of Americans, many of whom had witnessed this second horror on their television screens, began to speculate on the unknown and disturbing background of the assassination, the new President Lyndon Johnson wisely ordered a full Federal investigation, under the guidance of Supreme Court Justice Warren.

HIGHLIGHTS OF HIS ADMINISTRATION

ᵉᶳ Organization of the Peace Corps, March 1, 1961.

ᵉᶳ News of the first man sent into space, Russian Major Yuri Gagarin, who orbited the earth once, April 12, 1961.

ᵉᶳ Invasion of Cuba at Bay of Pigs, April 17, 1961, which proved a failure.

ᵉᶳ Cease-fire in Laos, May 1961.

ᵉᶳ Launching of Commander Alan B. Shepard Jr. into space from Cape Canaveral in a Mercury capsule and recovery in the Atlantic, May 5, 1961. This was followed, on July 21st, by a similar flight by Captain Virgil I. Grissom. Lt. Colonel John H. Glenn Jr. was the first American to orbit the earth, on February 20, 1962, when he made three circuits. Lt. Commander M. Scott Carpenter made another three-orbit flight, May 24th, and Commander Walter M. Schirra Jr. circled the earth six times, on October 3rd. On May 15–16, 1963, Major Leroy Gordon Cooper orbited the earth 22 times, completing the Mercury project.

ᵉᶳ The Kennedy conferences with de Gaulle in Paris, Khrushchev in Vienna, and Macmillan in London, May 30 to June 7, 1961.

ᵉᶳ The Berlin Wall, built between east and west sections of the city, August 13, 1961.

ᵉᶳ Announcement by the Russians of resumption of nuclear testing in the atmosphere, August 30, 1961.

ᵉᶳ Resumption by the United States of nuclear testing in the atmosphere, April 25, 1962.

ᵉᶳ The launching into space of Telstar I, the American Telephone & Telegraph Company's communications satellite, July 10, 1962.

ᵉᶳ Sending of Federal troops into Oxford, Miss., to subdue riots attending matriculation of the first Negro, James H. Meredith, at the University of Mississippi, September 30–October 1, 1962.

⋙ The emplacement of Russian medium-range nuclear missiles in Cuba and the landing there of Russian nuclear bombers, revealed by Kennedy, October 22, 1962. He announced an American blockade of Cuba to force withdrawal of these weapons. Premier Khrushchev agreed to withdraw the weapons and bombers and reduce Russian forces in Cuba. Kennedy announced the easing of the crisis on November 2nd.

⋙ The farmers' vote, for the first time since 1941, against the government's wheat control program, May 21, 1963.

⋙ Kennedy's request to Congress for a civil rights bill, June 19, 1963.

⋙ The treaty signed August 5, 1963, by Great Britain, the Soviet Union, and the United States, banning nuclear testing in the atmosphere, under water, and in outer space. Ratified by the U.S. Senate, September 24th.

⋙ The parade, August 28, 1963, of some 200,000 "peace marchers" in Washington, demanding civil rights for Negroes.

⋙ The direct telephone line, or "hot line" between Washington and Moscow, reserved for emergency use by the heads of government. Installed and operational on August 30, 1963.

⋙ A coup overturning the government of Ngo Dinh Diem and killing Diem in South Vietnam, November 1–2, 1963.

⋙ The assassination of President Kennedy in Dallas, Texas, at about 12:30 P.M., November 22, 1963, as he was driving to the Merchandise Mart to deliver a luncheon address.

LYNDON BAINES JOHNSON

THIRTY-SIXTH PRESIDENT

The circumstances of President Kennedy's death in Dallas were particularly grievous to the Vice President. As a Texan and a Democrat he had looked forward to this trip as a rekindling of the party in his state. The response to the President had been enthusiastic in Fort Worth that morning, and the crowds that gathered to watch the short motorcade crawl by on the way into Dallas were equally responsive. He could not have forgotten his own trouble in Dallas in the 1960 campaign, when he and his wife had been jostled and spat upon by a Nixon-Lodge crowd, but he certainly minimized such an outbreak of mob fever. Ironically, Kennedy's assassination eventually appeared to have no reference to Dallas or Texas politics, but that could not have been apparent to Vice President Johnson, riding two cars behind the President when the shots were fired. Thrown to the floor by a Secret Service man, a second after the cry "The President has been shot!" his car pursuing that of the dying President to the hospital, he partook as few men have in the horror of political assassination.

Less than two hours later Lyndon Johnson was sworn in as President, in the small conference room aboard the presidential plane at Love Field, outside Dallas. Then the plane, carrying also Kennedy's body and his widow, took off for Washington, where it arrived in the evening. Going direct to the White House executive offices, Johnson ended the fateful day of November 22nd, 1963, immersed in the business of the presidency. It was his good fortune to be the first Vice President adequately prepared for it. Functioning as President Kennedy's deputy, he had for nearly three years acted as a roving diplomat abroad, had kept his eye on national defense and the space program, and when in Washington had scarcely ever missed a cabinet meeting. In Kennedy's public appearances, Johnson was likely to be standing a little to one side or behind him. A tall man, with a firm jaw and still features, who favored a modified Stetson, his figure suggested the undying strain of the plainsman.

In fact, Johnson was the first man to bring some flavor of the West to the White House. A sentimental Texan, he looked homeward to the banks of the Pedernales River, not far from Austin, where his grandfather had settled a few years after Texas became a state. Brought up in agrarian liberalism by his father, he was alive to politics before he could vote. His father was strong in county politics and as a member of the state legislature, but his cash position was weak as a small farmer, and later, as a dealer in cattle and land in the village of Johnson City. Young Lyndon's first idea, when he graduated at fifteen from the Johnson City High School, was to go to work. His mother, a college-educated woman, did her best to turn his mind toward college. After three years, she won, and Lyndon quit his job as a laborer on the highway to enter Southwest State Teachers College at San Marcos. Here he applied himself with equal intensity to absorbing the courses and earning money, for both his own and a younger sister's education. He took many jobs, including that of secretary to the president of the college, taught three elementary grades in a school at Cotulla for a year, and still managed to graduate at the age of twenty-two, three years after he started.

Johnson was lucky in his first teaching appointment as instructor in history and speech at Sam Houston High School in Houston. He was luckier the following year when Richard Kleberg, of the King Ranch family, won a special election to Congress and offered him the job of administrative assistant in his Washington office. It was the open door to opportunity. In Washington he applied himself with typical intensity to absorbing Capitol politics, gravitating to Representative Sam Rayburn of Texas, who was impressed by the young man. On a visit to Austin he met a girl, Claudia Alta Taylor, a graduate in journalism of the University of Texas and daughter of a rich East Texan. Two months later Claudia ("Lady Bird") Taylor, still somewhat breathless from the Johnson campaign method, was Mrs. Lyndon Johnson. In 1935 Sam Rayburn proposed her husband as Texas administrator for the National Youth Administration, and Johnson returned to Austin to expend his enormous energy in finding education or work for some 33,000 of Texas's idle young people. Inevitably this work for the public good and his widening acquaintance in the state suggested the possibility of his running for public office. When the congressman of the Tenth District died in 1937, Johnson scraped together his savings, borrowed more from his father-in-law, and ran for election to the vacancy. Campaigning as a New Dealer, he won by a large plurality.

In the House of Representatives he had a reputation for whirlwind energy, unabashed persuasiveness, and unflagging concern for the folks back home. In 1941, with the blessing of Roosevelt, Johnson ran for the Senate in a special Texas election, but was defeated by the farmers' favorite, Wilbert Lee "Pass the Biscuits Pappy" O'Daniel, by a hatful of late returns. After Pearl Harbor, Lyndon joined the Navy as a reserve officer and was sent to the South Pacific to survey the handling and efficiency of military equipment, until President Roosevelt recalled members of Congress from military service. In 1948 he was tempted to try again for the Senate and won the Democratic nomination in a runoff primary. In those days Democratic nomination in Texas was equivalent to election.

Twelve years in the Senate developed Lyndon Johnson into one of the most impressive figures in the Democratic party. As party whip, and after 1954 as majority leader, his attention to the personal and legislative idiosyncrasies of the senators and his skill in maneuvering made him a power such as the Senate has seldom seen. He worked from dawn to dark daily, expending himself totally in the business he loved, until in 1955 a heart attack sent him to the hospital. A long, peaceful autumn, convalescing at his LBJ Ranch beside the Pedernales River, restored his health, and he was back as majority leader the following year. As the end of Eisenhower's two terms and the election of 1960 approached, the Johnson candidacy for the Democratic presidential nomination became a reality.

Johnson and his forces arrived at the convention in a confident humor. They had not fully believed how good the Kennedy organization was, and when its slick efficiency in securing delegates and controlling the convention was borne in on them, they were left gaping. They were angry too, as they might well be, for Johnson, strong in the South, piled up 409 votes to Kennedy's 806 in the balloting. After that, Johnson's readiness to accept the vice-presidential nomination startled his friends, but it was a good decision for the Democratic party. The Kennedy-Johnson ticket won narrowly in November, and undoubtedly part of the victory belonged to Lyndon Johnson.

Johnson picked up the torch of strong, humanitarian government handed down from Franklin Roosevelt to Harry Truman to John F. Kennedy. Besides his determination to carry through the Kennedy program of social reforms, known in his lap of the course as The Great Society, he brought to the presidency a kind of patriotic fundamentalism. This qualified him to follow loyally United States Government world policies but not to initiate them. He deferred in these matters to the military leadership and Kennedy's Secretary of Defense Robert McNamara, and to Kennedy's Secretary of State Dean Rusk.

The new President's first briefing was on the American sphere of influence in Southeast Asia, where a limited amount of economic and military aid had been invested in South Vietnam, a fragment of old French Indo-China, in order to check the spread of Communism in that part of the world. Three years of guerilla war by a Communist faction under the label National Liberation Front, popularly the Viet Cong, had made such progress that the central government and the American investment in its stability was threatened. Three weeks before Kennedy's death the government had been overthrown by a military junta and President Ngo Dinh Diem murdered, the act promising in spite of its bland cruelty a degree of political reform and tightening of the anti-Communist fighting organization. Johnson's Vietnam policy during his first months was to continue the Kennedy wait-and-see attitude, increasing the aid program to the Saigon government but forecasting an early withdrawal of the 17,000 American military troops in South Vietnam.

In the summer of 1964 Johnson had the confidence of his party, Congress, and as the presidential election was to show that fall, a large majority of the American voters. He was seen as a middle-of-the-road politician who would relieve both the taxpayers' burden and the curse of poverty on the lowest economic classes, a humane man who would make a fight for civil rights at home and confront the Communist world with an alert but reasonable firmness. In August he appeared to act with proper firmness after a minor incident between American and North Vietnamese naval forces. American destroyers cruising in the Gulf of Tonkin reported attacks by North Vietnamese gunboats on the 2nd and 4th. President

214

Johnson's reflexes were in good working order. On the instant he shot out bombers to attack North Vietnam in retaliation and sent to Congress a resolution giving him the power to repel attacks on United States armed forces and prevent future aggression. Senator Fulbright, Chairman of the Foreign Affairs Committee, escorted it quickly through the Senate, so that with the concurrence of the House it became law within the week. This "Tonkin Resolution" affirmed the President's independence of Congress in regard to Vietnam, but in August 1964, with political attention on the presidential elections, its full importance was not generally noted.

Johnson's nomination and election was a heady personal triumph. His opponent, Senator Barry Goldwater of Arizona, an old-school conservative and Air Force general, garnered the votes of those few in favor of outright war against Communism in South Vietnam, the "hawks" in journalistic slang. In the fervor of campaigning Johnson geared his appeal to win those in the majority who favored peace, the "doves" on the Vietnam question. The response was a record victory in terms of the popular vote. Yet with what appeared to be a clear mandate for non-belligerence in Vietnam, he embarked upon a war episode that was to make his administration one of the most ill-conceived and unpopular in American history.

Having more at heart internal improvements and reform than the checks and balances of foreign relations, Lyndon Johnson devoted himself in the first months after his inauguration to getting through Congress much of his program—a civil rights law protecting Negro voting rights, the promise of Federal aid in many directions, to schools and colleges, to economically distressed areas, to the poor and the aged, to the cities in need of slum clearance—a program, however, that was to suffer from anemia wherever it depended on large appropriations, which as time went on were pre-empted by the military. He included in his State of the Union message of January 1965 a clear statement of American responsibility in Southeast Asia. "Our own security is tied to the peace of Asia," he said.

On February 7 following, Johnson committed the full military effort of the United States to the war in Vietnam after an American Special Forces camp in Pleiku was attacked by the Viet Cong and eight men were killed and 108 wounded. In a matter of hours navy planes from carriers in the Tonkin Gulf were on their way to bomb North Vietnam in retaliation. From then on military operations grew and swelled rapidly, so that by the end of the year some 200,000 American men were serving in Vietnam, a number doubled by 1967 and reaching a half million by 1968, most of them draftees. To transport, supply, and provide fire power for such a force ever-increasing billions of dollars were appropriated by Congress, until in the summer of 1968 the war cost was estimated at more than $2 billion a month.

The war divided the American people in more bitterness than at any time since the Civil War and Reconstruction. Sharpening the division were the surging demands of black people for equal citizenship, spilling here and there in city slums into violence. Johnson's posture on their problems was fair and sympathetic. He was proud of his Civil Rights law protecting their voting rights and he sought, though without success, legislation to give them equal housing rights. He called Governor George Wallace of Alabama onto the carpet for the brutality of peace officers in breaking up a Civil Rights march from Selma to the capital, Montgomery, led by the Reverend Martin Luther King in March 1965, and he ordered in the National Guard to see that the march was peaceably accomplished. Yet he never secured the slightest co-operation or admission of his leadership from Negroes, partly because he was white but largely because they thought his friendship shallow.

If the Negroes were indifferent, the anti-war people attacked Johnson's leadership with deadly purpose. They accused him of duplicity in campaigning as the peace candidate and continuing to present his war management with a lack of candor. The phrase "credibility gap" took hold as an expression of the lack of confidence they felt in the administration. A rising young generation became for the first time a driving political force. They began by joining the "freedom marches" for Negro rights. As the war in Vietnam escalated they expressed their opposition to it by marching, picketing, and resisting the draft, until by the end of 1967 even Lyndon Johnson knew that, by and large, the country regarded the whole costly affair as a mistake.

In April 1968, American bombing of North Vietnam north of the 20th parallel was halted, and a tentative peace conference began in May at Paris between the United States and North Vietnam. In October Johnson ordered a total halt to the bombing of North Vietnam and began using persuasion and pressure to bring the South Vietnamese government into the Paris conference, which he accomplished early in December.

Meanwhile, on the home political front, the spontaneous anti-war movement had found a leader in Senator Eugene McCarthy, a Democrat-Farmer Laborite from Minnesota. In order to put the war issue to a test in the approaching presidential campaign he announced as a candidate for the Democratic nomination. In March 1968, the New Hampshire primary gave him an overwhelming victory and launched him on a dramatic bid for his party's support. His success inspired Robert Kennedy, younger brother of the dead President, to leap into the contest, so that Democrats now had the fascinating spectacle before their eyes of two of their most personable leaders vying for control of the party's anti-Johnson faction—until an assassin's bullet ended Robert Kennedy's life in June.

By the end of March 1968, Lyndon Johnson had decided in the bosom of his family that his only realistic and dignified course was to withdraw from politics. He therefore added as a postcript to a televised report on the Vietnam war this statement: "I shall not seek and I will not accept nomination of my party as your President." In the remaining ten months of office he took little part in politics or party, yielding to the suggestion that he not attend the Democratic convention in Chicago. As a private person on his luxurious Texas ranch, he survived the loss of public office for only a short time, becoming increasingly a heart invalid until his death in January 1973.

HIGHLIGHTS OF HIS ADMINISTRATION

✦§ Report of the President's commission on the assassination of President Kennedy (headed by Chief Justice Warren), issued September 27, 1964, named Lee Harvey Oswald as the sole culprit.

✦§ Kennedy-Johnson social laws enacted:
> $1.072 billion in aid to the Appalachian region, March 3, 1965.
> $1.3 in aid to elementary and secondary schools, April 11, 1965.
> Medical care for the aged (Medicare and Medicaid), July 30, 1965.
> Voting Rights law, August 6, 1965. Four-year $7.8 billion housing program, August 10, 1965.
> $665 million in aid to distressed areas, August 25, 1965.
> Doubling of the anti-poverty program to $1.6 billion, September 25, 1965.
> Five-year $4.7 billion grants and aid to colleges and scholarships, October 21, 1965.

Increase in the minimum wage to $1.60 an hour and extension of persons covered by 8,000,000, August 14, 1966.

✍§ 25th Amendment to the Constitution, providing succession of the Vice President in case of a President's disability and the method of filling the vice-presidential office when vacant, passed and sent to the states July 6, 1965. Ratified February 2, 1967.

✍§ Creation of a Housing and Urban Development Department in the Executive Branch, September 9, 1965.

✍§ Legislation enacted to set Federal standards in automobile safety and launch a $322 million highway safety program, September 9, 1966.

✍§ Creation of a Department of Transportation in the Executive Branch, October 15, 1966.

✍§ The war in Vietnam: Attack on American destroyers in the Gulf of Tonkin by North Vietnamese gunboats, August 2nd and 4th, 1964, prompted the President to send to Congress the Southeast Asia Resolution empowering him to repel aggression against United States armed forces. Rushed through Congress, it was signed on August 11. Used as authority for escalating the war, its passage was later condemned as precipitous and ill-considered by Senator J. William Fulbright and other opponents of the war policy.

Eight Americans were killed at a Special Forces camp at Pleiku, South Vietnam, on February 7, 1965. Johnson ordered retaliatory bombing of North Vietnam, thus yielding to the Air Force plan for systematic bombing of presumable Viet Cong supply sources.

First announcement of regular ground forces en route to South Vietnam, 3,500 Marines to Da Nang, March 7, 1965.

In June it was announced that 54,000 troops, Army, Marines, Air Force and Navy, were committed to the war. The number rose to 525,000 in 1968.

On May 10, 1968, peace talks began between the United States and North Vietnam in Paris, following a halt to American bombing of North Vietnam above the 20th parallel in April.

Total halt to bombing of North Vietnam announced by President Johnson in October 1968. South Vietnamese delegates joined peace talks in December.

✍§ Other Foreign Affairs: President Johnson sent a Marine force to the Dominican Republic after a left-wing anti-government coup, on April 28, 1965. Criticized for his intervention by the Organization of American States, he yielded to a peace-keeping international force.

The *Pueblo*, United States naval intelligence ship, was seized by North Koreans off their coast, on January 23, 1968. They charged violation of territorial waters, denied by the United States. Ship and crew remained in North Korean hands until released on December 23, 1968.

RICHARD MILHOUS NIXON

---◆---

THIRTY-SEVENTH PRESIDENT

On a sunny summer day in 1952 at Hampton Beach, New Hampshire, a serious young politician named Richard Nixon sat in a bedroom at a beachside hotel picking over the wording of an address he would shortly deliver accepting the Republican nomination for Vice President of the United States. Downstairs in the dining room a typical crowd of party faithful chattered pleasantly, ate lunch and awaited their candidate. After lunch he emerged from his retreat, went downstairs and made his speech to the audience, already exuberant in the conviction that this year the party would end twenty years of Democratic rule. If the man before them seemed wooden, possibly even mediocre, that was of little importance considering that they had at the head of the ticket the top general and hero of World War II, a man of iridescent political personality, Dwight D. Eisenhower.

Eisenhower's advisers had urged Nixon for the number two spot on the ticket largely because he had achieved national attention by his investigation of Alger Hiss, a former State Department official accused of liaison with the Communists. The Republican Convention had accepted him by acclamation. He had moved up fast in politics, covering the distance from small-town laywer to vice-presidential nominee in six years, impelled by determination to break away from the drab circumstances of his early life. His father, Francis A. Nixon, had been a man who never succeeded at anything. As a young man in Columbus, Ohio, he worked as motorman on a trolley car; at length he decided that California had better climate, possibly better opportunities, and moved out there, arriving at Whittier. There he met and married a Quaker girl, Hannah Milhous, and took to growing citrus in the neighboring village of Yorba Linda, where Richard was born, the second of five sons, on January 9, 1913. After some years of struggle, he gave up the ranch as a failure and moved back to Whittier, where he bought a small general store with a gas pump out front. Richard was nine at the time, and began to earn money at odd jobs and crop picking, not only because the family needed it but because his father believed that hard work was good for the soul. He entered Quaker Whittier College at seventeen and there proved his exceptional intellect as a scholar plus a talent for politics by winning every important student office and a scholarship to Duke University Law School.

Three years later, at twenty-four, with his law degree, Nixon went to New York hoping for an entry into a legal firm. Turned down wherever he looked, he was obliged to return to Whittier, where he was accepted by a local firm. The following five years were good ones. By all accounts he was popular, had a quick sense of humor, and a taste for parties. He began pairing off with a pretty teacher at the high school, Thelma Ryan, known as Pat. They were married in 1940. Then came World War II and Richard Nixon decided that the best thing for him was administrative work, so he went to Washington and got a job with the Office of Price Administration. After six months of office work, he was transferred to the Navy and there served as a Lieutenant Commander.

In 1946 a group of Republicans suggested to Nixon that he run for Congress against Jerry Voorhis, a Democrat of Labor-Liberal persuasion who had been Representative from the 12th California district for some years. When he agreed, they put him in the hands of a professional campaign manager, Murray Chotiner, whose simple formula for success was to find your opponent's weak point and attack that again and again until he was on the defensive and confused. Mr. Voorhis's weak point was an unsolicited endorsement by the C.I.O.'s National Political Action Committee, which to conservative Californians had a somewhat red tinge. It was a rough, cruel campaign, or, as Nixon said, "a fighting, rocking, socking" one, and he came out the winner. When, four years later, Nixon ran for the Senate against Helen Gahagan Douglas, a protegée of Eleanor Roosevelt and a Liberal, the Chotiner method operated on a larger, better publicized scale, earning Nixon the election, but also the nickname "Tricky Dick" among outraged Democrats.

When Nixon took his seat in the 80th Congress, President Truman had initiated containment of the Soviet Union abroad, or "cold war," and was deeply suspicious of Communist sympathizers at home. In Washington the effort to expose Communists and "fellow-travelers" was hectic, especially so on the House Committee to Investigate Un-American Activities. The young Congressman from California became a member of that Committee, and plunged into a study of the Communist menace. Therefore, when a moderately important former government official named Alger Hiss came before the Committee accused of being a Communist and of passing government secret papers to the Russians, Nixon had done his homework and plunged into the Hiss case with the zeal of a prosecutor, winning praise in some sectors of opinion and a great deal of attention in the press. Later Hiss, after two trials, was convicted of perjury and sentenced to five years in jail.

The presidential campaign of 1952 was just beginning to roll in September with Senator Nixon on his first speaking tour in northern California, when a sensational story about a "Nixon slush fund" erupted in the nation's press. The fund, it was alleged, had been secretly provided by rich Californians to supplement his Congressional salary. The impact of the story on Eisenhower was devastating, but, after counseling with his political advisers, he agreed on a fast check by accountants of Nixon finances and then a public statement by Nixon to clear himself. If he came out of it "as clean as a hound's tooth" he could stay on the ticket. The accountants' check showed nothing illegal, the $16,000 fund being no secret and intended for political purposes. Nixon, after three agonizing days of preparation, delivered a half-hour television speech of tried-and-true hokum that touched millions of American hearts. He declared that he had never been guilty of accepting political gifts, except once "a little spotted dog" which his elder daughter had named Checkers. At the end he appealed to his listeners to wire their support to the Republican National Committee. Telegrams poured in by the thousands and the incident passed into history when Eisenhower proclaimed him publicly as "my boy."

In the following eight years Nixon performed well his vice-presidential duties, whether they were to campaign vigorously for the administration or to make good-will tours abroad. Eisenhower's three illnesses during his second term gave Nixon a chance to show his intelligence and administrative talent in keeping the routines of government functioning. The President was so pleased with him that, after his last period as Acting President, he was awarded a signed statement confirming him in that role should anything further happen to suspend Eisenhower's capacity to perform his duties. As the end of his administration drew near Eisenhower made it clear that the Vice President had earned the Republican nomination for President in 1960 and should have it. And so it was done, unanimously, by the party convention.

Nixon's defeat by John F. Kennedy was a bitter one to accept, particularly as the popular vote showed a Kennedy plurality of only 118,574. Returning to California, he secured a lucrative position in a law firm, installed his wife and two daughters in a luxurious home, wrote an introspective book called *Six Crises* and planned for another try at the presidency. In his plans was the governorship of California, coming up for election in 1962, with the popular Democratic incumbent Edmund Brown sure to run. He was strongly advised against tackling Brown, particularly by his close personal friend and admirer Harry Robbins Haldeman, a young advertising man who had worked in the two previous Nixon campaigns; but when Nixon would not be dissuaded, Haldeman managed his campaign. It was a second major defeat, and in terms of his personal image, something of a disaster when, in a temporary nervous breakdown on election night, he chose to address the newspapermen awaiting his formal concession to Brown with bitterness and self-pity. The tag line, duly reported, was: ". . . just think how much you're going to be missing. You won't have Nixon to kick around anymore, because, gentlemen, this is my last press conference."

Following this Nixon made a shrewd move toward a return presidential engagement. He transferred his family to New York City, secured a lucrative partnership in a respected law firm, and in the next six years made a number of powerful friends, notably the banker Maurice Stans, who could raise money for his political activities at any time he needed it and in any quantity, and a lawyer, John N. Mitchell, of imposing toughness, who merged his law practice with Nixon's firm and became Nixon's campaign manager in 1968. More important, he made friends with the rank and file of the Republican Party from coast to coast, campaigning for presidential candidate Barry Goldwater in 1964 and in the off-year elections of 1966, covering no fewer than thirty-five states, speaking for party candidates from governors down to state representatives. And in 1968 he campaigned tirelessly for himself in the primary elections where he wanted to make a good showing in order to project a public image of success.

The year 1968 was not a good one for the Democrats. Their candidate with the widest party support, Senator Edmund Muskie of Maine, made a poor showing in the earliest primary, that of New Hampshire. President Johnson announced at the end of March that he would not run. The anti-war element that had long fought and bled for Eugene McCarthy appeared to be shifting toward Robert F. Kennedy, who also had considerable popularity among the rank and file of the party. Then Kennedy was murdered while celebrating his California primary victory at a Los Angeles hotel. The Democrats were thereafter divided and leaderless. At their national convention at Chicago in August, with a shambles of anti-war demonstrators and police going on in the streets outside its guarded perimeter, they nominated for president old-guard Democrat, Johnson's Vice President, Hubert Humphrey of Minnesota. Three weeks earlier, on August 7th, the Republicans in an orderly ceremony had nominated Richard Nixon, and after that his personal choice for Vice President, obscure Spiro T. Agnew, Governor of Maryland. In the campaign, Nixon, who felt his chief failure in 1960 was the poor projection of his image on television, worked meticulously to correct that and to use the medium to maximum advantage. In his speeches he came out strongly for the attitudes shared by most Americans: law and order, full employment, American prestige, and an end (with victory) to the war in Vietnam. Nixon won the election by a narrow margin, a margin that he was sure would have been larger had he captured the votes that went to third-party candidate George C. Wallace of Alabama, leader of conservative pro-segregation southerners, who came through with 46 electoral votes and just under 10,000,000 popular votes.

The Nixon administration top officials were chosen either from his political cronies and loyalists—John N. Mitchell, Attorney General, Maurice Stans, Secretary of Commerce—or, as "filler" in cabinet posts, from among little-know businessmen. The four independently worthy Republicans of cabinet rank were either ignored, fired or eased out of office by the end of Nixon's first term. Bob Haldeman became Chief of Staff and public relations man at the White House, and another loyal old campaigner, John D. Ehrlichman, signed on as counsel but was promoted in 1970 to director of the Domestic Council, a job that gave him the responsibility of filtering communications between the President and all cabinet secretaries who dealt with domestic affairs—such as the Secretaries of Interior, Labor, Health, Education and Welfare, etc. As for the Secretaries of State and Defense, they were subordinated to the President's Adviser on National Security, not by virtue of organization, but because that person was Henry Kissinger, an ex-Harvard professor with the virtuosity to become the President's whole team in foreign affairs and produce the victories the

225

President so ardently desired. In fact, from 1970 on, the real government of the United States, partly because of the declining vitality of Congress, was the Office of the President. Within it, besides the Ehrlichman and Kissinger domains, were such busy agencies as the C.I.A., the National Security Council, the Office of Management and Budget, plus ten more. This concentration of power, and its enclosure in the presidency, made secrecy practical, covert operations viable. By the end of Nixon's first term, of the three equal government branches set up by the founding fathers, only the Federal court system remained strong and independent, and it was a Federal district judge who opened up finally the wide-ranging misuse of power that became known generically as the Watergate Scandals.

Nixon felt that the first order of business when he took office was to bring American involvement in Indo-China to an end. Henry Kissinger presented the alternatives in such a way as to make only one possible: gradual withdrawal of American ground forces and continued pressure on North Vietnam and the rebel Viet Cong in South Vietnam to make peace, this to be accomplished without diminishing American prestige, or as it was called in the jargon of the day, "credibility" abroad. The naval and air forces were to remain in Indo-China in order to show American military power and as a tool for negotiation. The weak, corrupt, American-supported government of General Thieu in South Vietnam had some million men under arms, poor in discipline and morale. They were to take over the ground fighting as American troops withdrew, an operation labeled by the cover word, "Vietnamization." As Americans who had hoped for a quick end to the war became restive, seeing only a small withdrawal of troops by November 1969, the President addressed them on television. Persistently believing that opposition to the war was still only a minority movement, he made his appeal for trust and support to "the great silent majority of my fellow Americans," but even they were given to understand that "I have not and do not intend to announce the timetable of our program."

For some three years the American people feared that Nixon was fighting the Vietnam war as hard as his predecessor, resulting in a continuation of massive peace demonstrations fringed with violence. At the end of April 1970, Nixon announced that American troops had crossed the border into Cambodia. It proved to be a limited operation intended to disrupt North Vietnamese supply bases while the Americans turned over ground fighting to the South Vietnamese army; at home there arose a great protest at "an extension of the war." Demonstrations and some riots erupted on college campuses. In one such demonstration at Kent State University in Ohio, National Guardsmen fired into a mob of students, killing four of them, and this fuelled angrier protests than ever against the war.

226

The war was in fact winding down, with only episodic military action. In April 1972 North Vietnam mounted a full-scale invasion of South Vietnam from the north, and, as a kind of counter-attack, the United States mined Haiphong Harbor. In October, just before the presidential election, however, Kissinger publicly announced that in his opinion peace was "very near." On December 18th another horrifying move toward peace began with what was described as the most massive bombing of civilian areas in history, American B-52s laying down a blanket of destruction in the Hanoi-Haiphong sector, with thousands of sorties over a period of twelve days. In the silence that followed, peace came. A treaty was signed January 27th, 1973, Soviet Russia and China concurring, by which Vietnam as well as Cambodia and Laos were to work out their own political futures, with the total withdrawal of American forces. As if to create an image of victory, the Nixon administration made a television pageant of the returning American prisoners of war.

Resolution of the Vietnam dilemma was but a piece of what President Nixon might well have called his larger "game plan" for mitigating the long cold war between the United States and the Communist nuclear powers, China and the Soviet Union. In July 1971, Kissinger was in West Pakistan on a mission, when he seized the opportunity to fly secretly to Peking and complete arrangements for the President to visit China the following year. This was promptly made public, followed in October by an announcement that Nixon would also visit the Soviet Union. In the intervening months there occurred between the Soviet Union and the United States a confrontation without action in the war between Pakistan and India. Originating in a revolt by East Pakistan against the central government, situated across the bulk of India in West Pakistan, it caused India to support East Pakistan against her traditional enemy, West Pakistan. India signed a mutual defense agreement with Russia, secured Soviet arms and marched into East Pakistan to defeat the government troops, thus creating the new state Bangladesh. The American government protested Soviet support of India and announced its support of West Pakistan, but took no action beyond sending a small fleet into the Indian Ocean to show the flag.

In February 1972, President and Mrs. Nixon, with a large retinue, made a week-long visit to China, fully televised by satellite to the American people. The President talked with Communist Party Chairman Mao Tse-tung and Premier Chou En-lai and an agreement was signed, more friendly in the signing than in substance. The visit to Moscow in May was more productive, the President and Communist Party Secretary Leonid Brezhnev signing an agreement to limit the number of defensive anti-ballistic missiles, a non-agression pact and provision for a joint trade commission. Thus was inaugurated the policy of détente, and a beginning was made in limiting nuclear weapons of a defensive nature. Brezhnev returned Nixon's visit in June 1973, when they failed to make any advance from the beginning on a broader control of nuclear weapons, notably those of offensive nature.

Détente signified a lessening of the chance of direct confrontation with the Communist governments, but it was not intended to affect the practice on both sides of intervening in the affairs of other nations, overtly or covertly, to build or maintain their power in terms of global politics. Probably the Nixon administration's most significant achievement in that practice was Kissinger's indefatigable diplomacy in creating friendly relations with Egypt and other Arab states in the Middle East, while continuing to supply Israel with arms. The opportunity for diplomatic intervention came shortly after Kissinger's confirmation as Secretary of State in September, 1973. On October 8th, the Jewish holy day of Yom Kippur, Egypt and Syria, well supplied with sophisticated Soviet weapons, attacked Israel's border defenses, Egypt in the south on the Sinai Peninsula, Syria to the north on the Golan Heights, with initial success. Israel counterattacked, invading the Egyptian mainland across the Suez Canal, surrounding a large enemy force on Sinai, and starting down the road to Damascus in the north. The United States, because of Russian indirect involvement and on the chance that it might become direct, ordered an alert by all American nuclear forces around the world. Then Secretary Kissinger offered his services to produce a cease-fire. By shuttling back and forth between the capitals of the three countries, he produced a cease-fire and with remarkable celerity an agreement for all parties to sit down and work out a peace treaty. The important result for the United States was a moving toward friendly relations with the Arab states. In February diplomatic relations were resumed with Egypt, after a lapse of seven years, and in the following June President Nixon made an official tour of five Mid-east countries, pausing longest to discuss with President Anwar el-Sadat of Egypt what aid might be expected from the United States.

In domestic affairs President Nixon had the poorest record of legislation or other affirmative action of any president since Calvin Coolidge. The environmentalist lobby succeeded in having an Environmental Protection Agency established. But Nixon's interest in home problems was inextricably tangled in personal politics. During his first year in office he tried in the courts to have school desegregation stretched out or postponed, without success. And he wasted five months in a struggle with the Senate to place a conservative southerner of segregationist opinion on the Supreme Court.

All this was an unconcealed attempt to attract to himself the kind of southerners who had voted for Governor George Wallace of Alabama in 1968. But with the intricate national problems, such as welfare, taxation, and the universal hardship of increasing inflation with unemployment, he tended to delegate responsibility to the bureaucracy without putting forth the leadership necessary to produce solutions.

He was more involved in the challenge of the anti-war activists, who attacked his credibility. He tried jailing them and bringing them before the courts, but these methods only ended in frustration. He feared that they were the leading edge of anarchy and even rebellion. The critical press, such as the Washington *Post*, the New York *Times* and certain commentators on television, he also considered enemies beyond toleration. In June 1971, he was able to strike at both the anti-war people and the press with one punch. The New York *Times* began printing excerpts from a 1967 classified Defense Department report on the war in Indo-China, turned over to it by a former Defense Department employee, Daniel Ellsberg, who had become disillusioned and joined the anti-war movement. The President obtained a court order restraining the *Times* from further publication of the report, but the Supreme Court reversed the lower court's order, and the so-called Pentagon Papers were widely published and read. Ellsberg was indicted for violation of the espionage act and stealing government property. Nearly two years later, on May 11, 1973, a Federal District Judge in Los Angeles dismissed the charges against him, citing the government attorneys for misconduct in illegally withholding certain wiretap evidence from the defense attorneys. Two weeks before that Judge Byrne announced that he had received information from Washington that the office of Ellsberg's psychiatrist had been raided, apparently in an effort to get damaging personal information, by two men, Gordon Liddy and E. Howard Hunt. Liddy and Hunt were two men of the seven who had similarly burglarized the offices of the Democratic National Committee in the office-apartment complex known as Watergate the past June.

That "Watergate" crime, interrupted fortuitously by the police, had made a small splash in the news because three of these arrested had connections with the White House or the Committee to Re-elect the President or both. The men caught in the act were loaded with wiretapping equipment and $100 bills. The White House press secretary brushed off the incident as "a third-rate burglary," while most newspapers thought the proper word was "caper." But the Washington *Post* put two investigative reporters to work, and in the following months they found an amazing number of talkative sources who supplied in bits and pieces a story incomplete but suggestive of extensive covert operations—illegal wiretapping, a method of receiving illegal campaign contributions from corporations, sabotage of the leading Democratic candidate, Senator Muskie, before the 1972 primaries—and some of it was printable. They were able to identify to their own satisfaction those at high levels in the White House and the Committee for the Re-election of the President who directed these operations, but they lacked incontrovertible proof. The President outrode the scandal. In August he addressed the people on television, assuring them that "no one on the White House staff, no one in this administration, presently employed was involved in this very bizarre incident. What really hurts in matters of this sort is not the fact that they occur . . . What really hurts is if you try to cover it up." The people believed him, and in November he was re-elected by a landslide.

The seven Watergate burglars were indicted by a grand jury, the case against them being presented by U.S. attorneys, employees of the Department of Justice, formerly headed by Attorney General Mitchell, but now by an equally political Nixon loyalist, Richard Kleindienst. In January 1973, the seven went to trial, where five of them pleaded guilty; two were totally uncommunicative, or, in the jargon of the day, "stonewalled it." District Judge John J. Sirica took over the interrogation of the accused, probing for a clue to who hired and paid them, and in the end he expressed his dissatisfaction with the net information produced by the trial. There was, however, in prospect a congressional investigation. As that got under way, things began to happen in March. Most important was the performance of Nixon's nominee as director of the F.B.I., L. Patrick Gray, appearing before the Senate Judiciary Committee in confirmation hearings. As he had been acting director since J. Edgar Hoover's death the preceeding May, he was questioned sharply on the F.B.I.'s part in the investigation of Watergate. Loyal to the President but a blunderer, he revealed its negligence and ineptitude in the case.

In the White House inner sanctum, which had been hurting privately from the pain of covering up Watergate, Gray's testimony was taken as a disaster. John Dean, the President's Counsel and manager of the Watergate cover-up, sensed that he was about to be uncovered and began to tell all that he knew to the government attorneys in charge of the Watergate case. The Senate Select Committee on Presidential Campaign Activities (Chairman Sam Ervin) had picked up interesting information from one of the Watergate seven, who had finally decided to talk, in its preparation for open and televised hearings May 17th. In desperation the President decided to sever himself from those who would be tainted by the prospective revelations, not only about the Watergate burglary but about the wider conspiracy of which it was a part. On April 30th he announced the "resignations" of Dean, Haldeman, Ehrlichman, and Attorney General Kleindienst. Immediately the Senate voted for the appointment of a special Watergate prosecutor to press charges against all involved in the conspiracy. A new Attorney General, Elliot Richardson, chose Archibald Cox of the Harvard Law School, a man of the best legal ability and character.

So far as the bulk of Americans who got their news and entertainment from television were concerned, Sam Ervin's Watergate Committee hearings were of unprecedented importance. But they produced only one new piece of information. A low-level White House staffer, aide to Haldeman, testifying in July mentioned, almost casually, that the President had installed devices to record all his office conversations. There ensued a battle to get the tapes of his conversations, for the Committee, and, above all, for the Special Prosecutor. Nixon stood on executive privilege and refused them, then offered transcripts, which were refused. By October Prosecutor Cox had identified nine tapes that might be critical and subpoenaed them. Nixon tried to temporize, and when Cox remained firm demanded that Attorney General Richardson fire him. Richardson refused, as did his deputy. Both men resigned, and the next in rank, the Solicitor General, carried out the order. This occurred within a few hours on October 20th and was aptly memorialized by the press as "the Saturday night massacre."

In the midst of all this there passed from the scene, in quiet disgrace, the most controversial person in Nixon's official family, Vice President Spiro T. Agnew. He had announced in August that he was under investigation for receiving kickbacks from contractors while governor of Maryland. Now he had decided to resign and plead no contest on a charge of tax evasion. To replace him as Vice President, Nixon chose the popular Republican minority leader of the House, Gerald R. Ford, who was duly sworn in December 6th.

Nixon's angry dismissal of Archibald Cox had not served his cause, for the new Special Prosecutor, Leon Jaworski of Texas, was Cox's equal in tenacity. In March 1974 seven Nixon men, including Mitchell, Haldeman and Ehrlichman, were indicted on charges of covering up the Watergate scandal. The grand jury, in handing up the indictments to Judge Sirica, privately named the President as an unindicted co-conspirator. The matter of impeachment, long avoided by Congress, was now in the hands of the House Judiciary Committee. It subpoenaed all tapes and relevant documents, receiving instead 1,200 pages of edited transcripts, which it re-

231

jected. May 9th the Committee began public, televised debates on grounds for impeachment—a rare opportunity for Americans to see the democratic process in action. July 27th to July 30th three articles of impeachment were voted: 1, for obstructing justice by a cover-up; 2, for misuse of presidential power; 3, for defying the Committees' subpoenas for the tapes.

In the meantime Prosecutor Jaworski had appealed directly to the Supreme Court for an order requiring the President to hand over all tapes, and on July 24th it so ruled. On August 5th the White House complied, and there in a conversation with Haldeman six days after the Watergate burglary lay "the smoking gun," specific instructions from Nixon that the C.I.A. tell the F.B.I. not to trace the $100 bills found in the burglars' pockets, which had originated in a Nixon campaign contribution. Rather than face an impeachment trial in the Senate, Nixon resigned, as of noon August 9th. Retiring to his California villa, San Clemente, he gratefully received on September 8th a full pardon from his successor for all crimes that he had committed or may have committed.

HIGHLIGHTS OF HIS ADMINISTRATION

◄§ Watergate. A popular term signifying a wide conspiracy to arrogate to the President of the United States all political power, exposed and terminated by the Federal court system and Congress.

◄§ End of American war in Indo-China by signing of peace at Paris, January 27th, 1973. Terms: Withdrawal of all U.S. forces in Indo-China—in Laos and Cambodia as soon as a cease-fire could be achieved. In Cambodia U.S. Air Force continued bombing in support of the government against Communist rebels until August 15, 1973, when Congress cut off funds. Withdrawal of North Vietnam forces and demobilization of government and Viet Cong forces in South Vietnam. Creation of a national council of Reconciliation and Concord to oversee elections and an International Commission to Control and Supervise elections and the military terms. Fighting nevertheless continued, with the predictable military seizure by North Vietnam of South Vietnam. American casualties were 416,800 with 56,560 deaths.

◄§ Establishment of friendly relations with the People's Republic of China in 1972, in keeping with a policy of détente toward the Communist nuclear powers.

◄§ Signing with Soviet Union of limited agreement on control of defensive nuclear weapons, a non-aggression pact and trade pact in 1972, as furtherance of détente with Communist nuclear powers.

◄§ Reorganization of the Executive Office to expand it to fifteen offices and councils.

◄§ Rule by the Supreme Court that the death penalty is unconstitutional, June 29, 1972.

◄§ Devaluation of the dollar 10 per cent against the world's major currencies February 12, 1973.

GERALD RUDOLPH FORD

THIRTY-EIGHTH PRESIDENT

For the first time the 25th Amendment to the Constitution came into use with the resignation of Vice President Spiro Agnew in October 1973. By its terms the President nominates a new Vice President and both houses of Congress must confirm by a majority vote. President Nixon chose, of all Republicans, the one most likely to be confirmed by a Democratic Congress, the personally popular Gerald Ford, minority leader for the past eight years of the House of Representatives. With only a small dissent, he was confirmed and sworn into office December 6th. Eight months later when Nixon, like Agnew, left office in disgrace, Gerald Ford was sworn in as President, on August 9th, 1974.

At the time Ford had a record of unyielding conservativism, strongly supporting the war in South Vietnam, evidencing a laissez-faire attitude toward business and its control of the economic pattern, with, on the personal level, integrity and a conscientious modesty. Born July 14, 1913, in Omaha, Nebraska, he was taken by his mother, when his parents were

235

divorced, to Grand Rapids, Michigan, where he grew up. On his mother's remarriage, he was adopted by his stepfather and took his stepfather's name. As a student at the University of Michigan his favorite extra-curricular activity was football, which he played well. He made the University team, showing a capacity for doing well whatever he did and a taste for active outdoor sports as recreation. He graduated from Yale Law School and returned to Grand Rapids to start a law practice in 1941, but seven years later he was in politics for good when he ran and was elected to the House of Representatives. That same year he married Elizabeth Bloomer, a pretty young woman who had for a time performed with an elite modern dance group and was now ready to take up the occupation of housewife.

As President, Ford, in his first days, was most often labeled by the press as "average," an average man come to power, much like Harry Truman before him. He was aware of that comparison and liked it; also, like Truman, he was trapped at the beginning by what seemed to be the nature of his office into making fast decisions. Such was the one that caused a national shudder when he, without consultation, pardoned Richard Nixon for any crimes he might have committed. This, on September 8th, while Nixon aides such as Haldeman, Ehrichman and John Mitchell, who had implemented his policies, were facing criminal trial, appeared to many unjust and the gift of an unwarranted most-favored status should the future hold a possibility of Nixon's staging a comeback in public life. Ford explained the pardon as an effort to put Watergate behind him for the good of the country. Possibly another ill-considered act was his nomination of Nelson Rockefeller, a controversial man in Republican politics as well as public office, for Vice President. Congressional hearings, spread over four months, revealed most details of Rockefeller's finances and financially connected power, but chiefly that he was a distinguished adversary, for which quality he was eventually confirmed.

Ford's most popular contribution in his first year as President was a kind of antisepsis to the corruption of the Executive Office, primarily by his own frank and open personal style. Moreover he perceptibly reduced the power clique in the White House, although the bureaucracy remained, restoring cabinet officers to their traditional influence and dignity. He kept most of the top Nixon personnel, introducing only a few new men, but he re-adjusted and shuffled the Nixon holdovers with the new men, so that by the fall of 1975 he had a reasonably harmonious administration, making only one radical change. He resolved the long-standing conflict between National Security Adviser Henry Kissinger, also Secretary of State, and Secretary of Defense James R. Schlesinger by dismissing Schlesinger and narrowing Kissinger's authority to the State Department.

236

On broad national problems, such as inflation, unemployment and energy, Ford was at first inclined to advance positive proposals, challenging Congress to come up with its own proposals, but shortly, and concurrent with signs that all three of those problems were becoming less acute, settled into a cautious, virtually negative policy. On some insistent matters of controversy he attempted a unilateral resolution. One of these, of considerable interest, was amnesty for men who had refused to serve in the Vietnam War or had deserted. Some 130,000 of them were still refugees abroad, in jail or in hiding, many of them essentially conscientious objectors. Confirmed supporters of the war, such as Ford himself, and politicized alumni of the armed forces, such as the American Legion, opposed outright amnesty. The President therefore attempted a compromise, by which war resisters and deserters would receive clemency if they would turn themselves over to a program of serving up to two years in government-assigned duty as a penalty. A few accepted, but the bulk refused the concept that they should pay a penalty, and the program was a failure.

Ford's strongest adviser, as in the Nixon administration, remained Henry Kissinger, the man of détente and intricate diplomatic design, but there seemed less for him to do in a world quiescent for the time being. The inevitable Communist conquest of South Vietnam and Cambodia left Americans as mere spectators although, in the last days before Saigon fell, overwhelmed with concern for some 200,000 Vietnamese who had worked for Americans and clamored to be saved from the Communists. By air and ship, in the confusion of panic, the majority of these were transported across the Pacific to be re-settled by gradual stages in the United States. In the aftermath of the Communist occupation of Cambodia, in May 1975, there occurred a minor but inflammatory international incident similar to North Korea's seizure of the American intelligence ship *Pueblo* in 1968. In this case Cambodia seized an American merchant ship, the *Mayagüez*, near Tang Island off the Cambodian coast, claiming it had trespassed on Cambodian waters. With no diplomatic access to the new Communist government in Phnom Penh, and remembering that it took a year to negotiate the release of the *Pueblo*'s crew by the North Koreans, Ford decided to send in the Marines. With landings at Tang Island and air strikes at the Cambodian mainland, where, as it happened, the twenty-three *Mayagüez* crewmen had been taken, men and ship were readily released. The cost: fifty-six Americans killed or missing, fifty wounded.

In foreign affairs Ford continued the Nixon-Kissinger pattern of personal diplomacy, traveling to Europe; to Vladivostok by way of Japan and Korea for a conference with Leonid Brezhnev on nuclear offensive weapons that produced another paper agreement with no great bite to it; and to

China. At home he was embroiled with Congress in trying to contain inflation and prevent it from floating more Federal funds to relieve those suffering in the depression. In 1975 he used the veto and the tactical skill to make his veto stick on four bills he considered inflationary. As for politics, since Ford had long since declared his intention to run for election in 1976, it became necessary to cultivate party support for the nomination. In the summer of 1975 he fitted into his schedule short trips to Republican meetings of various types in a broad geographical distribution. It was on two such trips, both to California, that the shocking hazard of "the most powerful office in the world," asassination, nearly brought him to his end. The first incident was in Sacramento on September 5th, when, as he walked through a crowd talking to the people and shaking hands, a woman pointed a gun at him but failed to fire it. Seventeen days later in San Francisco, as he stepped from his hotel to his car, another woman pointed a gun and fired, but a quick-witted bystander lunged for her arm and apparently spoiled her aim. By necessity the President had to agree to tighter security and privately had to live with some of the contradictions of democracy, that an elected president might do well or might do badly, but regardless of either he might be suddenly dead.

LAWS GOVERNING
THE PRESIDENCY

THE CONSTITUTION: ARTICLE II

SECTION 1:

1. The Executive power shall be vested in a President of the United States of America. He shall hold his office during the term of four years, and together with the Vice President, chosen for the same term, be elected as follows:

2. Each State shall appoint, in such manner as the Legislature thereof may direct, a number of electors equal to the whole number of Senators and Representatives to which the State may be entitled in the Congress; but no Senator or Representative or person holding an office of trust or profit under the United States shall be appointed an elector.

The electors shall meet in their respective States and vote by ballot for two persons, of whom one at least shall not be an inhabitant of the same State with themselves. And they shall make a list of all the persons voted for, and of the number of votes for each, which list they shall sign and certify and transmit, sealed, to the seat of the Government of the United States, directed to the President of the Senate. The President of the Senate shall, in the presence of the Senate and House of Representatives, open all the certificates, and the votes shall then be counted. The person having the greatest number of votes shall be the President, if such number be a majority of the whole number of electors appointed, and if there be more than one who have such a majority, and have an equal number of votes, then the House of Representatives shall immediately choose by ballot one of them for President; and if no person have a majority, then from the five highest on the list the said House shall in like manner choose the President. But in choosing the President, the vote shall be taken by States, the representation from each State having one vote. A quorum, for this purpose, shall consist of a member or members from two-thirds of the States, and a majority of all the States shall be necessary to a choice. In every case, after the choice of the President, the person having the greatest number of votes of the electors shall be the Vice President. But if there should remain two or more who have equal votes, the Senate shall choose from them by ballot the Vice President.

3. The Congress may determine the time of choosing the electors and the day on which they shall give their votes, which day shall be the same throughout the United States.

4. No person except a natural born citizen, or a citizen of the United States at the time of the adoption of this Constitution, shall be eligible to the office of President; neither shall any person be eligible to that office who shall not have attained to the age of thirty-five years and been fourteen years a resident within the United States.

5. In case of the removal of the President from office, or of his death, resignation, or inability to discharge the powers and duties of the said office, the same shall devolve on the Vice President, and the Congress may by law provide for the case of removal, death, resignation, or inability, both of the President and Vice President, declaring what officer shall then act as President, and such officer shall act accordingly until the disability be removed or a President shall be elected.

6. The President shall, at stated times, receive for his services a compensation which shall neither be increased nor diminished during the period for which he shall have been elected, and he shall not receive within that period any other emolument from the United States or any of them.

7. Before he enter on the execution of his office he shall take the following oath or affirmation:

"I do solemnly swear (or affirm) that I will faithfully execute the office of President of the United States, and will, to the best of my ability, preserve, protect, and defend the Constitution of the United States."

SECTION 2:

1. The President shall be Commander-in-Chief of the Army and Navy of the United States, and of the militia of the several States when called into the actual service of the United States; he may require the opinion, in writing, of the principal officer in each of the executive departments upon any subject relating to the duties of their respective offices, and he shall have power to grant reprieves and pardons for offenses against the United States except in cases of impeachment.

2. He shall have power by and with the advice and consent of the Senate to make treaties, provided two-thirds of the Senators present concur; and he shall nominate and by and with the advice and consent of the Senate shall appoint ambassadors, other public ministers and consuls, judges of the Supreme Court, and all other officers of the United States whose appointments are not herein otherwise

provided for, and which shall be established by law; but the Congress may by law vest the appointment of such inferior officers as they think proper in the President alone, in the courts of law, or in the heads of departments.

3. The President shall have power to fill up all vacancies that may happen during the recess of the Senate by granting commissions, which shall expire at the end of their next session.

SECTION 3:

He shall from time to time give to the Congress information of the state of the Union, and recommend to their consideration such measures as he shall judge necessary and expedient; he may, on extraordinary occasions, convene both Houses, or either of them, and in case of disagreement between them with respect to the time of adjournment, he may adjourn them to such time as he shall think proper; he shall receive ambassadors and other public ministers; he shall take care that the laws be faithfully executed, and shall commission all the officers of the United States.

SECTION 4:

The President, Vice President, and all civil officers of the United States shall be removed from office on impeachment for and conviction of treason, bribery or other high crimes and misdemeanors.

XII AMENDMENT: *Ratified September 25, 1804*

The Electors shall meet in their respective States, and vote by ballot for President and Vice President, one of whom at least shall not be an inhabitant of the same State with themselves; they shall name in their ballots the person voted for as President, and in distinct ballots the person voted for as Vice President; and they shall make distinct lists of all persons voted for as President and of all persons voted for as Vice President, and of the number of votes for each, which lists they shall sign and certify, and transmit, sealed, to the seat of the Government of the United States, directed to the President of the Senate; the President of the Senate shall, in the presence of the Senate and House of Representatives, open all the certificates and the votes shall then be counted; the person having the greatest number of votes for President shall be the President, if such number be a majority of the whole number of Electors appointed; and if no person have such majority, then from the persons having the highest numbers, not exceeding three, on the list of those voted for as President, the House of Representatives shall choose immediately, by ballot, the President. But in choosing the President, the votes shall be taken by States, the representation from each State having one vote; a quorum for this purpose shall consist of a member or members from two-thirds of the States, and a majority of all the States shall be necessary to a choice. And if the House of Representatives shall not choose a President whenever the right of choice shall devolve upon them, before the fourth day of March next following, then the Vice President shall act as President, as in case of the death or other constitutional disability of the President. The person having the greatest number of votes as Vice President shall be the Vice President, if such number be a majority of the whole number of Electors appointed, and if no person have a

241

majority, then, from the two highest numbers on the list, the Senate shall choose the Vice President; a quorum for the purpose shall consist of two-thirds of the whole number of Senators, and a majority of the whole number shall be necessary to a choice. But no person constitutionally ineligible to the office of President shall be eligible to that of Vice President of the United States.

XX AMENDMENT: *Ratified February 6, 1933*

SECTION 1:

The terms of the President and Vice President shall end at noon on the 20th day of January, and the terms of Senators and Representatives at noon on the 3rd day of January, of the years in which such terms would have ended if this article had not been ratified; and the terms of their successors shall then begin.

SECTION 2:

The Congress shall assemble at least once in every year, and such meeting shall begin at noon on the 3rd day of January, unless they shall by law appoint a different day.

SECTION 3:

If, at the time fixed for the beginning of the term of the President, the President-elect shall have died, the Vice President-elect shall become President. If a President shall not have been chosen before the time fixed for the beginning of his term, or if the President-elect shall have failed to qualify, then the Vice President-elect shall act as President until a President shall have qualified; and the Congress may by law provide for the case wherein neither a President-elect nor a Vice President-elect shall have qualified, declaring who shall then act as President, or the manner in which one who is to act shall be selected, and such person shall act accordingly until a President or Vice President shall have qualified.

SECTION 4:

The Congress may by law provide for the case of the death of any of the persons from whom the House of Representatives may choose a President whenever the right of choice shall have devolved upon them, and for the case of the death of any of the persons from whom the Senate may choose a Vice President whenever the right of choice shall have devolved upon them.

SECTION 5:

Sections 1 and 2 shall take effect on the 15th day of October following the ratification of this article (Oct. 1933).

SECTION 6:

This article shall be inoperative unless it shall have been ratified as an amendment to the Constitution by the Legislatures of three-fourths of the several States within seven years from the date of its submission.

No person shall be elected to the office of the President more than twice, and no person who has held the office of President, or acted as President, for more than two years of a term to which some other person was elected President shall be elected to the office of the President more than once. But this Article shall not apply to any person holding the office of President when this Article was proposed by the Congress, and shall not prevent any person who may be holding the office of President, or acting as President, during the term within which this Article becomes operative from holding the office of President or acting as President during the remainder of such term.

LAW OF PRESIDENTIAL SUCCESSION: *July 18, 1947*

If by reason of death, resignation, removal from office, inability, or failure to qualify there is neither a President nor Vice President to discharge the powers and duties of the office of President, then the Speaker of the House of Representatives shall, upon his resignation as Speaker and as Representative, act as President. The same rule shall apply in the case of the death, resignation, removal from office, or inability of an individual acting as President.

If at the time when a Speaker is to begin the discharge of the powers and duties of the office of President there is no Speaker, or the Speaker fails to qualify as Acting President, then the President pro tempore of the Senate, upon his resignation as President pro tempore and as Senator, shall act as President.

An individual acting as President shall continue to act until the expiration of the then current Presidential term, except that (1) if his discharge of the powers and duties of the office is founded in whole or in part in the failure of both the President-elect and the Vice President-elect to qualify, then he shall act only until a President or Vice President qualifies, and (2) if his discharge of the powers and duties of the office is founded in whole or in part on the inability of the President or Vice President, then he shall act only until the removal of the disability of one of such individuals.

If, by reason of death, resignation, removal from office, or failure to qualify, there is no President pro tempore to act as President, then the officer of the United States who is highest on the following list, and who is not under disability to discharge the powers and duties of President, shall act as President: Secy. of State, Secy. of the Treasury, Secy. of Defense, Attorney General, Postmaster General, Secy. of the Interior, Secy. of Agriculture, Secy. of Commerce, Secy. of Labor.

ARTICLE XXV: *Passed by Congress July 6, 1965. Ratified February 10, 1967.*

SECTION 1:

In case of the removal of the President from office or his death or resignation, the Vice President shall become President.

SECTION 2:

Whenever there is a vacancy in the office of the Vice President, the President shall nominate a Vice President who shall take the office upon confirmation by a majority vote of both houses of Congress.

Whenever the President transmits to the President pro tempore of the Senate and the Speaker of the House of Representatives his written declaration that he is unable to discharge the powers and duties of his office, and until he transmits to them a written declaration to the contrary, such powers and duties shall be discharged by the Vice President as Acting President.

Whenever the Vice President and a majority of either the principal officers of the executive departments, or of such other body as Congress may by law provide, transmit to the President pro tempore of the Senate and the Speaker of the House of Representatives their written declaration that the President is unable to discharge the powers and duties of his office, the Vice President shall immediately assume the powers and duties of the office of Acting President.

Thereafter, when the President transmits to the President pro tempore of the Senate and the Speaker of the House of Representatives his written declaration that no inability exists, he shall resume the powers and duties of his office unless the Vice President and a majority of either the principal officers of the executive department, or of such other body as Congress may by law provide, transmit within four days to the President pro tempore of the Senate and the Speaker of the House of Representatives their written declaration that the President is unable to discharge the powers and duties of his office. Thereupon Congress shall decide the issue, assembling within 48 hours for that purpose if not in session. If the Congress, within 21 days after receipt of the latter written declaration, or, if Congress is not in session, within 21 days after Congress is required to assemble, determines by two-thirds vote of both houses that the President is unable to discharge the powers and duties of his office, the Vice President shall continue to discharge the same as Acting President; otherwise, the President shall resume the powers and duties of his office.

SALIENT FACTS
ABOUT EACH PRESIDENT

---◆◇◆---

1.* GEORGE WASHINGTON *(Federalist)* 1789–1797

Born February 22, 1732,** at Pope's Creek, Westmoreland Co., Virginia
Son of Augustine and Mary Ball Washington
Married Mrs. Martha Dandridge Custis, January 6, 1759
Major, lieutenant colonel, and colonel, Virginia militia, 1752–58
Elected to Virginia House of Burgesses, 1758
Member First Continental Congress, 1774
Took command Continental Army, Cambridge, Massachusetts, July 3, 1775
Elected President unanimously, February 4, 1789
Appointed lieutenant general and commander-in-chief U.S. Army, July 3, 1798
Died December 14, 1799

LANDMARKS
Mount Vernon, Washington's home, near Washington
His Birthplace, reconstructed, in Westmoreland Co., Virginia

* Numbering the Presidents is officially done by terms in office. Because Cleveland
  had two terms in office, with Harrison between, this system makes him the 22nd
  and 24th President, and gives us 36 Presidents for only 35 men.
** But February 11, 1731, based on Julian Calendar.

VICE PRESIDENT
John Adams

CABINET

SECRETARY OF STATE: (acting) John Jay, 1789; Thomas Jefferson, September 26, 1789; Edmund Randolph, January 2, 1794; Timothy Pickering, August 20, 1795

SECRETARY OF THE TREASURY: Alexander Hamilton, September 11, 1789; Oliver Wolcott, Jr., February 2, 1795

SECRETARY OF WAR: Henry Knox, September 12, 1789; Timothy Pickering, January 2, 1795; James McHenry, January 27, 1796

ATTORNEY GENERAL:† Edmund Randolph, September 26, 1789; William Bradford, January 27, 1794; Charles Lee, December 10, 1795

POSTMASTER GENERAL:†† Samuel Osgood, September 26, 1789; Timothy Pickering, August 12, 1791; Joseph Habersham, February 25, 1795

1789 ELECTORAL VOTE

Each elector cast two votes. The candidate with the most votes was declared President, the candidate with the next highest number of votes the Vice President. All electors in 1789 and in 1792 cast one vote for Washington, therefore he was considered elected unanimously both times. John Adams in both years received most of the electors' second votes.

George Washington	69	George Clinton	3
John Adams	34	Samuel Huntington	2
John Jay	9	John Milton	2
Robert H. Harrison	6	James Armstrong	1
John Rutledge	6	Edward Telfair	1
John Hancock	4	Benjamin Lincoln	1

† Officially not a cabinet member until 1814.
†† Officially not a cabinet member until 1829.

2. JOHN ADAMS (*Federalist*) 1797–1801

Born October 30, 1735, at Braintree (now Quincy), Massachusetts
Son of John and Susanna Boylston Adams
Married Abigail Smith, October 25, 1764; 5 children
Lawyer
Harvard College, Cambridge, Massachusetts, graduated 1755
Member, Massachusetts legislature, 1768, revolutionary congress, 1774, and constitutional conventions, 1779 and 1820
Member First Continental Congress, 1774; Second Continental Congress, 1775
Commissioner to France, 1778
Minister to the Netherlands, 1780; to England, 1785–88
Vice President of the U.S., 1789–97
Died July 4, 1826

LANDMARK

Adams National Historic Site, the Adams home in Quincy, Massachusetts. Open to the public April 19 to November 10

VICE PRESIDENT

Thomas Jefferson (*Republican*)

CABINET

SECRETARY OF STATE: Timothy Pickering (from Washington admin.), dismissed May 12, 1800; John Marshall, May 13, 1800

SECRETARY OF THE TREASURY: Oliver Wolcott, Jr. (from Washington admin.); Samuel Dexter, January 1, 1801

SECRETARY OF WAR: James McHenry (from Washington admin.); Samuel Dexter, May 13, 1800

ATTORNEY GENERAL: Charles Lee (from Washington admin.)

POSTMASTER GENERAL: Joseph Habersham (from Washington admin.)

SECRETARY OF THE NAVY: Benjamin Stoddert, May 21, 1798

1796 ELECTORAL VOTE

John Adams	71	John Jay	5
Thomas Jefferson	68	James Iredell	3
Thomas Pinckney	59	John Henry	2
Aaron Burr	30	Samuel Johnson	2
Samuel Adams	15	George Washington	2
Oliver Ellsworth	11	Charles Cotesworth Pinckney	1
George Clinton	7		

3. THOMAS JEFFERSON (*Republican*) 1801–1809

Born April 13, 1743, at Shadwell, Virginia
Son of Peter and Jane Randolph Jefferson
Married Mrs. Martha Wayles Skelton, January 1, 1772; 6 children
Lawyer, writer, architect, planter
College of William and Mary, Williamsburg, Virginia, graduated 1762
Member, Virginia House of Burgesses, 1769–74
Member Continental Congress, 1775 and 1776. Chairman, Committee to draft the Declaration of Independence
Governor of Virginia, 1779–81
Minister plenipotentiary to France, 1784, and Minister, 1785–89
Secretary of State, 1789–93
Vice President, 1797–1801
Rector, University of Virginia, March 29, 1819
Died July 4, 1826

LANDMARK
Monticello, Jefferson home, near Charlottesville, Virginia

VICE PRESIDENT, *First Term*
Aaron Burr
Born February 6, 1756, Newark, New Jersey
Served in the Continental Army, 1775–79
Attorney general, New York State, 1789–90
Member U.S. Senate, 1791–97
Killed Alexander Hamilton in a duel, July 11, 1804
Arrested and tried for treason, but acquitted, 1807
Died September 14, 1836

VICE PRESIDENT, *Second Term*
George Clinton
Born July 26, 1739, at Little Britain, New York
Member Continental Congress, 1775–76
Brigadier general of militia, 1775–77
Governor of New York, 1777–95 and 1801–04
Died April 20, 1812

CABINET
SECRETARY OF STATE: James Madison, March 5, 1801
SECRETARY OF THE TREASURY: Samuel Dexter (from Adams admin.); Albert Gallatin, May 14, 1801
SECRETARY OF WAR: Henry Dearborn, March 5, 1801
ATTORNEY GENERAL: Levi Lincoln, March 5, 1801; John Breckenridge, August 7, 1805; Caesar Augustus Rodney, January 20, 1807
POSTMASTER GENERAL: Joseph Habersham (from Adams admin.); Gideon Granger, November 28, 1801
SECRETARY OF THE NAVY: Benjamin Stoddert (from Adams admin.); Robert Smith, July 15, 1801

1800 ELECTORAL VOTE
Thomas Jefferson (*Republican*) 73; Aaron Burr (*Republican*) 73; John Adams

(*Federalist*) 65; Charles Cotesworth Pinckney (*Federalist*) 64; John Jay (*Federalist*) 1

Since Jefferson and Burr were tied, the election was referred to the House of Representatives to elect one of the two, voting by states on the basis of one vote to each state. On the 36th ballot, February 17, 1801, 10 states voted for Jefferson, 4 for Burr, and 2 not voting. This made Jefferson President and Burr Vice President.

1804 ELECTORAL VOTE

The first election after ratification of the XII Amendment: each elector now voted for a President and a Vice President

Thomas Jefferson (*Republican*) 162; Charles Cotesworth Pinckney (*Federalist*) 14

4. JAMES MADISON (*Republican*) 1809–1817

Born March 16, 1751, at Port Conway, Virginia
Son of James and Eleanor Rose Conway Madison
Married Mrs. Dolly (or Dolley) Payne Todd, September 15, 1794
Lawyer, scholar
College of New Jersey (Princeton), Princeton, New Jersey, graduated 1771
Member Virginia legislature, 1776–77 and 1784–86
Member Continental Congress, 1780–83 and 1786–88
Member and chief recorder Constitutional Convention, 1787
Member U.S. House of Representatives, 1789–97
Secretary of State, 1801–09
Rector, University of Virginia, 1826
Died June 28, 1836

VICE PRESIDENT, *First Term*
George Clinton (died in office, April 20, 1812)

VICE PRESIDENT, *Second Term*
Elbridge Gerry (died in office)
Born July 17, 1744, at Marblehead, Massachusetts
Member Continental Congress, 1776–81 and 1782–85
Member Constitutional Convention, 1787
Member U.S. House of Representatives, 1789–93
Mission to France, 1797
Governor of Massachusetts, 1810–11. His name originated slang word "gerrymander" from his redistricting of Massachusetts to favor Republicans, while he was governor.
Died November 23, 1814

CABINET

SECRETARY OF STATE: Robert Smith, March 6, 1809; James Monroe, April 2, 1811

SECRETARY OF THE TREASURY: Albert Gallatin (from Jefferson admin.); George Washington Campbell, February 9, 1814; Alexander James Dallas, October 6, 1814; William Harris Crawford, October 22, 1816

SECRETARY OF WAR: William Eustis, March 7, 1809; John Armstrong, January 13, 1813; James Monroe, September 27, 1814; Alexander James Dallas, ad interim, March 14, 1815; William Harris Crawford, August 1, 1815

ATTORNEY GENERAL: Caesar Augustus Rodney (from Jefferson admin.); William Pinkney, December 11, 1811; Richard Rush, February 10, 1814

POSTMASTER GENERAL: Gideon Granger (from Jefferson admin.); Return Jonathan Meigs, Jr., March 17, 1814

SECRETARY OF THE NAVY: Robert Smith (from Jefferson admin.); Paul Hamilton, March 7, 1809; William Jones, January 12, 1813; Benjamin Williams Crowninshield, December 19, 1814

1808 ELECTORAL VOTE
James Madison (*Republican*) 122; Charles Cotesworth Pinckney (*Federalist*) 47; George Clinton (*Republican*) 6

1812 ELECTORAL VOTE
James Madison (*Republican*) 128; De Witt Clinton (*Federalist*) 89

5. JAMES MONROE (*Republican*) 1817–1825

Born April 28, 1758, Westmoreland Co., Virginia
Son of Spence and Elizabeth Jones Monroe
Married Elizabeth Kortright, February 16, 1786; 3 children
Lawyer, soldier
College of William and Mary, Williamsburg. Did not graduate
Served in Continental Army, 1775–78. Promoted to major
Military commissioner of Virginia with rank of lieutenant colonel, 1780
Member Virginia House of Delegates, 1782
Member Continental Congress, 1783–86
Member Virginia Assembly, 1786 and 1810
Member U.S. Senate, 1790–94
Minister to France, 1794–96
Governor of Virginia, 1799–1803 and 1811
Envoy Extraordinary and minister plenipotentiary to France, 1803, and to England
the same year
Mission to Spain, 1804–05
Mission to England, 1806, to negotiate a treaty
Secretary of State, 1811–17
Secretary of War, 1814
Regent, University of Virginia, 1826
Died July 4, 1831

LANDMARKS
Monroe's estate, Ash Lawn, near Charlottesville, Virginia
Monroe's Law Office, Fredericksburg, Virginia

VICE PRESIDENT, *First and Second Terms*
Daniel D. Tompkins
Born June 21, 1774 at Fox Meadows (Scarsdale), New York
Lawyer
Columbia College, graduated 1795
Member New York State Assembly, 1803
Governor of New York, 1807–17
Died June 11, 1825

CABINET
SECRETARY OF STATE: John Quincy Adams, March 5, 1817

SECRETARY OF THE TREASURY: William Harris Crawford (from Madison admin.)

SECRETARY OF WAR: George Graham (acting), March 4, 1817; John Caldwell Calhoun, October 8, 1817

ATTORNEY GENERAL: Richard Rush (from Madison admin.); William Wirt, November 13, 1817

POSTMASTER GENERAL: Return Jonathan Meigs (from Madison admin.); John McLean, July 1, 1823

SECRETARY OF THE NAVY: Benjamin Williams Crowninshield (from Madison admin.); Smith Thompson, November 9, 1818; Samuel Lewis Southard, September 16, 1823

1816 ELECTORAL VOTE

James Monroe (*Republican*) 183; Rufus King (*Federalist*) 34

1820 ELECTORAL VOTE

James Monroe (*Republican*) 231; John Quincy Adams (*Federalist*) 1

6. JOHN QUINCY ADAMS (*Republican*) 1825–1829

Born July 11, 1767, at Braintree (Quincy), Massachusetts
Son of John and Abigail Smith Adams
Married Louisa Catherine Johnson, July 26, 1797; 4 children
Lawyer
Secretary to Minister to Russia Francis Dana, 1781
Harvard College, Cambridge, Massachusetts, graduated 1788
Minister to the Netherlands, 1794
Sent to Sweden, 1798, to negotiate a commercial treaty
Member Massachusetts Senate, 1802
Member U.S. Senate, 1803–08
Minister to Russia, 1809–14
A commissioner to negotiate Treaty of Ghent ending the War of 1812 with England, 1814
Minister to England, 1815–17
Secretary of State, 1817–25
Member U.S. House of Representatives, 1831–48
Died February 23, 1848

LANDMARK: (*See under John Adams*)

VICE PRESIDENT
John Caldwell Calhoun
Born March 18, 1782, Abbeville District, South Carolina
Yale College, New Haven, Connecticut, graduated 1804
Member U.S. House of Representatives, 1811–17
Secretary of War, 1817–25
Vice President, 1825–29 and 1829–32
Member U.S. Senate, 1832–43 and 1845–50
Secretary of State, 1844–45
Died March 31, 1850

CABINET
SECRETARY OF STATE: Henry Clay, March 7, 1825
SECRETARY OF THE TREASURY: Richard Rush, March 7, 1825
SECRETARY OF WAR: James Barbour, March 7, 1825; Peter Buell Porter, March 26, 1828
ATTORNEY GENERAL: William Wirt (from Monroe admin.)
POSTMASTER GENERAL: John McLean (from Monroe admin.)
SECRETARY OF THE NAVY: Samuel Lewis Southard (from Monroe admin.)

1824 ELECTION	ELECTORAL VOTE	POPULAR VOTE
John Quincy Adams (*Republican*)	84	105,321
Andrew Jackson (*Democrat*)	99	155,872
William Harris Crawford (*Democratic-Republican*)	41	44,282
Henry Clay (*Democratic-Republican*)	37	46,587

Since no candidate had the majority of electoral votes, the election was referred to the House of Representatives, where Adams was elected, with 13 votes against 7 for Jackson and 4 for Crawford.

7. ANDREW JACKSON (*Democrat*) 1829–1837

Born March 15, 1767, at Waxhaw, South Carolina
Son of Andrew and Elizabeth Hutchinson Jackson
Married Mrs. Rachel Donelson Robards, 1791
Planter, lawyer, soldier, merchant
Solicitor, Superior Court district of Mero (west Tennessee), 1789
Judge Advocate, Davidson Regiment of militia, 1792
Delegate to Tennessee constitutional convention, 1796
Member U.S. House of Representatives, 1796–97
Member U.S. Senate, 1797–98 and 1823–25
Judge Supreme Court of Tennessee, 1798–1804
Major general, militia for western Tennessee, 1801
Commander, expedition against the Creek Indians, 1813–14
Victorious commander, defense of New Orleans, 1814–15
Commander, expedition against the Seminole Indians, 1818
Governor of Florida, 1821
Died June 8, 1845

LANDMARK
The Hermitage, Jackson home, near Nashville

VICE PRESIDENT, *First Term*
John Caldwell Calhoun

VICE PRESIDENT, *Second Term*
Martin Van Buren

CABINET

SECRETARY OF STATE: Martin Van Buren, March 6, 1829; Edward Livingston, May 24, 1831; Louis McLane, May 29, 1833; John Forsyth, June 27, 1834

SECRETARY OF THE TREASURY: Samuel Delucenna Ingham, March 6, 1829; Louis McLane, August 8, 1831; William John Duane, May 29, 1833; Roger Brooke Taney, September 23, 1833; Levi Woodbury, June 27, 1834

SECRETARY OF WAR: John Henry Eaton, March 9, 1829; Lewis Cass, August 1, 1831; Benjamin Franklin Butler, March 3, 1837

ATTORNEY GENERAL: John Macpherson Berrien, March 9, 1829; Roger Brooke Taney, July 20, 1831; Benjamin Franklin Butler, November 15, 1833

POSTMASTER GENERAL: William Taylor Barry, March 9, 1829; Amos Kendall, May 1, 1835

SECRETARY OF THE NAVY: John Branch, March 9, 1829; Levi Woodbury, May 23, 1831; Mahlon Dickerson, June 30, 1834

1828 ELECTION	ELECTORAL VOTE	POPULAR VOTE
Andrew Jackson (*Democrat*)	178	647,231
John Quincy Adams (*Whig*)	83	509,097

1832 ELECTION	ELECTORAL VOTE	POPULAR VOTE
Andrew Jackson (*Democrat*)	219	687,502
Henry Clay (*Whig*)	49	530,189
John Floyd (*Independent Democratic*)	11	
William Wirt (*Anti-Masonic*)	7 ·	

8. MARTIN VAN BUREN *(Democrat)* 1837–1841

Born December 5, 1782, at Kinderhook, New York
Son of Abraham and Mary Hoes Van Buren
Married Hannah Hoes, February 21, 1807; 4 children
Member New York Senate, 1813–20
Attorney general, New York State, 1815–19
Member U.S. Senate, 1821–28
Governor of New York, January 1, 1829–March 12, 1829
Secretary of State, 1829–31
Vice President, 1833–37
Nominee of Free Soil party for the presidency, 1848
Died July 24, 1862

VICE PRESIDENT

Richard Mentor Johnson
Born October 17, 1780, at Floyd's Station, Kentucky
Member Kentucky House of Representatives, 1804–07; 1819; 1841–42
Member U.S. House of Representatives, 1807–19 and 1829–37
Colonel Kentucky Volunteers in the War of 1812
Member U.S. Senate, 1819–29
Died November 19, 1850

CABINET

SECRETARY OF STATE: John Forsyth (from Jackson admin.)

SECRETARY OF THE TREASURY: Levi Woodbury (from Jackson admin.)

SECRETARY OF WAR: Joel Roberts Poinsett, March 7, 1837

ATTORNEY GENERAL: Benjamin Franklin Butler (from Jackson admin.); Felix Grundy, September 1, 1838; Henry Dilworth Gilpin, January 11, 1840

POSTMASTER GENERAL: Amos Kendall (from Jackson admin.); John Milton Niles, May 25, 1840

SECRETARY OF THE NAVY: Mahlon Dickerson (from Jackson admin.); James Kirke Paulding, July 1, 1838

1836 ELECTION	ELECTORAL VOTE	POPULAR VOTE
Martin Van Buren *(Democrat)*	170	762,678
William Henry Harrison *(Whig)*	73	548,007
Hugh Lawson White *(Whig)*	26	
Daniel Webster *(Whig)*	14	
Willie Person Mangum *(Whig)*	11	

In the vote for Vice President no candidate had a majority. The vote: Richard Mentor Johnson *(Democrat)* 147; Francis Granger *(Whig)* 77; John Tyler *(Whig)* 47; William Smith *(Whig)* 23. Election referred to the Senate; Johnson elected, 33 to 16.

9. WILLIAM HENRY HARRISON (*Whig*) March 4–April 4, 1841

Born February 9, 1773, at Berkeley, Charles City Co., Virginia
Son of Benjamin and Elizabeth Bassett Harrison
Married Anna Tuthill Symmes, November 25, 1795; 10 children
Hampden-Sydney College, Hampden-Sydney, Virginia. Did not graduate. Studied
medicine at the University of Pennsylvania
Member U.S. Army, 1791–98, resigning with rank of captain
Secretary of the Northwest Territory, 1798–99
Member U.S. House of Representatives, 1799–1800 and 1816–19
Territorial governor of Indiana, 1801–13
Commander U.S. forces at the Battle of Tippecanoe, November 7, 1811
Major general, War of 1812, in command of the Northwest, 1813
Member U.S. Senate, 1825–28
Minister to Colombia, 1828–29
Whig nominee for President, 1836
Died April 4, 1841

LANDMARKS
Berkeley Plantation, boyhood home, Charles City, Virginia
Grouseland, Harrison home, Vincennes, Indiana
Tomb at North Bend, Ohio

VICE PRESIDENT
John Tyler

CABINET
SECRETARY OF STATE: Daniel Webster, March 5, 1841

SECRETARY OF THE TREASURY: Thomas Ewing, March 5, 1841

SECRETARY OF WAR: John Bell, March 5, 1841

ATTORNEY GENERAL: John Jordan Crittenden, March 5, 1841

POSTMASTER GENERAL: Francis Granger, March 6, 1841

SECRETARY OF THE NAVY: George Edmund Badger, March 5, 1841

1840 ELECTION	ELECTORAL VOTE	POPULAR VOTE
William Henry Harrison (*Whig*)	234	1,275,017
Martin Van Buren (*Democrat*)	60	1,128,702

10. JOHN TYLER (*Whig*) 1841 (April 6)–1845

Born March 29, 1790, Charles City Co., Virginia
Son of John and Mary Marot Armistead Tyler
Married, first, Letitia Christian, March 29, 1813; 8 children
Married, second time, Julia Gardiner, June 26, 1844; 7 children
Lawyer
College of William and Mary, Williamsburg, Virginia, graduated 1807
Member Virginia House of Delegates, 1811–16; 1823–25; 1839
Member U.S. House of Representatives, 1817–21
Governor of Virginia, 1825–27
Member U.S. Senate, 1827–36
Chancellor College of William and Mary, 1859
Member Virginia convention that voted for secession, 1861
Delegate to Confederate Congress, 1861
Died January 18, 1862

LANDMARK
Sherwood Forest, Tyler's home near Charles City, Virginia

CABINET
SECRETARY OF STATE: Daniel Webster (from Harrison admin.); Hugh Swinton Legaré (ad int.), May 9, 1843; Abel Parker Upshur, June 24, 1843; John Caldwell Calhoun, March 6, 1844

SECRETARY OF THE TREASURY: Thomas Ewing (from Harrison admin.); Walter Forward, September 13, 1841; John Canfield Spencer, March 3, 1843; George Mortimer Bibb, June 15, 1844

SECRETARY OF WAR: John Bell (from Harrison admin.); John Canfield Spencer, October 12, 1841; James Madison Porter, March 8, 1843; William Wilkins, February 15, 1844

ATTORNEY GENERAL: John Jordan Crittenden (from Harrison admin.); Hugh Swinton Legaré, September 13, 1841; John Nelson, July 1, 1843

POSTMASTER GENERAL: Francis Granger (from Harrison admin.); Charles Anderson Wickliffe, September 13, 1841

SECRETARY OF THE NAVY: George Edmund Badger (from Harrison admin.); Abel Parker Upshur, September 13, 1841; David Henshaw, July 24, 1843; Thomas Walker Gilmer, February 15, 1844; John Young Mason, March 14, 1844

11. JAMES KNOX POLK (*Democrat*) 1845–1849

Born November 2, 1795, near Little Sugar Creek, Mecklenburg Co., North Carolina
Son of Samuel and Jane Knox Polk
Married Sarah Childress, January 1, 1824
University of North Carolina, graduated 1818
Admitted to the bar at Columbia, Tennessee, 1820
Member Tennessee House of Representatives, 1823–25
Member U.S. House of Representatives, 1825–39 (Speaker, 1835 on)
Governor of Tennessee, 1839–41
Died June 15, 1849

LANDMARK
James K. Polk home, Columbia, Tennessee

VICE PRESIDENT
George Mifflin Dallas
Born July 10, 1792, Philadelphia, Pennsylvania
Princeton, graduated 1810
Solicitor of United States Bank, 1815–17
Mayor of Philadelphia, 1829
U.S. district attorney, eastern Pennsylvania district, 1829–31
Member U.S. Senate, 1831–33
Attorney general, Pennsylvania, 1833–35
Minister to Russia, 1837–39
Minister to Great Britain, 1856–61
Died December 31, 1864

CABINET
SECRETARY OF STATE: James Buchanan, March 6, 1845

SECRETARY OF THE TREASURY: Robert James Walker, March 6, 1845

SECRETARY OF WAR: William Learned Marcy, March 6, 1845

ATTORNEY GENERAL: John Young Mason, March 6, 1845; Nathan Clifford, October 17, 1846; Isaac Toucey, June 21, 1848

POSTMASTER GENERAL: Cave Johnson, March 6, 1845

SECRETARY OF THE NAVY: George Bancroft, March 10, 1845; John Young Mason, September 9, 1846

1844 ELECTION	ELECTORAL VOTE	POPULAR VOTE
James Knox Polk (*Democrat*)	170	1,337,243
Henry Clay (*Whig*)	105	1,299,068
James Gillespie Birney (*Liberty party*)		62,300

12. ZACHARY TAYLOR (*Whig*) 1849–(July 9) 1850

Born November 24, 1784, at Montebello, Orange Co., Virginia
Son of Lieutenant Colonel Richard and Sarah Dabney Strother Taylor
Married Margaret Mackall Smith, June 21, 1810; 6 children
Enlisted in the army, 1806
Commissioned first lieutenant 7th Infantry, May 3, 1808
Served in the War of 1812, the Black Hawk War in 1832, and the Seminole War, in 1837
Commander, U.S. Army on the Rio Grande in War with Mexico, 1846–47
Died in the presidency, July 9, 1850

VICE PRESIDENT
Millard Fillmore

CABINET (*all but John Clayton appointed March 8, 1849*)
SECRETARY OF STATE: John Middleton Clayton, March 7, 1849
SECRETARY OF THE TREASURY: William Morris Meredith
SECRETARY OF WAR: George Washington Crawford
ATTORNEY GENERAL: Reverdy Johnson
POSTMASTER GENERAL: Jacob Collamer
SECRETARY OF THE NAVY: William Ballard Preston
SECRETARY OF THE INTERIOR: Thomas Ewing

1848 ELECTION	ELECTORAL VOTE	POPULAR VOTE
Zachary Taylor (*Whig*)	163	1,360,101
Lewis Cass (*Democrat*)	127	1,220,544
Martin Van Buren (*Free Soil* party)		291,263

13. MILLARD FILLMORE (*Whig*) 1850 (July 10)–1853

Born January 7, 1800, in Cayuga Co., New York
Son of Nathaniel and Phoebe Millard Fillmore
Married, first, Abigail Powers, February 5, 1826; 2 children
Married, second, Mrs. Caroline Carmichael McIntosh, February 10, 1858
Began practicing law in East Aurora, New York 1823
Member New York State Assembly, 1829–31. Elected by Anti-Masons
Member U.S. House of Representatives, 1833–35 and 1837–43
Controller of New York State, 1848–49
Vice President, March 4, 1849–July 9, 1850
Candidate for presidency on "Know-Nothing" party ticket, 1856
Died March 8, 1874

CABINET

SECRETARY OF STATE: John Middleton Clayton (from Taylor admin.); Daniel Webster, July 22, 1850; Edward Everett, November 6, 1852

SECRETARY OF THE TREASURY: William Morris Meredith (from Taylor admin.); Thomas Corwin, July 23, 1850

SECRETARY OF WAR: George Washington Crawford (from Taylor admin.); Major General Winfield Scott (ad int.) July 24, 1850; Charles Magill Conrad, August 15, 1850

ATTORNEY GENERAL: Reverdy Johnson (from Taylor admin.); John Jordan Crittenden, July 22, 1850

POSTMASTER GENERAL: Jacob Collamer (from Taylor admin.); Nathan Kelsey Hall, July 23, 1850; Samuel Dickinson Hubbard, August 31, 1852

SECRETARY OF THE NAVY: William Ballard Preston (from Taylor admin.); William Alexander Graham, July 22, 1850; John Pendleton Kennedy, July 22, 1852

SECRETARY OF THE INTERIOR: Thomas Ewing (from Taylor admin.); Thomas McKean Thompson McKennan, August 15, 1850; Alexander Hugh Holmes Stuart, September 12, 1850

14. FRANKLIN PIERCE (*Democrat*) 1853–1857

Born November 23, 1804, at Hillsboro, New Hampshire
Son of General Benjamin and Anna Kendrick Pierce
Married Jane Means Appleton, November 10, 1834; 3 children
Bowdoin College, Brunswick, Maine, graduated 1824
Member New Hampshire House of Representatives, 1829–33 (Speaker 1832)
Member U.S. House of Representatives, 1833–37
Member U.S. Senate, 1837–42
Retired from politics to practice law at Concord, New Hampshire
Served in War with Mexico, 1846–47; resigned from army, 1848
President New Hampshire State Constitutional Convention in 1850
Died October 8, 1869

LANDMARK
Pierce Homestead, Hillsboro, New Hampshire. Open daily June 9 to October 12

VICE PRESIDENT
William Rufus King
Born April 7, 1786, Sampson Co., North Carolina
University of North Carolina, graduated 1803
Member U.S. House of Representatives, 1811–16
Member U.S. Senate, 1819–44 and 1848–52
Minister to France, 1844–46
Died April 18, 1853

CABINET (*all appointed March 7, 1853*)
SECRETARY OF STATE: William Learned Marcy
SECRETARY OF THE TREASURY: James Guthrie
SECRETARY OF WAR: Jefferson Davis
ATTORNEY GENERAL: Caleb Cushing
POSTMASTER GENERAL: James Campbell
SECRETARY OF THE NAVY: James Cochran Dobbin
SECRETARY OF THE INTERIOR: Robert McClelland

1856 ELECTION	ELECTORAL VOTE	POPULAR VOTE
Franklin Pierce (*Democrat*)	254	1,601,474
Winfield Scott (*Whig*)	42	1,386,578
John Parker Hale (*Free Soil party*)		155,825

15. JAMES BUCHANAN (*Democrat*) 1857–1861

Born April 23, 1791, at Cove Gap, Pennsylvania
Son of James and Elizabeth Speer Buchanan
Lawyer
Dickinson College, Carlisle, Pennsylvania, graduated 1809
Member of Pennsylvania House of Representatives, 1814–15
Member U.S. House of Representatives, 1821–31
Minister to Russia, 1832–33
Member U.S. Senate, 1834–45
Secretary of State, 1845–49
Minister to Great Britain, 1853
Died June 1, 1868

LANDMARK
Wheatland, Buchanan's home, Lancaster, Pennsylvania, a restoration. Open March 15 to November 30

VICE PRESIDENT
John Cabell Breckinridge
Born January 21, 1821, near Lexington, Kentucky
Centre College, Danville, Kentucky, graduated 1839
Member U.S. House of Representatives, 1851–55
Candidate for presidency on Southern Democratic (pro-slavery) ticket, 1860
Member U.S. Senate, March 4 to December 4, 1861
Served in Confederate Army during the Civil War
Confederate Secretary of War, 1865
Died May 17, 1875

CABINET
SECRETARY OF STATE: Lewis Cass, March 6, 1857; Jeremiah Sullivan Black, December 17, 1860
SECRETARY OF THE TREASURY: Howell Cobb, March 6, 1857; Philip Francis Thomas, December 12, 1860; John Adams Dix, January 11, 1861
SECRETARY OF WAR: John Buchanan Floyd, March 6, 1857; Joseph Holt (ad int.) January 18, 1861
ATTORNEY GENERAL: Jeremiah Sullivan Black, March 6, 1857; Edwin McMasters Stanton, December 20, 1860
POSTMASTER GENERAL: Aaron Venable Brown, March 6, 1857; Joseph Holt, March 14, 1859; Horatio King, January 1, 1861
SECRETARY OF THE NAVY: Isaac Toucey, March 6, 1857
SECRETARY OF THE INTERIOR: Jacob Thompson, March 6, 1857

1856 ELECTION	ELECTORAL VOTE	POPULAR VOTE
James Buchanan (*Democrat*)	174	1,927,995
John Frémont (*Republican*)	114	1,391,555
Millard Fillmore (*American,* or *"Know-Nothing,"* party) 8		874,534

262

16. ABRAHAM LINCOLN (*Republican*) 1861–(April 15) 1865

Born February 12, 1809, in Hardin Co., Kentucky
Son of Thomas and Nancy Hanks Lincoln
Married Mary Todd, November 4, 1842; 4 children
Lawyer
Volunteered for Black Hawk War, 1832
Unsuccessful candidate Illinois House of Representatives, 1832
Member Illinois General Assembly, 1835–36
Member U.S. House of Representatives, 1847–49
Defeated by Stephen A. Douglas, 1858, for U.S. Senate
Died April 15, 1865, the morning after he was shot by the assassin John Wilkes Booth

LANDMARKS
The reputed cabin where Lincoln was born, near Hodgenville, Kentucky
The Lincoln Home, Springfield, Illinois (8th and Jackson Sts.)
Lincoln Tomb, Oak Ridge Cemetery, Springfield
New Salem State Park, near Petersburg, Illinois, has the rebuilt village of New Salem, where Lincoln lived as a young man
William Petersen House, where Lincoln died, Washington, D.C., opposite Lincoln Museum (Ford's Theatre)

VICE PRESIDENT, *First Term*
Hannibal Hamlin
Born August 27, 1809, at Paris Hill, Maine
As a young man, edited *The Jeffersonian* weekly, at Paris, Maine
Member, Maine House of Representatives, as a Democrat, 1836–40 (Speaker three times)
Member U.S. House of Representatives, 1843–47
Member U.S. Senate, 1848–56
Governor of Maine, January 8 to February 20, 1857, resigning to serve in U.S. Senate as a Republican, March 1857–January 1861
Collector of the Port of Boston, 1865–66
Member U.S. Senate, 1869–81
Minister to Spain, 1881–83
Died July 4, 1891

VICE PRESIDENT, *Second Term*
Andrew Johnson

CABINET
SECRETARY OF STATE: William Henry Seward, March 5, 1861
SECRETARY OF THE TREASURY: Salmon Portland Chase, March 5, 1861; William Pitt Fessenden, July 1, 1864; Hugh McCulloch, March 7, 1865
SECRETARY OF WAR: Simon Cameron, March 5, 1861; Edwin McMasters Stanton, January 15, 1862
ATTORNEY GENERAL: Edward Bates, March 5, 1861; James Speed, December 2, 1864
POSTMASTER GENERAL: Montgomery Blair, March 5, 1861; William Dennison, July 24, 1864

SECRETARY OF THE NAVY: Gideon Welles, March 5, 1861

SECRETARY OF THE INTERIOR: Caleb Blood Smith, March, 1861; John-Palmer Usher, January 1, 1863

1860 ELECTION	ELECTORAL VOTE	POPULAR VOTE
Abraham Lincoln (*Republican*)	180	1,866,352
John C. Breckinridge (*Southern Democrat*)	72	845,763
Stephen A. Douglas (*Northern Democrat*)	12	1,375,157
John Bell (*Constitution Union Party*)	39	589,581

1864 ELECTION		
(*Eleven Confederate States not voting*)		
Abraham Lincoln (*Republican*)	212	2,216,067
George B. McClellan (*Democrat*)	21	1,808,725

17. ANDREW JOHNSON (*Democrat*) 1865 (April 15)–1869

Born December 29, 1808, at Raleigh, North Carolina
Son of Jacob and Mary McDonough Johnson
Married Eliza McCardle, May 5, 1827; 5 children
Tailor in early life, as apprentice in North Carolina, on his own in Greeneville, Tennessee
Alderman of Greeneville, 1828–29
Mayor of Greeneville, 1830–33
Member Tennessee legislature, 1835–37 and 1839–41
Elected to Tennessee Senate, 1841
Member U.S. House of Representatives, 1843–53
Governor of Tennessee, 1853–57
Member U.S. Senate, 1857–62 and March 4 to July 31, 1875
Military governor of Tennessee, 1862–65
Died July 31, 1875

LANDMARKS:
Johnson homestead and tailor shop, and his tomb in the Andrew Johnson National Cemetery, Greeneville

CABINET

SECRETARY OF STATE: William Henry Seward (from Lincoln admin.)

SECRETARY OF THE TREASURY: Hugh McCulloch (from Lincoln admin.)

SECRETARY OF WAR: Edwin McMasters Stanton (from Lincoln admin.); Ulysses Simpson Grant (ad int.) August 12, 1867–January 13, 1868; Stanton reinstated January 13, 1868; John McAllister Schofield, May 28, 1868

ATTORNEY GENERAL: James Speed (from Lincoln admin.); Henry Stanbery, July 23, 1866; William Maxwell Evarts, July 15, 1868

POSTMASTER GENERAL: William Dennison (from Lincoln admin.); Alexander Williams Randall, July 17, 1866

SECRETARY OF THE NAVY: Gideon Welles (from Lincoln admin.)

SECRETARY OF THE INTERIOR: James Palmer Usher (from Lincoln admin.); James Harlan, May 15, 1865; Orville Hickman Browning, July 27, 1866

18. ULYSSES SIMPSON GRANT (*Republican*) 1869–1877

Born April 27, 1822, at Point Pleasant, Ohio
Christened Hiram Ulysses, but Grant did not bother to correct error made when appointed to West Point
Son of Jesse Root and Hannah Simpson Grant
Married Julia Dent, August 22, 1848; 4 children
U.S. Military Academy, graduated 1843
Served in the Mexican War, 1846–47. Resigned from army, 1853
Commissioned colonel of the 21st Illinois Volunteers, 1861; assigned to commands, southeast Missouri and western Kentucky
Promoted major general and placed in command of west Tennessee, 1862
Commander, Mississippi campaign, 1863
Assumed command U.S. armies as lieutenant general, March 1864
In command of the campaign in Virginia, 1864–65, ending with Lee's surrender at Appomattox, April 9, 1865
Received rank of General of the Army from Congress, 1866
Secretary of War (ad int.) August 12, 1867–January 13, 1868
Defeated for Republican nomination for President, 1880
Began publishing his best-selling *Memoirs*, 1885
Died July 23, 1885

LANDMARKS:
Ulysses S. Grant Home, East Galena, Illinois
Grant Birthplace, Pt. Pleasant, Ohio. Open April–Oct., except Mondays
Grant's Tomb, New York City (Riverside Drive). Open to the public daily

VICE PRESIDENT, *First Term*
Schuyler Colfax
Born March 23, 1823, New York, New York
Moved to South Bend, Indiana and published influential St. Joseph Valley *Register* from 1845
Member U.S. House of Representatives, 1855–69 (Speaker from 1863)
Charged with condoning the Crédit Mobilier fraud, 1873, he retired from politics
Died January 13, 1885

VICE PRESIDENT, *Second Term*
Henry Wilson (name assumed on reaching manhood)
Born February 16, 1812, Farmington, New Hampshire. Named Jeremiah Jones Colbaith
Farm apprentice until 21, learned shoemaker's trade in Natick, Massachusetts, and used his earnings to go to school. Built up a shoe factory and prospered
Became strong abolitionist. Published Boston *Republican* as voice of the Free Soil party
Member Massachusetts House of Representatives, 1841–42, and Massachusetts Senate, 1844–46 and 1850–52
President of the Free Soil National Convention, 1852
Member U.S. Senate, 1855–73. Leader for Reconstruction
Died November 22, 1875

CABINET

SECRETARY OF STATE: Elihu Benjamin Washburne, March 5, 1869; Hamilton Fish, March 11, 1869

SECRETARY OF THE TREASURY: George Sewall Boutwell, March 11, 1869; William Adams Richardson, March 17, 1873; Benjamin Helm Bristow, June 2, 1874; Lot Myrick Morrill, June 21, 1876

SECRETARY OF WAR: John Aaron Rawlins, March 11, 1869; William Tecumseh Sherman, September 9, 1869; William Worth Belknap, October 25, 1869; Alphonso Taft, March 8, 1876; James Donald Cameron, May 22, 1876

ATTORNEY GENERAL: Ebenezer Rockwood Hoar, March 5, 1869; Amos Tappan Akerman, June 23, 1870; George Henry Williams, January 10, 1872; Edward Pierrepont, May 15, 1875; Alphonso Taft, May 22, 1876

POSTMASTER GENERAL: John Angel James Creswell, March 5, 1869; James William Marshall, July 3, 1874; Marshall Jewell, August 24, 1874; James Noble Tyner, July 12, 1876

SECRETARY OF THE NAVY: Adolph Edward Borie, March 5, 1869; George Maxwell Robeson, June 25, 1869

SECRETARY OF THE INTERIOR: Jacob Dolson Cox, March 5, 1869; Columbus Delano, November 1, 1870; Zachariah Chandler, October 19, 1875

1868 ELECTION	ELECTORAL VOTE	POPULAR VOTE
Ulysses S. Grant (*Republican*)	214	3,015,071
Horatio Seymour (*Democrat*)	80	2,709,615

1872 ELECTION		
Ulysses S. Grant (*Republican*)	286	3,597,070
Horace Greeley (*Democrat-Liberal Republican*)		2,834,079

Since Greeley died, November 29, 1872, his electoral votes were split: Thomas Andrew Hendricks, 42; Benpamin Gratz Brown, 18; Charles Jones Jenkins, 2; David Davis, 1; 3 votes for Greeley were not counted. Among minor parties, votes were recorded for: Charles O'Conor (Straight-Out Democrat, opposed to Liberal Republicans) 29,489; James Black (Prohibition) 5,608.

19. RUTHERFORD BIRCHARD HAYES (*Republican*) 1877–1881

Born October 4, 1822, at Delaware, Ohio
Son of Rutherford and Sophia Birchard Hayes
Married Lucy Ware Webb, December 30, 1852; 8 children
Kenyon College, Gambier, Ohio, graduated 1842. Harvard Law School, 1845
Served all during Civil War. Breveted major general
Member U.S. House of Representatives, 1865–67
Governor of Ohio, 1868 and 1876–77
Died January 17, 1893

LANDMARK
Hayes Library and Museum, Fremont, Ohio, on grounds of Spiegel Grove, the Hayes estate

VICE PRESIDENT
William Almon Wheeler
Born June 30, 1819, Malone, New York
U.S. district attorney, Franklin County, New York 1847–49
Member New York State Assembly, 1850–51; New York State Senate, 1858–59
Member U.S. House of Representatives, 1861–63 and 1869–77
Died June 4, 1887

CABINET
SECRETARY OF STATE: William Maxwell Evarts, March 12, 1877

SECRETARY OF THE TREASURY: John Sherman, March 8, 1877

SECRETARY OF WAR: George Washington McCrary, March 12, 1877; Alexander Ramsey, December 10, 1879

ATTORNEY GENERAL: Charles Devens, March 12, 1877

POSTMASTER GENERAL: David McKendree Key, March 12, 1877; Horace Maynard, June 2, 1880

SECRETARY OF THE NAVY: Richard Wigginton Thompson, March 12, 1877; Nathan Goff, Jr., January 6, 1881

SECRETARY OF THE INTERIOR: Carl Schurz, March 12, 1877

1876 ELECTION	ELECTORAL VOTE	POPULAR VOTE
Rutherford B. Hayes (*Republican*)	185	4,033,950
Samuel J. Tilden (*Democrat*)	184	4,284,757
Peter Cooper (*Greenback*)		81,737
Green Clay Smith (*Prohibition*)		9,522
James B. Walker (*American*)		2,636

Twenty electoral votes were disputed in this election. One was of an ineligible elector in Oregon, the rest in three Southern states (Florida, South Carolina, and Louisiana) where enforced "carpet-bag" Republican rule still existed under the Reconstruction laws. An electoral commission of 15 men, 5 each from the Supreme Court, the Senate, and the House of Representatives, voted along party lines. The decision, 8 to 7, gave the 20 disputed votes to Hayes.

20. JAMES ABRAM GARFIELD (*Republican*) March 4, 1881–September 19, 1881

Born November 19, 1831, at Orange, Ohio
Son of Abram and Eliza Ballou Garfield
Married Lucretia Rudolph, November 11, 1858; 7 children
Teacher, lawyer
William College, Williamstown, Massachusetts, graduated 1856
President, Hiram College, Hiram, Ohio, 1857–61
Member Ohio State Senate, 1859
Served in the Civil War. Promoted to major general
Elected to U.S. House of Representatives, 1862. Resigned from the army to take his seat and served, 1863–80
Shot by a disappointed office seeker, Charles J. Guiteau, July 2, 1881
Died September 19, 1881

LANDMARK
The Garfield home, Lawnfield, Mentor, Ohio. Closed Mondays

VICE PRESIDENT
Chester Alan Arthur

CABINET (*all appointed March 5, 1881*)
SECRETARY OF STATE: James Gillespie Blaine
SECRETARY OF THE TREASURY: William Windom
SECRETARY OF WAR: Robert Todd Lincoln
ATTORNEY GENERAL: Wayne MacVeagh
POSTMASTER GENERAL: Thomas Lemuel James
SECRETARY OF THE NAVY: William Henry Hunt
SECRETARY OF THE INTERIOR: Samuel Jordan Kirkwood

1880 ELECTION	ELECTORAL VOTE	POPULAR VOTE
James A. Garfield (*Republican*)	214	4,449,053
Winfield S. Hancock (*Democrat*)	155	4,442,030
James B. Weaver (*Greenback Labor*)		308,578
Neal Dow (*Prohibition*)		10,305
John W. Phelps (*American*)		700

21. CHESTER ALAN ARTHUR (*Republican*) 1881 (September 20)–1885

Born October 5, 1830, at Fairfield, Vermont
Son of William and Malvina Stone Arthur
Married Ellen Lewis Herndon, October 25, 1859; 3 children
Union College, Schenectady, New York, graduated 1848
Studied law in New York City, 1848–53
Judge advocate of militia, New York State, 1857
Quartermaster general of New York State and chief engineer of militia on governor's staff, 1862
Collector of the Port of New York, 1871–78. Removed by order of President Hayes
Republican candidate for President, 1884
Died November 18, 1886

CABINET

SECRETARY OF STATE: James Gillespie Blaine (from Garfield admin.); Frederick Theodore Frelinghuysen, December 12, 1881

SECRETARY OF THE TREASURY: William Windom (from Garfield admin.); Charles James Folger, October 27, 1881; Walter Quintin Gresham, September 24, 1884; Hugh McCulloch, October 28, 1884

SECRETARY OF WAR: Robert Todd Lincoln (from Garfield admin.)

ATTORNEY GENERAL: Wayne MacVeagh (from Garfield admin.); Benjamin Harris Brewster, December 19, 1881

POSTMASTER GENERAL: Thomas Lemuel James (from Garfield admin.); Timothy Otis Howe, December 20, 1881; Walter Quintin Gresham, April 3, 1883; Frank Hatton, September 25, 1884

SECRETARY OF THE NAVY: William Henry Hunt (from Garfield admin.); William Eaton Chandler, April 12, 1882

SECRETARY OF THE INTERIOR: Samuel Jordan Kirkwood (from Garfield admin.); Henry Moore Teller, April 6, 1882

22. & 24. GROVER CLEVELAND (*Democrat*) 1885–1889 and 1893–1897

Born March 18, 1837, at Caldwell, New Jersey
Full name Stephen Grover Cleveland
Son of Richard Falley and Anne Neal Cleveland
Married Frances Folsom, June 2, 1886; 5 children
Studied law and worked as clerk in Buffalo law firm, 1855–59
Assistant district attorney Erie Co., New York, 1863–65
Sheriff Erie Co., 1871–73
Mayor of Buffalo, 1882
Governor of New York, 1883–85
Defeated as Democratic candidate for the presidency, 1888
Trustee, Princeton University, 1901
Died June 24, 1908

LANDMARK
Cleveland's birthplace, Caldwell, New Jersey. Closed Mondays

VICE PRESIDENT, *First Term*
Thomas Andrews Hendricks
Born September 7, 1819, near Zanesville, Ohio
South Hanover College, Hanover, Indiana, graduated 1841
Member U.S. House of Representatives, 1851–55
Commissioner, General Land Office, 1855–59
Member U.S. Senate, 1863–69
Elected governor of Indiana, 1872
Defeated as Democratic candidate for the vice-presidency, on the Tilden ticket, 1876
Died November 25, 1885

VICE PRESIDENT, *Second Term*
Adlai Ewing Stevenson
Born October 23, 1835, Christian Co., Kentucky
Master in chancery, 1860–64
Member U.S. House of Representatives, 1875–77 and 1879–81
First assistant postmaster general, 1885–89
Appointed by McKinley to visit Europe and try to secure adoption of a bimetallic currency standard
Died June 14, 1914

CABINET, *First Term*
SECRETARY OF STATE: Thomas Francis Bayard, March 6, 1885
SECRETARY OF THE TREASURY: Daniel Manning, March 6, 1885; Charles Stebbins Fairchild, April 1, 1887
SECRETARY OF WAR: William Crowninshield Endicott, March 6, 1885
ATTORNEY GENERAL: Augustus Hill Garland, March 6, 1885
POSTMASTER GENERAL: William Freeman Vilas, March 6, 1885; Donald McDonald Dickinson, January 16, 1888
SECRETARY OF THE NAVY: William Collins Whitney, March 6, 1885
SECRETARY OF THE INTERIOR: Lucius Quintus Cincinnatus Lamar, March 6, 1885; William Freeman Vilas, January 16, 1888
SECRETARY OF AGRICULTURE: Norman Jay Colman, February 13, 1889

CABINET, *Second Term*

SECRETARY OF STATE: Walter Quintin Gresham, March 6, 1893; Richard Olney, June 8, 1895

SECRETARY OF THE TREASURY: John Griffin Carlisle, March 6, 1893

SECRETARY OF WAR: Daniel Scott Lamont, March 6, 1893

ATTORNEY GENERAL: Richard Olney, March 6, 1893; Judson Harmon, June 8, 1895

POSTMASTER GENERAL: Wilson Shannon Bissell, March 6, 1893; William Lyne Wilson, March 1, 1895

SECRETARY OF THE NAVY: Hilary Abner Herbert, March 6, 1893

SECRETARY OF THE INTERIOR: Hoke Smith, March 6, 1893; David Rowland Francis, September 1, 1896

SECRETARY OF AGRICULTURE: Julius Sterling Morton, March 6, 1893

1884 ELECTION	ELECTORAL VOTE	POPULAR VOTE
Grover Cleveland (*Democrat*)	219	4, 911,017
James G. Blaine (*Republican*)	182	4,848,334
Benjamin F. Butler (*Greenback and Anti-Monopoly*)		175,370
John P. St. John (*Prohibition*)		150,369
1892 ELECTION		
Grover Cleveland (*Democrat*)	277	5,554,414
Benjamin Harrison (*Republican*)	145	5,190,802
James B. Weaver (*People's*)	22	1,027,329
John Bidwell (*Prohibition*)		264,138
Simon Wing (*Socialist Labor*)		21,512

23. BENJAMIN HARRISON (*Republican*) 1889–1893

Born August 20, 1833, at North Bend, Ohio
Son of John Scott and Elizabeth Ramsey Irwin Harrison, and grandson of President William Henry Harrison
Married Caroline Lavinia Scott, October 20, 1853 (2 children); second wife, Mrs. Mary Scott Lord Dimmick, April 6, 1896 (1 child)
Lawyer
Miami University, Oxford, Ohio, graduated 1852
Reporter, Indiana Supreme Court, 1860 and 1864–68
Served in the Civil War 1862–65. Breveted brigadier general
Member U.S. Senate, 1881–87
Defeated as Republican candidate for presidency in 1892
Died March 13, 1901

LANDMARK
Benjamin Harrison's home, Indianapolis

VICE PRESIDENT
Levi Parsons Morton
Born May 16, 1824, at Shoreham, Vermont
Became a merchant in Hanover, New Hampshire, 1843; Boston banker, 1850
Founded banking firm of Levi P. Morton & Co., New York City, 1863, which helped float the government's Civil War loan
Member U.S. House of Representatives, 1879–81
Minister to France, 1881–85
Governor of New York, 1895–97
Died May 16, 1920

CABINET
SECRETARY OF STATE: James Gillespie Blaine, March 5, 1889; John Watson Foster, June 29, 1892

SECRETARY OF THE TREASURY: William Windom, March 5, 1889; Charles Foster, February 24, 1891

SECRETARY OF WAR: Redfield Proctor, March 5, 1889; Stephen Benton Elkins, December 22, 1891

ATTORNEY GENERAL: William Henry Harrison Miller, March 5, 1889

POSTMASTER GENERAL: John Wanamaker, March 5, 1889

SECRETARY OF THE NAVY: Benjamin Franklin Tracy, March 5, 1889

SECRETARY OF THE INTERIOR: John Willock Noble, March 5, 1889

SECRETARY OF AGRICULTURE: Jeremiah McLain Rusk, March 5, 1889

1888 ELECTION	ELECTORAL VOTE	POPULAR VOTE
Benjamin Harrison (*Republican*)	233	5,444,337
Grover Cleveland (*Democrat*)	168	5,540,050
Clinton B. Fisk (*Prohibition*)		249,506
Alson J. Streeter (*Union Labor*)		146,935
Robert H. Cowdrey (*United Labor*)		2,818
James L. Curtis (*American*)		1,612

25. WILLIAM McKINLEY (*Republican*) 1897–(September 14) 1901

Born January 29, 1843, at Niles, Ohio
Son of William and Nancy Campbell Allison McKinley
Married Ida Saxton, January 25, 1871; 2 children
Served in Civil War, with 23rd Ohio Volunteers
Practiced law at Canton, Ohio, from 1867 (Prosecuting attorney, Stark Co.)
Member U.S. House of Representatives, 1877–83, and 1885–91
Governor of Ohio, 1892–96
Shot by an anarchist, at Buffalo, New York, September 6, 1901
Died September 14, 1901

LANDMARKS
McKinley Memorial, Westlawn Cemetery, Canton
Memorial and museum, Niles

VICE PRESIDENT, *First Term*
Garret Augustus Hobart
Born June 3, 1844, at Long Branch, New Jersey
Rutgers College, New Brunswick, New Jersey, graduated 1863
Prosecuting attorney of Passaic Co., New Jersey
Member New Jersey Assembly, 1872–76 (Speaker, 1874)
Member New Jersey Senate, 1876–82 (its president, 1881–82)
Died November 21, 1899

VICE PRESIDENT, *Second Term*
Theodore Roosevelt

CABINET
SECRETARY OF STATE: John Sherman, March 5, 1897; William Rufus Day, April 26, 1898; John Hay, September 20, 1898

SECRETARY OF THE TREASURY: Lyman Judson Gage, March 5, 1897

SECRETARY OF WAR: Russell Alexander Alger, March 5, 1897; Elihu Root, August 1, 1899

ATTORNEY GENERAL: Joseph McKenna, March 5, 1897; John William Griggs, January 25, 1898; Philander Chase Knox, April 5, 1901

POSTMASTER GENERAL: James Albert Gary, March 5, 1897; Charles Emory Smith, April 21, 1898

SECRETARY OF THE NAVY: John Davis Long, March 5, 1897

SECRETARY OF THE INTERIOR: Cornelius Newton Bliss, March 5, 1897; Ethan Allen Hitchcock, December 21, 1898

SECRETARY OF AGRICULTURE: James Wilson, March 5, 1897

1896 ELECTION	ELECTORAL VOTE	POPULAR VOTE
William McKinley (*Republican*)	271	7,035,638
William Jennings Bryan (*Democrat*)	176	6,467,946
William Jennings Bryan (*Populist*)		222,583
John McA. Palmer (*National Democrat*)		133,148
Joshua Levering (*Prohibition*)		132,007
Charles H. Matchett (*Socialist Labor*)		36,274
Charles E. Bentley (*National*)		13,969

1900 ELECTION	ELECTORAL VOTE	POPULAR VOTE
William McKinley (*Republican*)	292	7,219,530
William Jennings Bryan (*Democrat*)	155	6,358,071
John G. Woolley (*Prohibition*)		208,914
Eugene V. Debs (*Social-Democrat*)		87,814
Wharton Barker (*People's, Anti-Fusionist*)		50,373
Joseph F. Malloney (*Socialist Labor*)		39,739
Seth H. Ellis (*Union Reform*)		5,700
Jonah Fitz R. Leonard (*United Christian*)		5,500

26. THEODORE ROOSEVELT (*Republican*) 1901 (September 14)–1909

Born October 27, 1858, in New York City
Son of Theodore and Martha Bulloch Roosevelt
Married Alice Hathaway Lee, October 27, 1880 (1 child); second wife, Edith Kermit Carow, December 2, 1886 (5 children)
Harvard College, Cambridge, Massachusetts, graduated 1880
Member New York State Assembly, 1882–84
Member U.S. Civil Service Commission, 1889–95
Police Commissioner, New York City, 1895–97
Assistant secretary of the Navy, 1897–98
Helped organize First Volunteer U.S. Cavalry for service, War with Spain. Commanded regiment in Cuba at siege of Santiago, 1898
Governor of New York, 1899–1901
Candidate for President on Progressive ("Bull Moose") ticket, 1912; defeated
As a writer, he produced a long list of books and magazine articles. Best-known books: *Autobiography, The Winning of the West, History of New York, African Game Trails*
Died January 6, 1919

LANDMARKS
Theodore Roosevelt Museum, New York City. Closed Mondays
Sagamore Hill, Oyster Bay, Long Island. Closed Tuesdays
The Theodore Roosevelt Monument, Mt. Roosevelt, near Deadwood, South Dakota
Theodore Roosevelt National Memorial Park, western North Dakota

VICE PRESIDENT
Charles Warren Fairbanks
Born May 11, 1852, near Unionville Centre, Ohio
Ohio Wesleyan University, Delaware, Ohio, graduated 1872
Member U.S. Senate, 1897–1905
Member Joint U.S.–British High Commission to settle Fur Seal and other controversies with Canada, McKinley administration
Candidate for Vice President on the Republican ticket, 1916
Died June 4, 1918

CABINET
SECRETARY OF STATE: John Hay (from McKinley admin.); Elihu Root, July 7, 1905; Robert Bacon, January 27, 1909

SECRETARY OF THE TREASURY: Lyman Judson Gage (from McKinley admin.); Leslie Mortier Shaw, January 9, 1902; George Bruce Cortelyou, January 15, 1907

SECRETARY OF WAR: Elihu Root (from the McKinley admin.); William Howard Taft, January 11, 1904; Luke Edward Wright, June 29, 1908

ATTORNEY GENERAL: Philander Chase Knox (from McKinley admin.); William Henry Moody, July 1, 1904; Charles Joseph Bonaparte, December 12, 1906

POSTMASTER GENERAL: Charles Emory Smith (from McKinley admin.); Henry Clay Payne, January 9, 1902; Robert John Wynne, October 10, 1904; George Bruce Cortelyou, March 6, 1905; George von Lengerke Meyer, January 15, 1907

SECRETARY OF THE NAVY: John Davis Long (from McKinley admin.); William Henry Moody, April 29, 1902; Paul Morton, July 1, 1904; Charles Joseph Bonaparte, July 1, 1905; Victor Howard Metcalf, December 12, 1906; Truman Handy Newberry, December 1, 1908

SECRETARY OF THE INTERIOR: Ethan Allen Hitchcock (from the McKinley admin.) ; James Rudolph Garfield, January 15, 1907

SECRETARY OF AGRICULTURE: James Wilson (from the McKinley admin.)

SECRETARY OF COMMERCE AND LABOR: George Bruce Cortelyou, February 16, 1903; Victor Howard Metcalf, July 1, 1904; Oscar Solomon Straus, December 12, 1906

1904 ELECTION	ELECTORAL VOTE	POPULAR VOTE
Theodore Roosevelt (*Republican*)	336	7,628,834
Alton Brooks Parker (*Democrat*)	140	5,084,491
Eugene V. Debs (*Socialist*)		402,283
Silas Comfort Swallow (*Prohibition*)		258,536
Thomas E. Watson (*People's*)		117,183
Charles H. Corregan (*Socialist Labor*)		31,249
Austin Holcomb (*Continental*)		1,000

27. WILLIAM HOWARD TAFT (*Republican*) 1909–1913

Born September 15, 1857, at Cincinnati, Ohio
Son of Alphonso and Louise Maria Torrey Taft
Married Helen Herron, June 19, 1886; 3 children
Yale College, New Haven, Connecticut, graduated 1878
Cincinnati Law School, graduated 1880
Judge, Superior Court of Cincinnati, 1887–90
U.S. Solicitor General, 1890–92
Judge, U.S. Circut Court, 1892–1900
President of Philippines Commission, 1900–01
Governor General, Philippine Islands, 1901–04
Secretary of War, 1904–08
Professor of law, Yale University, New Haven, Connecticut, 1913–21
Chief Justice of the U.S. Supreme Court, 1921–30
Died March 8, 1930

VICE PRESIDENT

James Schoolcraft Sherman
Born October 24, 1855, at New Hartford, New York
Hamilton College, Clinton, New York, graduated 1878
Mayor of Utica, 1884–85
Member U.S. House of Representatives, 1887–91 and 1893–1909
Renominated in 1912, he died 3 days before the election
Died October 30, 1912

CABINET

SECRETARY OF STATE: Philander Chase Knox, March 5, 1909

SECRETARY OF THE TREASURY: Franklin MacVeagh, March 5, 1909

SECRETARY OF WAR: Jacob McGavock Dickinson, March 5, 1909; Henry Lewis Stimson, May 16, 1911

ATTORNEY GENERAL: George Woodward Wickersham, March 5, 1909

POSTMASTER GENERAL: Frank Harris Hitchcock, March 5, 1909

SECRETARY OF THE NAVY: George von Lengerke Meyer, March 5, 1909

SECRETARY OF THE INTERIOR: Richard Achilles Ballinger, March 5, 1909; Walter Lowrie Fisher, March 7, 1911

SECRETARY OF AGRICULTURE: James Wilson (from Roosevelt admin.)

SECRETARY OF COMMERCE AND LABOR: Charles Nagel, March 5, 1909

1908 ELECTION	ELECTORAL VOTE	POPULAR VOTE
William H. Taft (*Republican*)	321	7,679,006
William Jennings Bryan	162	6,409,106
Eugene V. Debs (*Socialist*)		420,793
Eugene W. Chafin (*Prohibition*)		253,840
Thomas L. Hisgen (*Independence*)		82,872
Thomas E. Watkins (*People's*)		29,100
August Gillhaus (*Socialist Labor*)		14,021

28. WOODROW WILSON (*Democrat*) 1913–1921

Born December 28, 1856, at Staunton, Virginia
Full name Thomas Woodrow Wilson
Son of Joseph Ruggles and Jessie Janet Woodrow Wilson
Married Ellen Louise Axson, June 24, 1885 (3 children); second wife, Mrs. Edith
Bolling Galt, December 18, 1915
Princeton College, Princeton, New Jersey, graduated 1879
University of Virginia Law School; did not graduate
Admitted to the bar, 1882, and practiced law at Atlanta, 1882–83
Ph.D. Johns Hopkins University, 1886
Taught history and government, Bryn Mawr, 1885; Wesleyan, Middletown, Connecticut, 1888–90; Princeton, 1890–1902
President, Princeton University, 1902–10
Governor of New Jersey, 1911–13
Collapsed, September 26, 1919, while on presidential speaking tour
Awarded Nobel Peace Prize, December 10, 1920
Died February 3, 1924

LANDMARK
The Manse, Wilson's birthplace, Staunton, Virginia

VICE PRESIDENT
Thomas Riley Marshall
Born March 14, 1854, at North Manchester, Indiana
Wabash College, Crawfordsville, Indiana, graduated 1873
Governor of Indiana, 1909–13; sponsored reform laws
Popular as a wit and after-dinner speaker during vice-presidency
Died June 1, 1925

CABINET
SECRETARY OF STATE: William Jennings Bryan, March 5, 1913; Robert Lansing, June 9, 1915; Bainbridge Colby, March 22, 1920

SECRETARY OF THE TREASURY: William Gibbs McAdoo, March 5, 1913; Carter Glass, December 6, 1918; David Franklin Houston, January 31, 1920

SECRETARY OF WAR: Lindley Miller Garrison, March 5, 1913; Newton Diehl Baker, March 7, 1916

ATTORNEY GENERAL: James Clark McReynolds, March 5, 1913; Thomas Watt Gregory, August 29, 1914; Alexander Mitchell Palmer, March 5, 1919

POSTMASTER GENERAL: Albert Sidney Burleson, March 5, 1913

SECRETARY OF THE NAVY: Josephus Daniels, March 5, 1913

SECRETARY OF THE INTERIOR: Franklin Knight Lane, March 5, 1913; John Barton Payne, February 28, 1920

SECRETARY OF AGRICULTURE: David Franklin Houston, March 5, 1913; Edwin Thomas Meredith, January 31, 1920

SECRETARY OF COMMERCE: William Cox Redfield, March 5, 1913; Joshua Willis Alexander, December 11, 1919

SECRETARY OF LABOR: William Bauchop Wilson, March 5, 1913

279

1912 ELECTION	ELECTORAL VOTE	POPULAR VOTE
Woodrow Wilson (*Democrat*)	435	6,286,214
Theodore Roosevelt (*Progressive*)	88	4,216,020
William H. Taft (*Republican*)	8	3,483,922
Eugene V. Debs (*Socialist*)		900,672
Eugene W. Chafin (*Prohibition*)		206,275
Arthur E. Reimer (*Socialist Labor*)		28,750
1916 ELECTION		
Woodrow Wilson (*Democrat*)	277	9,129,606
Charles Evans Hughes (*Republican*)	254	8,538,221
Allan L. Benson (*Socialist*)		585,113
James F. Hanly (*Prohibition*)		220,506
Arthur E. Reimer (*Socialist Labor*)		13,403

29. WARREN GAMALIEL HARDING (*Republican*) 1921–(August 2) 1923

Born November 2, 1865, at Corsica, Ohio
Son of George Tryon and Phoebe Elizabeth Dickerson Harding
Married Mrs. Florence Kling De Wolfe
Ohio Central College, Iberia, Ohio, attended 1879–82
Bought Marion, Ohio, *Star*, 1884, with two partners. He developed this into a successful newspaper
Member Ohio Senate, 1899–1903
Lieutenant-governor of Ohio, 1904–05
Member U.S. Senate, 1915–21
Died in office, August 2, 1923

LANDMARKS

The Harding Memorial; the Harding Home & Museum, Marion

VICE PRESIDENT

Calvin Coolidge

CABINET

SECRETARY OF STATE: Charles Evans Hughes, March 4, 1921

SECRETARY OF THE TREASURY: Andrew William Mellon, March 4, 1921

SECRETARY OF WAR: John Wingate Weeks, March 5, 1921

ATTORNEY GENERAL: Harry Micajah Daugherty, March 5, 1921

POSTMASTER GENERAL: William Harrison Hays, March 5, 1921; Hubert Work, March 4, 1922; Harry Stewart New, February 27, 1923

SECRETARY OF THE NAVY: Edwin Denby, March 5, 1921

SECRETARY OF THE INTERIOR: Albert Bacon Fall, March 5, 1921; Hubert Work, February 27, 1923

SECRETARY OF AGRICULTURE: Henry Cantwell Wallace, March 5, 1921

SECRETARY OF COMMERCE: Herbert Clark Hoover, March 5, 1921

SECRETARY OF LABOR: James John Davis, March 5, 1921

1920 ELECTION	ELECTORAL VOTE	POPULAR VOTE
Warren G. Harding (*Republican*)	404	16,152,200
James M. Cox (*Democrat*)	127	9,147,353
Eugene V. Debs (*Socialist*)		919,799
Parley P. Christensen (*Farmer Labor*)		265,411
Aaron S. Watkins (*Prohibition*)		189,408
William W. Cox (*Socialist Labor*)		31,715
Robert C. Macauley (*Single Tax*)		5,837

30. CALVIN COOLIDGE (*Republican*) 1923 (August 3)–1929

Born July 4, 1872, at Plymouth, Vermont
Full name John Calvin Coolidge
Son of John Calvin and Victoria Josephine Moor Coolidge
Married Grace Anna Goodhue, October 4, 1905; 2 children
Amherst College, Amherst, Massachusetts, graduated 1895
Practiced law in Northampton, Massachusetts, from 1897
Member City Council, Northampton, 1899–1901
Clerk of the court, Hampshire Co., 1903–04
Member Massachusetts House of Representatives, 1907–08
Mayor of Northampton, 1910–11
Member Massachusetts Senate, 1912–15 (its president, 1914–15)
Lieutenant-governor of Massachusetts, 1916–18
Governor of Massachusetts, 1919–20
Died January 5, 1933

LANDMARK
Coolidge Homestead, Plymouth Notch, Vermont. Open May–October

VICE PRESIDENT
Charles Gates Dawes
Born August 27, 1865, at Marietta, Ohio
U.S. Comptroller of the Currency, 1898–1901
Engaged in banking in Chicago, Illinois, 1902–25
Chief of procurement, American Expeditionary Force, World War I
Director of the U.S. Bureau of the Budget, 1921
President of the German reparations commission, which presented the "Dawes Plan" for international payments, 1923
Ambassador to the Court of St. James's, 1929–32
Delegate to London Naval Conference, 1930
President of Reconstruction Finance Corp., 1932
Died April 23, 1951

CABINET
SECRETARY OF STATE: Charles Evans Hughes (from Harding admin.); Frank Billings Kellogg, February 16, 1925

SECRETARY OF THE TREASURY: Andrew William Mellon (from Harding admin.)

SECRETARY OF WAR: John Wingate Weeks (from Harding admin.); Dwight Filley Davis, October 13, 1925

ATTORNEY GENERAL: Harry Micajah Daugherty (from Harding admin.); Harlan Fiske Stone, April 7, 1924; John Garibaldi Sargent, March 17, 1925

POSTMASTER GENERAL: Harry Stewart New (from Harding admin.)

SECRETARY OF THE NAVY: Edwin Denby (from Harding admin.); Curtis Dwight Wilbur, March 18, 1924

SECRETARY OF THE INTERIOR: Hubert Work (from Harding admin.); Roy Owen West, July 25, 1928

SECRETARY OF AGRICULTURE: Henry Cantwell Wallace (from Harding admin.); Howard Mason Gore, October 26, 1924; William Marion Jardine, February 18, 1925

SECRETARY OF COMMERCE: Herbert Clark Hoover (from Harding admin.); William Fairfield Whiting, August 21, 1928

SECRETARY OF LABOR: James John Davis (from Harding admin.)

1924 ELECTION	ELECTORAL VOTE	POPULAR VOTE
Calvin Coolidge (*Republican*)	382	15,725,016
John W. Davis (*Democrat*)	136	8,385,586
Robert M. LaFollette (*Progressive*)	13	4,822,856
Herman P. Faris (*Prohibition*)		57,520
Frank T. Johns (*Socialist Labor*)		36,428
William Z. Foster (*Communist*)		36,386
Gilbert O. Nations (*American*)		23,967
William J. Wallace (*Commonwealth Land*)		1,582

31. HERBERT CLARK HOOVER (*Republican*) 1929–1933

Born August 10, 1874, at West Branch, Iowa
Son of Jesse Clark and Hulda Randall Minthorn Hoover
Married Lou Henry, February 10, 1899; 2 children
Mining engineer
Stanford University, Stanford, California, graduated 1895
Managed Australian mines for Bewick, Moreing & Co., London, 1897–99
Chief engineer, Chinese Imperial Bureau of Mines, 1899
Consultant and mgr. on mining and industrial projects, 1900–14
Chairman Commission for Relief in Belgium, 1915–18
U.S. Food Administrator, 1917–19
Chairman Supreme Economic Conference, in Paris, 1919
Secretary of Commerce, 1921–28
Chairman Commission on Organization of the Executive Branch of the Government, 1947–49 and 1953–55

LANDMARK
Hoover birthplace, West Branch, Iowa

VICE PRESIDENT
Charles Curtis
Born January 25, 1860, Topeka, Kansas
Prosecuting attorney, Shawnee Co., Kansas, 1885–89
Member U.S. House of Representatives, 1893–1907
Member U.S. Senate, 1907–13 and 1915–29
Died February 8, 1936

CABINET
SECRETARY OF STATE: Henry Lewis Stimson, March 4, 1929

SECRETARY OF THE TREASURY: Andrew William Mellon (from Coolidge admin.);
Ogden Livingston Mills, February 10, 1932

SECRETARY OF WAR: James William Good, March 5, 1929; Patrick Jay Hurley,
December 9, 1929

ATTORNEY GENERAL: William De Witt Mitchell, March 5, 1929

POSTMASTER GENERAL: Walter Folger Brown, March 5, 1929

SECRETARY OF THE NAVY: Charles Francis Adams, March 5, 1929

SECRETARY OF THE INTERIOR: Ray Lyman Wilbur, March 5, 1929

SECRETARY OF AGRICULTURE: Arthur Mastick Hyde, March 5, 1929

SECRETARY OF COMMERCE: Robert Patterson Lamont, March 5, 1929; Roy Dikeman
Chapin, August 8, 1932

SECRETARY OF LABOR: James John Davis (from Coolidge admin.); William Nuckles
Doak, December 8, 1930

1928 ELECTION	ELECTORAL VOTE	POPULAR VOTE
Herbert C. Hoover (*Republican*)	444	21,392,190
Alfred E. Smith (*Democrat*)	87	15,016,443
Norman Thomas (*Socialist*)		267,420
William Z. Foster (*Communist*)		48,770
Verne L. Reynolds (*Socialist Labor*)		21,603
William F. Varney (*Prohibition*)		20,106
Frank E. Webb (*Farmer Labor*)		6,390

32. FRANKLIN DELANO ROOSEVELT (*Democrat*) 1933–(April 12) 1945

Born January 30, 1882, at Hyde Park, New York
Son of James and Sara Delano Roosevelt
Married Anna Eleanor Roosevelt, March 17, 1905; 6 children
Harvard College, Cambridge, Massachusetts, graduated 1903
Columbia University law school, did not graduate
Practiced law in New York City, 1907–10
Member New York State Senate, 1911–13
Assistant secretary of the Navy, 1913–20
Defeated as candidate for Vice President on Cox ticket, 1920
Suffered attack of poliomyelitis that left him crippled, 1921
Governor of New York, 1929–33
Died in presidency, April 12, 1945

LANDMARKS

Roosevelt home and library, Hyde Park, New York. Home open daily except Mondays
"The Little White House" at Warm Springs Foundation, Warm Springs, Georgia, where Roosevelt died

VICE PRESIDENT, *First and Second Terms*

John Nance Garner
Born November 22, 1868, near Detroit, Red River Co., Texas
Judge, Uvalde Co., 1893–96
Member Texas House of Representatives, 1898–1902
Member U.S. House of Representatives, 1903–33 (Speaker, 1931)

VICE PRESIDENT, *Third Term*

Henry Agard Wallace
Born October 7, 1888, Adair Co., Iowa
Iowa State College, Ames, Iowa, graduated 1910
Breeder of high-yielding variety of corn
Editor of *Wallace's Farmer*, 1924–29
Secretary of Agriculture, 1933–40
Secretary of Commerce, 1945–46
Candidate for President on Progressive party ticket, 1948

VICE PRESIDENT, *Fourth Term*

Harry S. Truman

CABINET

SECRETARY OF STATE: Cordell Hull, March 4, 1933; Edward Riley Stettinius, November 30, 1944

SECRETARY OF THE TREASURY: William Hartman Woodin, March 4, 1933; Henry Morgenthau, Jr., January 1, 1934

SECRETARY OF WAR: George Henry Dern, March 4, 1933; Harry Hines Woodring, September 25, 1936; Henry Lewis Stimson, July 10, 1940

ATTORNEY GENERAL: Homer Stille Cummings, March 4, 1933; Frank Murphy, January 2, 1939; Robert Houghwout Jackson, January 18, 1940; Francis Biddle, September 5, 1941

POSTMASTER GENERAL: James Aloysius Farley, March 4, 1933; Frank Comerford Walker, September 10, 1940

SECRETARY OF THE NAVY: Claude Augustus Swanson, March 4, 1933; Charles Edison (acting) August 5, 1939; Frank Knox, July 10, 1940; James Vincent Forrestal, May 18, 1944

SECRETARY OF THE INTERIOR: Harold Le Claire Ickes, March 4, 1933

SECRETARY OF AGRICULTURE: Henry Agard Wallace, March 4, 1933; Claude Raymond Wickard, August 27, 1940

SECRETARY OF COMMERCE: Daniel Calhoun Roper, March 4, 1933; Harry Lloyd Hopkins, December 24, 1938; Jesse Holman Jones, September 16, 1940; Henry Agard Wallace, March 1, 1945

SECRETARY OF LABOR: Frances Perkins, March 4, 1933

1932 ELECTION	ELECTORAL VOTE	POPULAR VOTE
Franklin D. Roosevelt (*Democrat*)	472	22,821,857
Herbert C. Hoover (*Republican*)	59	15,761,841
Norman Thomas (*Socialist*)		881,951
William Z. Foster (*Communist*)		102,785
William D. Upshaw (*Prohibition*)		81,869
William H. Harvey (*Liberty*)		53,425
Verne L. Reynolds (*Socialist Labor*)		33,276
Jacob S. Coxey (*Farmer Labor*)		7,309

1936 ELECTION		
Franklin D. Roosevelt (*Democrat*)	523	27,751,597
Alfred M. Landon (*Republican*)	8	16,679,583
William Lemke (*Union*)		892,793
Norman Thomas (*Socialist*)		187,720
Earl R. Browder (*Communist*)		80,159
David L. Colvin (*Prohibition*)		37,847
John W. Aiken (*Socialist Labor*)		12,777

1940 ELECTION		
Franklin D. Roosevelt (*Democrat*)	449	27,243,466
Wendell Willkie (*Republican*)	82	22,304,755
Norman Thomas (*Socialist*)		99,557
Roger W. Babson (*Prohibition*)		57,812
Earl R. Browder (*Communist*)		46,251
John W. Aiken (*Socialist Labor*)		9,458

1944 ELECTION		
Franklin D. Roosevelt (*Democrat*)	432	25,602,505
Thomas E. Dewey (*Republican*)	99	22,006,278
Norman Thomas (*Socialist*)		80,518
Claude A. Watson (*Prohibition*)		74,758
Edward A. Teichert (*Socialist Labor*)		45,336

33. HARRY S. TRUMAN (*Democrat*) 1945 (April 12)–1953

Born May 8, 1884, at Lamar, Missouri
Son of John Anderson and Martha Ellen Young Truman
Married Elizabeth Virginia (Bess) Wallace, June 28, 1919; 1 child
Farmer, businessman
Graduated from high school, 1901; worked as clerk, Kansas City
Managed mother's family farm, 1906–17. During this time, he was a member National Guard, a Mason (founder of the local lodge); also helped to secure a Farm Bureau in Jackson Co. and organize farm clubs for boys and girls
Served in France, World War I, in Field Artillery
Elected Judge for eastern Jackson Co., Missouri for two years, 1922
Elected in 1926 and 1930 as presiding judge of the county court
Member U.S. Senate, 1935–45. Chairman Special Senate Committee to Investigate the National Defense Program, 1941–44
Died December 26, 1972

LANDMARK
Truman Library and Museum, Independence, Missouri

VICE PRESIDENT
Alben William Barkley
Born November 24, 1877, near Lowes, Graves Co., Kentucky
Marvin College, Clinton, Kentucky, graduated 1897
Prosecuting attorney, 1905–09; county judge, 1909–13, McCracken Co., Kentucky
Member U.S. House of Representatives, 1913–27
Member U.S. Senate, 1927–49 (Majority leader, 1937–48)
Member U.S. Senate, 1955–56
Died April 30, 1956

CABINET
SECRETARY OF STATE: Edward Riley Stettinius (from Roosevelt admin.); James Francis Byrnes, July 2, 1945; George Catlett Marshall, January 8, 1947; Dean Gooderham Acheson, January 19, 1949

SECRETARY OF THE TREASURY: Henry Morgenthau, Jr. (from Roosevelt admin.); Frederick Moore Vinson, July 18, 1945; John Wesley Snyder, June 12, 1946

SECRETARY OF DEFENSE: James Vincent Forrestal, July 26, 1947; Louis Arthur Johnson, March 23, 1949; George Catlett Marshall, September 21, 1950; Robert Abercrombie Lovett, September 17, 1951

SECRETARY OF WAR: Henry Lewis Stimson (from Roosevelt admin.); Robert Porter Patterson, September 26, 1945; Kenneth Claiborne Royall, July 21, 1947 (served until new Department of Defense organized)

ATTORNEY GENERAL: Francis Biddle (from Roosevelt admin.); Thomas Campbell Clark, June 15, 1945; James Howard McGrath, August 19, 1949

POSTMASTER GENERAL: Frank Comerford Walker (from Roosevelt admin.); Robert Emmet Hannegan, May 8, 1945; Jesse Monroe Donaldson, December 16, 1947

SECRETARY OF THE NAVY: James Vincent Forrestal (from Roosevelt admin.; served until new Department of Defense organized)

SECRETARY OF INTERIOR: Harold Le Claire Ickes (from Roosevelt admin.); Julius Albert Krug, March 6, 1946; Oscar Littleton Chapman, December 1, 1949

SECRETARY OF AGRICULTURE: Claude Raymond Wickard (from Roosevelt admin.) ; Clinton Presba Anderson, June 2, 1945; Charles Franklin Brannan, May 29, 1948

SECRETARY OF COMMERCE: Henry Agard Wallace (from Roosevelt admin.) ; William Averell Harriman, September 28, 1946; Charles Sawyer, May 6, 1948

SECRETARY OF LABOR: Frances Perkins (from Roosevelt admin.) ; Lewis Baxter Schwellenbach, June 1, 1945; Maurice Joseph Tobin, August 13, 1948

1948 ELECTION	ELECTORAL VOTE	POPULAR VOTE
Harry S. Truman (*Democrat*)	303	24,105,812
Thomas E. Dewey (*Republican*)	189	21,970,065
James Strom Thurmond (*States' Rights Democrat*)	39	1,169,021
Henry A. Wallace (*Progressive*)		1,156,103
Norman Thomas (*Socialist*)		139,009
Claude A. Watson (*Prohibition*)		103,216
Edward A. Teichert (*Socialist Labor*)		29,061
Farrell Dobbs (*Socialist Workers*)		13,613

34. DWIGHT DAVID EISENHOWER (*Republican*) 1953–1961

Born October 14, 1890, at Denison, Texas
Son of David Jacob and Ida Elizabeth Stover Eisenhower
Married Mamie Geneva Doud, July 1, 1916; 2 children
United States Military Academy, West Point, New York, graduated 1915
Stationed at various army posts, 1915–25
Command and General Staff School, Ft. Leavenworth, Kansas, 1925–26, graduating first in his class
War Department, Washington, 1929–33
With General MacArthur in the Philippines, 1935–39
Chief of Staff, Third Army, 1941
Attached to General Staff, War Dept., in charge of Operations Division, 1942
Appointed Commanding General European Theatre of Operations, June 25, 1942, with temporary rank of Lieutenant General
Supreme Commander of Allied Expeditionary Force, December 24, 1943; directed landings in Normandy beginning June 6, 1944; given temporary rank of General of The Armies, December 1944
Accepted surrender of German Army at Rheims, May 7, 1945
Chief of Staff, U.S. Army 1945–48
President of Columbia University, 1948–50
Supreme Allied Commander under the North Atlantic Treaty Organization (NATO), Paris, 1950–52
Died March 28, 1969

LANDMARK
Eisenhower boyhood home, Museum and Library, Abilene, Kansas

VICE PRESIDENT
Richard Milhous Nixon

CABINET
SECRETARY OF STATE: John Foster Dulles, January 21, 1953; Christian Archibald Herter, April 17, 1959

SECRETARY OF THE TREASURY: George Magoffin Humphrey, January 21, 1953; Robert Bernard Anderson, July 29, 1957

SECRETARY OF DEFENSE: Charles Erwin Wilson, January 28, 1953; Neil Hosler McElroy, October 9, 1957

ATTORNEY GENERAL: Herbert Brownell, Jr., January 21, 1953; William Pierce Rogers, January 27, 1958

POSTMASTER GENERAL: Arthur Ellsworth Summerfield, January 21, 1953

SECRETARY OF THE INTERIOR: Douglas McKay, January 21, 1953; Frederick Andrew Seaton, June 8, 1956

SECRETARY OF AGRICULTURE: Ezra Taft Benson, January 21, 1953

SECRETARY OF COMMERCE: Sinclair Weeks, January 21, 1953; Lewis Lichtenstein Strauss, November 13, 1958

SECRETARY OF LABOR: Martin Patrick Durkin, January 21, 1953; James Paul Mitchell, October 8, 1953

SECRETARY OF HEALTH, EDUCATION AND WELFARE: Oveta Culp Hobby, April 11, 1953; Marion Bayard Folsom, August 1, 1955; Arthur Sherwood Flemming, August 1, 1958

1952 ELECTION	ELECTORAL VOTE	POPULAR VOTE
Dwight D. Eisenhower (*Republican*)	442	33,936,252
Adlai E. Stevenson (*Democrat*)	89	27,314,992
Vincent W. Hallinan (*Progressive*)		135,007
Stuart Hamblen (*Prohibition*)		72,769
Eric Hass (*Socialist Labor*)		30,376
Darlington Hoopes (*Socialist*)		19,685
Farrell Dobbs (*Socialist Workers*)		10,306

1956 ELECTION		
Dwight D. Eisenhower (*Republican*)	457	35,585,316
Adlai E. Stevenson (*Democrat*)	73	26,031,322
(*One Democratic vote cast for Walter B. Jones of Alabama*)		
Thomas C. Andrews (*States' Rights*)		109,961
Dr. Enoch A. Holtwick (*Prohibition*)		41,937
Eric Hass (*Socialist Labor*)		41,159
William E. Jenner (*Texas Constitution Party*)		30,999
Farrell Dobbs (*Socialist Workers*)		5,549
Henry Krajewski (*American Third Party*)		1,829
Darlington Hoopes (*Socialist*)		846

35. JOHN FITZGERALD KENNEDY (*Democrat*) 1961–(November 22) 1963

Born May 29, 1917, in Brookline, Massachusetts
Son of Joseph Patrick and Rose Fitzgerald Kennedy
Married Jacqueline Bouvier, September 12, 1953; 3 children
Harvard College, Cambridge, Massachusetts, graduated 1940
Published *Why England Slept*, 1940
Served in the Navy, World War II, as commander of a PT boat
Member U.S. House of Representatives, 1947–53
Member U.S. Senate, 1953–61
Published his book *Profiles in Courage*, 1956, for which he won the Pulitzer Prize
Assassinated in Dallas, Texas, November 22, 1963

MEMORIAL PLANNED
The John F. Kennedy Library, Boston, Massachusetts

VICE PRESIDENT
Lyndon Baines Johnson

CABINET
SECRETARY OF STATE: Dean Rusk, January 21, 1961

SECRETARY OF THE TREASURY: Clarence Douglas Dillon, January 21, 1961

SECRETARY OF DEFENSE: Robert Strange McNamara, January 21, 1961

ATTORNEY GENERAL: Robert Francis Kennedy, January 21, 1961

POSTMASTER GENERAL: James Edward Day, January 21, 1961; John A. Gronouski, September 9, 1963

SECRETARY OF THE INTERIOR: Stewart Lee Udall, January 21, 1961

SECRETARY OF AGRICULTURE: Orville Lothrop Freeman, January 21, 1961

SECRETARY OF COMMERCE: Luther Hartwell Hodges, January 21, 1961

SECRETARY OF LABOR: Arthur Joseph Goldberg, January 21, 1961; William Willard Wirtz, August 30, 1962

SECRETARY OF HEALTH, EDUCATION AND WELFARE: Abraham Alexander Ribicoff, January 21, 1961; Anthony Joseph Celebrezze, July 14, 1962

1960 ELECTION	ELECTORAL VOTE	POPULAR VOTE
John F. Kennedy (*Democrat*)	303	34,227,096
Richard M. Nixon (*Republican*)	219	34,108,546
(*Senator Harry F. Byrd received 15 electoral votes, 14 from protesting Democratic, 1 from a Republican elector*)		
Eric Hass (*Socialist Labor*)		46,560
Rutherford B. Decker (*Prohibition*)		46,203
Orval E. Faubus (*National States' Rights*)		44,977
Farrell Dobbs (*Socialist Workers*)		39,541

36. LYNDON BAINES JOHNSON (*Democrat*) November 22, 1963–1969

Born August 27, 1908, near Stonewall, Texas
Son of Samuel Ealy and Rebekah Baines Johnson
Married Claudia Alta (Lady Bird) Taylor, November 17, 1934; 2 children
Southwest State Teachers College, San Marcos, Texas, graduated 1930
Taught history and speech at Sam Houston High School, Houston, Texas, 1930–31
Secretary to Congressman Richard M. Kleberg, 1931–35
Texas State administrator for the National Youth Administration, 1935–37
Member U.S. House of Representatives 1937–49
Served in World War II one year, until recalled by the President. Lieutenant Commander in the Naval Reserve.
Member U.S. Senate, 1949–61 (Majority leader 1955–61)
Vice President, 1961–November 22, 1963
Died January 22, 1973

VICE PRESIDENT
Hubert Horatio Humphrey
Born May 27, 1911, at Wallace, South Dakota
Denver College of Pharmacy, graduated 1933
University of Minnesota, graduated 1939, *magna cum laude*
Louisiana State University, M.A., 1940
Instructor University of Minnesota, 1940–41
Superintendent WPA Workers Education Service, State Director for War Production Training, Assistant State Director of the War Manpower Commission (in sequence), 1941–43
Ran for Mayor of Minneapolis, 1943. Defeated
Taught political science. Macalester College, St. Paul, Minnesota, 1944
Elected Mayor of Minneapolis, 1945 (two terms)
United State Senator, 1949–65
Defeated by Richard M. Nixon in 1968 presidential election

CABINET (*all from Kennedy administration*)
SECRETARY OF STATE: Dean Rusk
SECRETARY OF THE TREASURY: Clarence Douglas Dillon
SECRETARY OF DEFENSE: Robert Strange McNamara
ATTORNEY GENERAL: Robert Francis Kennedy
POSTMASTER GENERAL: John A. Gronouski
SECRETARY OF THE INTERIOR: Stewart Lee Udall
SECRETARY OF AGRICULTURE: Orville Lothrop Freeman
SECRETARY OF COMMERCE: Luther Hartwell Hodges
SECRETARY OF LABOR: William Willard Wirtz
SECRETARY OF HEALTH, EDUCATION AND WELFARE: Anthony Joseph Celebrezze

37. RICHARD MILHOUS NIXON (*Republican*) 1969–August 9, 1974

Born January 9, 1913, at Yorba Linda, California
Son of Francis A. and Hannah Milhous Nixon
Married Thelma Ryan, June 21, 1940; 2 children
Whittier College, Whittier, California, graduated 1934
Duke University Law School, graduated 1937
Law practice, Whittier, 1937–42
Office of Price Administration, January–August, 1942
U.S. Navy, August 1942 to end of war. Discharged as lieutenant commander
U.S. House of Representatives, 1947–51
U.S. Senate, 1951–53
Vice President, 1953–61
Private law practice, 1961–69
Resigned August 9, 1974

VICE PRESIDENT, *First*
Spiro Theodore Agnew
Born November 9, 1918, at Baltimore, Maryland
Son of Theodore Spiro and Margaret Akers Agnew
Attended Johns Hopkins. Graduated University of Baltimore Law School, 1947
County Executive, Baltimore Co., 1962–66
Governor of Maryland, 1967–69
Charged with taking kickbacks from contractors while governor of Maryland and with income tax evasion, he pled no contest to the tax evasion and resigned, October 10, 1973, from the vice-presidency

VICE PRESIDENT, *Second*
Gerald Rudolph Ford. After nomination by the President and confirmation by Congress, he took office December 6, 1973

CABINET
SECRETARY OF STATE: William P. Rogers, January 22, 1969–September 3, 1973; Henry A. Kissinger, September 22, 1973

SECRETARY OF THE TREASURY: David M. Kennedy, January 22, 1969–February 1, 1971; John B. Connally, Jr., February 11, 1971; George P. Shultz, June 12, 1972; William E. Simon, April 17, 1974

SECRETARY OF DEFENSE: Melvin R. Laird, January 22, 1969; Elliot L. Richardson, February 2, 1973; James R. Schlesinger, July 2, 1973

ATTORNEY GENERAL: John N. Mitchell, January 22, 1969; Richard G. Kleindienst, June 12, 1972–April 30, 1973; Elliot L. Richardson, May 25, 1973–October 20, 1973; William B. Saxbe, January 4, 1974

SECRETARY OF THE INTERIOR: Walter J. Hickel, January 24, 1969–November 25, 1970; Rogers C.B. Morton, January 29, 1971

POSTMASTER GENERAL: Winton M. Blount, January 22, 1969–July 1, 1971. (The post office then became an independent agency.)

SECRETARY OF AGRICULTURE: Clifford M. Hardin, January 22, 1969–November 11, 1971; Earl L. Butz, December 2, 1971

SECRETARY OF COMMERCE: Maurice H. Stans, January 22, 1969; Peter G. Peterson, February 21, 1972; Frederick B. Dent, February 2, 1973

SECRETARY OF LABOR: George P. Shultz, January 22, 1969–July 1, 1970; James D. Hodgson, July 2, 1970; Peter J. Brennan, February 2, 1973

SECRETARY OF HEALTH, EDUCATION AND WELFARE: Robert H. Finch, January 22, 1969–June 23, 1970; Elliot L. Richardson, June 24, 1970; Casper W. Weinberger, February 12, 1973

SECRETARY OF HOUSING AND URBAN DEVELOPMENT: George W. Romney, January 22, 1969; James T. Lynn, February 2, 1973

SECRETARY OF TRANSPORTATION: John A. Volpe, January 22, 1969; Claude S. Brinegar, February 2, 1973

1968 ELECTION	ELECTORAL VOTE	POPULAR VOTE
Richard M. Nixon (*Republican*)	301	30,721,046
Hubert H. Humphrey (*Democrat*)	191	30,587,809
George C. Wallace (*Southern*)	46	9,585,028
1972 ELECTION		
Richard M. Nixon (*Republican*)	520	47,169,911
George McGovern (*Democrat*)	17	29,170,383
John G. Schmitz (*American Independent Party*)		1,099,482

38. GERALD RUDOLPH FORD (*Republican*) 1974–

Born July 14, 1913, in Omaha, Nebraska

Son of Leslie and Dorothy Gardner King. Given name: Leslie King, Jr. On divorce and second marriage of mother, adopted by and given the name of his stepfather

Married Elizabeth Bloomer Warren (born Elizabeth Bloomer), October 18, 1948; 4 children

University of Michigan, graduated 1935 (in football, named Most Valuable Player 1934 team)

Yale University Law School, graduated 1941

Served in U.S. Navy 1942–46, demobilized as Lieutenant Commander

Law practice, Grand Rapids, Michigan, 1946–48

Elected to House of Representatives from 5th Michigan district, 1948

House Minority Leader 8 years

Nominated as Vice President by Nixon on resignation of Vice President Agnew, October 13, 1973; confirmed in Senate 92–3, in the House 387–35; sworn into office December 6, 1973

VICE PRESIDENT

Nelson Aldrich Rockefeller

Born July 8, 1908, at Bar Harbor, Maine

Son of John Davison, Jr., and Abby Greene Aldrich Rockefeller

Graduated Dartmouth College, 1930

Director Rockefeller Center Inc., 1931–58

Co-ordinator of Inter-American Affairs, 1940–44

Assistant Secretary of State, 1944–45

Under-Secretary of Health, Education and Welfare, 1953–54

Governor of New York, 1958–73

CABINET

SECRETARY OF STATE: Henry A. Kissinger (from Nixon admin.)

SECRETARY OF THE TREASURY: William E. Simon (from Nixon admin.)

SECRETARY OF DEFENSE: James R. Schlesinger (from Nixon admin.); Donald H. Rumsfeld, November 2, 1975

ATTORNEY GENERAL: William B. Saxbe (from Nixon admin.); Edward H. Levi, January 15, 1975

SECRETARY OF THE INTERIOR: Rogers C.B. Morton (from Nixon admin.); Stanley K. Hathaway, April 4, 1975; Thomas S. Kleppe, October 9, 1975

SECRETARY OF AGRICULTURE: Earl L. Butz (from Nixon admin.)

SECRETARY OF COMMERCE: Frederick B. Dent (from Nixon admin.); Rogers C.B. Morton, May 1, 1975; Elliot L. Richardson, February 2, 1976

SECRETARY OF LABOR: Peter J. Brennan (from Nixon admin.); John T. Dunlop, February 9, 1975–January 13, 1976; William J. Usery, January 19, 1976

SECRETARY OF HEALTH, EDUCATION AND WELFARE: Casper W. Weinberger (from Nixon admin.); David Mathews, June 27, 1975

SECRETARY OF HOUSING AND URBAN DEVELOPMENT: James T. Lynn (from Nixon admin.); Carla A. Hills, February 14, 1975

SECRETARY OF TRANSPORTATION: Claude S. Brinegar (from Nixon admin.); William T. Coleman, Jr., January 15, 1975

SELECTED BIBLIOGRAPHY

———◆———

THE PRESIDENCY:

AGAR, HERBET. *People's Choice.* Georgia: Dunwoody Press, 1968

BINKLEY, WILFRED E. *American Political Parties, Their Natural History.* New York: Alfred A. Knopf, 1943, 1958

BOOTH, EDWARD T. *Country Life in America as Lived by Ten Presidents of the United States.* New York: Alfred A. Knopf, 1947

COHN, DAVID L. *The Fabulous Democrats: A History of the Democratic Party in Text and Pictures.* Foreword by The Hon. Sam Rayburn. New York: G. P. Putnam's Sons, 1956

DURANT, JOHN and ALICE. *Pictorial History of American Presidents.* New York: A. S. Barnes & Co., 1955

FAULKNER, HAROLD U. *Politics, Reform and Expansion 1890–1900.* New York: Harper and Brothers, 1959

FISHER, LOUIS. *Presidential Spending Power.* Princeton, N.J.: Princeton University Press, 1975

FURMAN, BESS. *White House Profile.* Indianapolis: The Bobbs-Merrill Co., 1951

HALBERSTAM, DAVID. *The Best and the Brightest.* New York: Random House, 1969

HARRIMAN, W. AVERELL and ELIE ABEL. *Special Envoy.* New York: Random House, 1975

HOFSTADTER, RICHARD. *The American Political Tradition and the Men Who Made It.* New York: Alfred A. Knopf, 1951. Also *The Age of Reform; from Bryan to F.D.R.* New York: Alfred A. Knopf, 1956

HOOVER, IRWIN H. (IKE). *Forty-two Years in the White House.* Boston: Houghton Mifflin Co., 1934

HYMAN, SIDNEY. *The American President.* New York: Harper and Brothers, 1954

JENSEN, AMY (LA FOLLETTE). *The White House and Its Thirty-Three Families.* New York: McGraw-Hill Book Co., 1962

JONES, CRANSTON. *Homes of the American Presidents.* (With photos.) New York: McGraw-Hill Book Co., 1962

KANE, JOSEPH N. *Facts About the Presidents.* New York: The H. W. Wilson Co., 1959

KENT, FRANK R. *The Democratic Party, a History.* New York: The Century Co., 1928

MAYER, GEORGE H. *The Republican Party, 1854–1964.* New York: Oxford University Press, 1964

NEUSTADT, RICHARD E. *Presidential Power; the Politics of Leadership.* New York: John Wiley & Sons, 1960

PETERSON, SVEND. *A Statistical History of the American Presidential Elections.* New York: Frederick Ungar Publishing Co., 1963

POLSBY, NELSON and AARON B. WILDAVSKY. *Presidential Elections: Strategies of American Electoral Politics.* New York: Charles Scribner's Sons, 1964

ROSEBOOM, EUGENE H. *A History of Presidential Elections.* New York: The Macmillan Co., 1957

ROSSITER, CLINTON. *The American Presidency.* New York: Harcourt, Brace & Co., 1956. Also *Conservatism in America; the Thankless Persuasion.* New York: Alfred A. Knopf, 1962

STANWOOD, EDWARD. *A History of the Presidency.* (2 v.) Boston: Houghton Mifflin Co., 1916

THOMAS, HELEN. *Dateline White House.* New York: Macmillan, 1975

UMBREIT, KENNETH B. *Founding Fathers; Men Who Shaped Our Tradition.* New York: Harper and Brothers, 1941

THE PRESIDENTS:

WASHINGTON:

CUNLIFFE, MARCUS. *George Washington, Man and Monument.* Boston: Little, Brown & Co., 1958

FITZPATRICK, JOHN C. *George Washington Himself.* Indianapolis: The Bobbs-Merrill Co., 1933

FORD, PAUL L. *The True George Washington.* Philadelphia: J. B. Lippincott Co., 1896; reprinted as *George Washington,* 1924

FREEMAN, DOUGLAS S. *George Washington.* (7 v.; v. 7 eds. John A. Carroll and Mary W. Ashworth.) New York: Charles Scribner's Sons, 1948–57

HAWORTH, PAUL L. *George Washington, Country Gentleman.* Indianapolis: The Bobbs-Merrill Co., 1925 (republication of *George Washington, Farmer.* 1915)

IRVING, WASHINGTON. *Life of George Washington.* (5 v.) New York: G. P. Putnam & Co., 1855–59. Several following editions.

NETTELS, CURTIS P. *George Washington and American Independence*. Boston: Little, Brown & Co., 1951

SEARS, LOUIS M. *George Washington*. New York: Thomas Y. Crowell Co., 1932

JOHN ADAMS:

ADAMS, ABIGAIL. *Letters of Mrs. Adams, the Wife of John Adams*. (2 v.) 3rd ed. with Introd. by Charles Francis Adams. Boston: C. C. Little & J. Brown, 1840–44

ADAMS, JAMES T. *The Adams Family*. Boston: Little, Brown & Co., 1930

The Adams Papers, Diary and Autobiography of John Adams. (vols. I–IV) ed. L. H. Butterfield. Cambridge, Mass.: Belknap Press of Harvard University Press, 1961

The Book of Abigail and John. Selected letters of the Adams Family, 1762–1784. Ed. L. H. Butterfield, Marc Friedlander and Mary-Jo Kline. Cambridge, Mass.: Harvard University Press, 1975

BOWEN, CATHERINE D. *John Adams and the American Revolution*. Boston: Little, Brown & Co., 1950

HARASZTI, ZOLTAN. *John Adams and the Prophets of Progress*. Cambridge, Mass.: Harvard University Press, 1952

KURTZ, STEPHEN G. *The Presidency of John Adams; the Collapse of Federalism, 1795–1800*. Philadelphia: The University of Pennsylvania Press, 1957

SMITH, PAGE. *John Adams*. (2 v.) New York: Doubleday & Co., 1962

JEFFERSON:

BOWERS, CLAUDE G. *The Young Jefferson, 1743–1789* and *Jefferson in Power* and *Jefferson and Hamilton*. Boston: Houghton Mifflin Co., 1925–45

CHINARD, GILBERT. *Thomas Jefferson: The Apostle of Americanism*. Ann Arbor, Mich.: University of Michigan Press, 1939, 1957

FRARY, I. T. *Thomas Jefferson, Architect and Builder*. Richmond: Garrett & Massie, 1950

JEFFERSON, THOMAS. *Autobiography*. With Introd. by Dumas Malone (memoirs from childhood through the Declaration of Independence). New York: G. P. Putnam's Sons, 1959

KOCH, ADRIENNE. *Jefferson and Madison; the Great Collaboration*. New York: Alfred A. Knopf, 1950

MALONE, DUMAS. *Jefferson and His Time*. (4 volumes.) Boston: Little, Brown & Co., 1948–62

MADISON:

ANTHONY, KATHARINE. *Dolly Madison, Her Life and Times*. Garden City, N.Y.: Doubleday & Co., 1949

BRANT, IRVING. James Madison. (6 v.) Indianapolis: The Bobbs-Merrill Co., 1941–61

HUNT, GAILLARD. *Madison*. New York: Doubleday, Page & Co., 1902

KOCH, ADRIENNE (see under Jefferson)

MONROE:

CRESSON, W. P. *James Monroe*. Chapel Hill, N.C.: University of North Carolina Press, 1946

STYRON, ARTHUR. *The Last of the Cocked Hats: James Monroe & the Virginia Dynasty*. Norman, Okla.: University of Oklahoma Press, 1945

J. Q. ADAMS:

ADAMS, JAMES T. (see under John Adams)

ADAMS, JOHN QUINCY. *Diary, 1794–1845.* Ed. Allan Nevins. New York: Charles Scribner's Sons, 1951

Selected Writings of John Quincy and John Adams. Eds. Adrienne Koch and William Peden. New York: Alfred A. Knopf, 1946

BEMIS, SAMUEL F. *John Quincy Adams and the Foundations of American Foreign Policy* and *John Quincy Adams and the Union.* (2 v.) New York: Alfred A. Knopf, 1949, 1956

EAST, ROBERT A. *John Quincy Adams; The Critical Years: 1785–1794.* New York: Bookman Associates, 1962

JACKSON:

BASSETT, JOHN S. *The Life of Andrew Jackson.* (2 v.) Garden City, N.Y.: Doubleday, Page & Co., 1911. (2 v. in 1.) New York: The Macmillan Co., 1931

JAMES, MARQUIS. *Andrew Jackson, The Border Captain* and *Andrew Jackson, Portrait of a President.* Indianapolis: The Bobbs-Merrill Co., 1933, 1937

SCHLESINGER, ARTHUR M., JR. *The Age of Jackson.* Boston: Little, Brown & Co., 1949

VAN DEUSEN, GLYNDON G. *The Jacksonian Era, 1828–1848.* New York: Harper and Brothers, 1959

WARD, JOHN W. *Andrew Jackson, Symbol for an Age.* New York: Oxford University Press, 1955

VAN BUREN:

BANCROFT, GEORGE. *Martin Van Buren to the End of His Public Career.* New York: Harper and Brothers, 1889

LYNCH, DENNIS T. *An Epoch and a Man, Martin Van Buren and His Times.* New York: H. Liveright, 1929

SHEPARD, EDWARD M. *Martin Van Buren.* Boston: Houghton Mifflin Co., 1888, 1916

VAN BUREN, MARTIN. *Autobiography.* Ed. John C. Fitzpatrick. Washington: Govt. Printing Office, 1920

W. H. HARRISON:

CLEAVES, FREEMAN. *Old Tippecanoe: William Henry Harrison and His Time.* New York: Charles Scribner's Sons, 1939

GREEN, JAMES A. *William Henry Harrison, His Life and Times.* Richmond: Garrett & Massie, 1941

TYLER:

CHITWOOD, OLIVER P. *John Tyler, Champion of the Old South.* New York: D. Appleton-Century, 1939

SEAGER, ROBERT. *And Tyler Too; A Biography of John and Julia Gardiner Tyler.* New York: McGraw-Hill Book Co., 1963

POLK:

JENKINS, JOHN S. *Life of James Knox Polk, Late President of the United States.* 1850

McCORMAC, EUGENE I. *James K. Polk; a Political Biography.* Berkeley, Calif.: University of California Press, 1922

Polk; the Diary of a President, 1845–1849. Ed. Allan Nevins. New York: Long-
mans, Green & Co., 1952

TAYLOR:

HAMILTON, HOLMAN. *Zachary Taylor, Soldier of the Republic* and *Zachary Taylor,
Soldier in the White House.* Indianapolis: The Bobb-Merrill Co., 1941–51

McKINLEY, SILAS BENT and SILAS BENT. *Old Rough and Ready, the Life and Times
of Zachary Taylor.* New York: Vanguard Press, 1946

FILLMORE:

CHAMBERLAIN, IVORY. *Biography of Millard Fillmore.* Buffalo, N.Y.: Thomas &
Lathrop, 1856

GRIFFIS, WILLIAM E. *Millard Fillmore.* Ithaca, N.Y.: Andrus & Church, 1915

RAYBACK, ROBERT J. *Millard Fillmore; Biography of a President.* Buffalo, N.Y.:
Buffalo Historical Soc., 1959

PIERCE:

NICHOLS, ROY F. *Franklin Pierce, Young Hickory of the Granite Hills.* Philadelphia:
University of Pennsylvania Press, 1958

BUCHANAN:

AUCHAMPAUGH, PHILIP G. *James Buchanan and His Cabinet on the Eve of Secession.* Lancaster, Pa.: Privately printed, 1926

CURTIS, GEORGE T. *Life of James Buchanan.* (2 v.) New York: Harper and
Brothers, 1883

KLEIN, PHILIP S. *President James Buchanan, a Biography.* University Park:
Pennsylvania State University Press, 1962

LINCOLN:

BISHOP, JAMES A. *The Day Lincoln Was Shot.* New York: Harper and Brothers,
1955

DUFF, JOHN J. *A. Lincoln: Prairie Lawyer.* New York: Rinehart, 1960

*The Living Lincoln: The Man, His Mind, His Times, and the War He Fought, Re-
constructed from His Own Writings.* Eds. Paul M. Angle and Earl S. Miers.
New Brunswick, N.J.: Rutgers University Press, 1955

LUTHIN, REINHARD H. *The Real Abraham Lincoln.* New York: Prentice-Hall, 1960

NICOLAY, JOHN C. and JOHN HAY. *Abraham Lincoln.* (10 v.) 1890. Also *A Short Life
of Abraham Lincoln.* (1 v.) New York: Century Co., 1902

RANDALL, JAMES G. *Lincoln the President.* (4 v.: 4th v. with Richard N. Current.)
New York: Dodd, Mead & Co., 1946–55

ROSCOE, THEODORE. *The Web of Conspiracy: The Complete Story of the Men Who
Murdered Abraham Lincoln.* Englewood Cliffs, N.J.: Prentice-Hall, 1959

SANDBURG, CARL. *Abraham Lincoln, The Prairie Years.* New York: Harcourt, Brace
& Co., 1926

STEPHENSON, NATHANIEL W. *Lincoln.* Indianapolis: The Bobbs-Merrill Co., 1922

TARBELL, IDA. *The Life of Abraham Lincoln.* (2 v.) New York: The Macmillan Co.,
1917

THOMAS, BENJAMIN P. *Abraham Lincoln: a Biography.* New York: Alfred A.
Knopf, 1952

ANDREW JOHNSON:

LOMASK, MILTON. *Andrew Johnson: President on Trial.* New York: Farrar, Straus and Cudahy, 1960

McKITRICK, ERIC L. *Andrew Johnson and Reconstruction.* Chicago: University of Chicago Press, 1960

STRYKER, LLOYD P. *Andrew Johnson; A Study in Courage.* New York: The Macmillan Co., 1929

WINSTON, ROBERT W. *Andrew Johnson, Plebian and Patriot.* New York: H. Holt & Co., 1928

GRANT:

CATTON, BRUCE. *U.S. Grant and the American Military Tradition.* Boston: Little, Brown & Co., 1954. Also *Grant Moves South.* (v. 2 in 3-v. series: see under Lewis.) Boston: Little, Brown & Co., 1960

COOLIDGE, LOUIS A. *Ulysses S. Grant.* Boston: Houghton Mifflin Co., 1922

GRANT, U.S. *Personal Memoirs.* (2 v.) New York: Charles L. Webster & Co., 1885–86

Mr. Lincoln's General: U.S. Grant. Illus. autobiography from his *Memoirs.* Ed. Roy Meredith. New York: E. P. Dutton & Co., 1959

HESSELTINE, WILLIAM B. *Ulysses S. Grant, Politician.* New York: Frederick Ungar Publishing Co., 1957, 1935

LEWIS, LLOYD. *Captain Sam Grant.* (v. 1 in 3-v. series: see under Catton.) Boston: Little Brown & Co., 1950

NEVINS, ALLAN. *Hamilton Fish: The Inner History of the Grant Administration.* (2 v.) New York: Frederick Ungar Publishing Co., 1957, 1936

HAYES:

BARNARD, HARRY. *Rutherford B. Hayes and His America.* Indianapolis: The Bobbs-Merrill Co., 1954

ECKENRODE, H. J. and POCAHONTAS W. WRIGHT. *Rutherford B. Hayes, Statesman of Reunion.* New York: Dodd, Mead & Co., 1930

WILLIAMS, CHARLES R. *Life of Rutherford B. Hayes.* (2 v.) Boston: Houghton Mifflin Co., 1914

WILLIAMS, T. HARRY. *Hayes: The Diary of a President, 1875–1881.* New York: McKay Publishing Co., 1964

GARFIELD:

CALDWELL, ROBERT G. *James A. Garfield, Party Chieftain.* New York: Dodd, Mead & Co., 1931

CONWELL, RUSSELL H. *The Life, Speeches and Public Services of James A Garfield.* Boston: B. B. Russell, 1881

SMITH, THEODORE C. *The Life and Letters of James Abram Garfield.* (2 v.) New Haven, Conn.: Yale University Press, 1925

ARTHUR:

HOWE, GEORGE F. *Chester A. Arthur: A Quarter Century of Machine Politics.* New York: Frederick Ungar Publishing Co., 1957, 1935

CLEVELAND:

LYNCH, DENNIS T. *Grover Cleveland, a Man Four-Square.* New York: H. Liveright, 1932

McELROY, ROBERT M. *Grover Cleveland: the Man and the Statesman.* New York: Harper and Brothers, 1923

MERRILL, HORACE S. *Bourbon Leader: Grover Cleveland and the Democratic Party.* Boston: Little, Brown & Co., 1957

NEVINS, ALLAN. *Grover Cleveland: A Study in Courage.* New York: Dodd, Mead & Co., 1932

BENJAMIN HARRISON:

SIEVERS, HARRY J. (v. 1.) *Benjamin Harrison, Hoosier Warrior (1833–1865)* and (v. 2.) *Benjamin Harrison, Hoosier Statesman. From the Civil War to the White House, 1865–1888.* Chicago: Henry Regnery Co., 1952–59

WALLACE, LEWIS. *Life of Gen. Ben Harrison.* Philadelphia: Hubbard Brothers, 1888

McKINLEY:

CROLY, HERBERT. *Marcus Alonzo Hanna: His Life and Work.* New York: The Macmillan Co., 1912

LEECH, MARGARET. *In the Days of McKinley.* New York: Harper and Brothers, 1959

OLCOTT, CHARLES S. *Life of William McKinley.* (2 v.) Boston: Houghton Mifflin Co., 1916

THEODORE ROOSEVELT:

BISHOP, JOSEPH B. *Theodore Roosevelt and His Time, Shown in His Own Letters.* (2 v.) New York: Charles Scribner's Sons, 1920

BLUM, JOHN M. *The Republican Roosevelt.* New York: Atheneum, 1962

HAGEDORN, HERMANN. *The Roosevelt Family of Sagamore Hill.* New York: The Macmillan Co., 1954

PRINGLE, HENRY F. *Theodore Roosevelt, a Biography.* New York: Harcourt, Brace & Co., 1956, 1931

PUTNAM, CARLETON. *Theodore Roosevelt, the Formative Years, 1858–1886.* (First of 3 v.) New York: Charles Scribner's Sons, 1958

ROOSEVELT, THEODORE. *An Autobiography.* New York: The Macmillan Co., 1914

TAFT:

BUTT, ARCHIBALD W. *Taft and Roosevelt, the Intimate Letters of Archie Butt.* (2 v.) Garden City, N.Y.: Doubleday, Doran & Co., 1930

DUFFY, HERBERT S. *William Howard Taft.* New York: Minton, Balch & Co., 1930

PRINGLE, HENRY F. *The Life and Times of William Howard Taft, a Biography.* (2 v.) New York: Farrar & Rinehart, 1939

WILSON:

DODD, WILLIAM E. *Woodrow Wilson and His Work.* New York: Peter Smith Publishers, 1932, 1920

KERNEY, JAMES. *The Political Education of Woodrow Wilson.* New York: The Century Co., 1926

LINK, ARTHUR S. *Wilson* (3 v.) Princeton: Princeton University Press, 1947–60. Also *Woodrow Wilson, a Brief Biography.* Cleveland: World Publishing Co., 1963. Also *Woodrow Wilson and the Progressive Era, 1910–1917.* New York: Harper and Brothers, 1954

McADOO, ELEANOR WILSON. *The Woodrow Wilsons.* New York: The Macmillan Co., 1937

TUMULTY, JOSEPH P. *Woodrow Wilson as I Know Him.* Garden City, N.Y.: Doubleday, Page & Co., 1925, 1921

WILSON, EDITH BOLLING. *My Memoir.* Indianapolis: The Bobbs-Merrill Co., 1939

HARDING:

ADAMS, SAMUEL H. *Incredible Era, the Life and Times of Warren Gamaliel Harding.* Boston: Houghton Mifflin Co., 1939

BRITTON, NAN. *The President's Daughter.* New York: Boni & Liveright, 1927

JOHNSON, WILLIS F. *The Life of Warren G. Harding.* 1923

NOGGLE, BURL. *Teapot Dome: Oil and Politics in the 1920's.* Baton Rouge, La.: Louisiana State University Press, 1962

RUSSELL, FRANCIS. *The Shadow of Blooming Grove—Warren G. Harding in His Times.* New York-Toronto: McGraw-Hill Book Company, 1968

SINCLAIR, ANDREW. *The Available Man—Warren Gamaliel Harding.* New York: The Macmillan Company, 1965

COOLIDGE:

COOLIDGE, CALVIN. *Autobiography.* New York: Cosmopolitan Book Corp., 1929

FUESS, CLAUDE M. *Calvin Coolidge, the Man from Vermont.* Boston: Little, Brown & Co., 1940

WHITE, WILLIAM ALLEN. *A Puritan in Babylon, The Story of Calvin Coolidge.* New York: The Macmillan Co., 1939

HOOVER:

HINSHAW, DAVID. *Herbert Hoover, American Quaker.* New York: Farrar, Straus and Cudahy, 1950

HOOVER, HERBERT. *Memoirs.* (3 v.) New York: The Macmillan Co., 1951–52

HYDE, ARTHUR M. and RAY LYMAN WILBUR. *The Hoover Policies.* New York: Charles Scribner's Sons, 1937

LYONS, EUGENE. *Our Unknown Ex-President, a Portrait of Herbert Hoover.* Garden City, N.Y.: Doubleday & Co., 1948. Republished as *The Herbert Hoover Story*, 1959

WARREN, HARRIS G. *Hoover and the Great Depression.* New York: Oxford University Press, 1959

F. D. ROOSEVELT:

BURNS, JAMES MAC GREGOR. *Roosevelt: The Lion and the Fox.* New York: Harcourt, Brace & Co., 1956

FREIDEL, FRANK B. *Franklin D. Roosevelt.* (6 v., of which 3 published.) Boston: Little, Brown & Co., 1952–56

LEUCHTENBURG, WILLIAM E. *Franklin D. Roosevelt and the New Deal, 1932–1940.* New York: Harper and Brothers, 1963

LINDLEY, ERNEST K. *Franklin D. Roosevelt, a Career in Progressive Democracy.* Indianapolis: The Bobbs-Merrill Co., 1931

MICHELSON, CHARLES. *The Ghost Talks.* New York: G. P. Putnam's Sons, 1944

PERKINS, FRANCES. *The Roosevelt I Knew.* New York: The Viking Press, 1946

ROOSEVELT, ELEANOR. *Autobiography.* New York: Harper and Brothers, 1961

SHERWOOD, ROBERT E. *Roosevelt and Hopkins, an Intimate History*. New York: Harper and Brothers, 1950

TULLY, GRACE G. *F.D.R. My Boss*. New York: Charles Scribner's Sons, 1949

TRUMAN:

ALLEN, ROBERT S. and WILLIAM V. SHANNON. *The Truman Merry-go-round*. New York: The Vanguard Press, 1950

DANIELS, JONATHAN. *The Man of Independence*. Philadelphia: J. B. Lippincott Co., 1950

McNAUGHTON, FRANK and WALTER HEYMEYER. *Harry Truman, President*. New York: Whittlesey House, McGraw-Hill Book Co., 1948

STEINBERG, ALFRED. *The Man from Missouri; The Life and Times of Harry S. Truman*. New York: G. P. Putnam's Sons, 1962

TRUMAN, HARRY S. *Memoirs*. (2 v.) Garden City, N.Y.: Doubleday & Co., 1955–56. Also *Mr. Citizen*. New York: Geis Associates, 1960

EISENHOWER:

ADAMS, SHERMAN. *Firsthand Report; The Story of the Eisenhower Administration*. New York: Harper and Brothers, 1961

BUTCHER, CAPT. HARRY C., U.S.N.R. *My Three Years with Eisenhower*. New York: Simon & Schuster, 1946

EISENHOWER, DWIGHT D. *Crusade in Europe*. New York: Doubleday & Co., 1955, 1948. Also *The White House Years, The Mandate for Change, 1953–56*. Garden City, N.Y.: Doubleday & Co., 1963

GUNTHER, JOHN. *Eisenhower, the Man and the Symbol*. New York: Harper and Brothers, 1952

PUSEY, MERLO JOHN. *Eisenhower, the President*. New York: The Macmillan Co., 1956

KENNEDY:

BURNS, JAMES MAC GREGOR. *John Kennedy: A Political Profile*. New York: Harcourt, Brace & Co., 1960

DONOVAN, ROBERT J. *PT 109, John F. Kennedy in World War II*. New York: McGraw-Hill Book Co., 1961

FAY, PAUL B. *The Pleasure of his Company*. New York: Harper & Row, 1966

KENNEDY, JOHN F. *Profiles in Courage*. New York: Harper and Brothers, 1956. Also *Why England Slept*. New York: W. Funk, Inc., 1961, 1940

LASKY, VICTOR. *John F. Kennedy: What's Behind the Image?* Washington: Free World Press, 1960

MANCHESTER, WILLIAM R. *Portrait of a President: John F. Kennedy in Profile*. Boston: Little, Brown & Co., 1962

SIDEY, HUGH. *John F. Kennedy, President*. New York: Antheneum Publishers, 1964, 1963

SORENSON, THEODORE C. *Decision-Making in the White House*. New York: Columbia University Press, 1963

SORENSON, THEODORE. *Kennedy*. New York: Harper & Row, 1965

TREGASKIS, RICHARD W. *John F. Kennedy: War Hero*. New York: Dell Publishing Co., 1962

WHITE, THEODORE H. *The Making of the President, 1960*. New York: Atheneum Publishers, 1961

LYNDON JOHNSON:

CALIFANO, JOSEPH A., JR. *A Presidential Nation.* New York: W. W. Norton & Co., 1975

PROVENCE, HARRY. *Lyndon B. Johnson.* New York: Fleet Publishing Corp., 1964

SHERRILL, ROBERT. *The Accidental President.* New York: Grossman Publishers, 1967

WHITE, WILLIAM S. *The Professional: Lyndon B. Johnson.* Boston: Houghton Mifflin Co., 1964

NIXON:

BERNSTEIN, CARL and BOB WOODWARD. *All the President's Men.* New York: Simon & Schuster, 1974. Also Warner Paperback Library Edition, 1975

BRESLIN, JIMMY. *How the Good Guys Finally Won.* New York: The Viking Press, 1975

CONGRESSIONAL QUARTERLY. *Watergate: Chronology of a Crisis.* Washington, 1975

DREW, ELIZABETH. *Washington Journal: The Events of 1973–1974.* New York: Random House, 1975

EVANS, ROWLAND, JR., and ROBERT D. NOVAK. *Nixon in the White House; The Frustration of Power.* New York: Random House, 1971

McGINNISS, JOE. *The Selling of the President 1968.* New York: Trident Press, 1969. Also New York: Pocket Books, 1970

RATHER, DAN and GARY PAUL GATES. *The Palace Guard.* New York: Harper & Row, 1974. Also New York: Warner Paperback Library, 1975

SAFIRE, WILLIAM. *Before the Fall; an Inside View of the pre-Watergate White House.* Garden City, N.Y.: Doubleday, 1975

WHITE, THEODORE H. *Breach of Faith: the Fall of Richard Nixon.* New York: Atheneum Publishers. Reader's Digest Press, 1975

WILLS, GARRY. *Nixon Agonistes; the Crisis of the Self-Made Man.* New York: Houghton, Mifflin Co., 1969, 1970. Also a Signet Book from New American Library, Sept. 1971

WITCOVER, JULES. *The Resurrection of Richard Nixon.* New York: G. P. Putnam's Sons, 1970

	DATE DUE		
102			
MAY 1 9 '89 Herb			
NOV 2 8 '89 Mores			

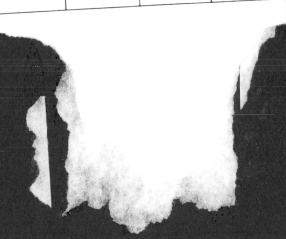